TOOLS STUDENTS NEED TO BE
SKILLFUL WRITERS

BUILDING BETTER SENTENCES

PHYLLIS HOSTMEYER

CORWIN
A SAGE Company

CORWIN
A SAGE Company

FOR INFORMATION:

Corwin
A SAGE Company
2455 Teller Road
Thousand Oaks, California 91320
(800) 233-9936
www.corwin.com

SAGE Publications Ltd.
1 Oliver's Yard
55 City Road
London EC1Y 1SP
United Kingdom

SAGE Publications India Pvt. Ltd.
B 1/I 1 Mohan Cooperative Industrial Area
Mathura Road, New Delhi 110 044
India

SAGE Publications Asia-Pacific Pte. Ltd.
3 Church Street
#10-04 Samsung Hub
Singapore 049483

Acquisitions Editor: Jessica Allan
Associate Editor: Julie Nemer
Editorial Assistant: Lisa Whitney
Permissions Editors: Jason Kelley and Karen Ehrmann
Project Editor: Veronica Stapleton
Copy Editor: Trey Thoelcke
Typesetter: C&M Digitals (P) Ltd.
Proofreader: Annie Lubinsky
Indexer: Molly Hall
Cover Designer: Rose Storey

Printed in the United States of America

Library of Congress Cataloging-in-Publication Data

Hostmeyer, Phyllis, author.

Tools students need to be skillful writers : building better sentences/ Phyllis Hostmeyer.

pages cm
Includes bibliographical references and index.

ISBN 978-1-4129-8904-6 (pbk.)

1. English language—Sentences—Study and teaching (Elementary) 2. English language—Composition and exercises—Study and teaching (Elementary) I. Title.

LB1576.H673 2012
372.6—dc23   2012017421

This book is printed on acid-free paper.

12 13 14 15 16 10 9 8 7 6 5 4 3 2 1

Contents

Preface

Tools Students Need to Be Skillful Writers: Building Better Sentences is not intended to be a comprehensive list of rules to be followed by students and teachers. It is not intended to be a textbook or a scripted program.

Tools Students Need to Be Skillful Writers is intended to be a sourcebook of sentence-level grammar activities that will give students explicit practice and confidence in writing a variety of sentence types effectively. It is a book of practical ideas to be shared by real teachers as they help students to study and practice the craft of writing. It is intended to follow standard written English and provide insights into the courtesies of consistent and accurate mechanics, spelling, and usage. And, perhaps most importantly, it is intended to honor the expertise of teachers as decision makers as they celebrate the art of teaching.

With the advent of high-stakes testing in the 1980s, I, like many teachers, was required to teach writing formulas. I attended one or two forty-five-minute after-school workshops with presenters who flew through formulas that assigned a numerical value to every sentence. Each presenter promised, "If students simply follow the formula, they will create high-scoring essays." But the rigid formulas bothered me. Students were held to a specific number of paragraphs, a specific number of sentences per paragraph, and mandated transition words that often did not accurately express the relationship among the ideas. The strict formulas lacked creativity, student choice, purpose, and authenticity. My philosophy of education revolved around student choice and decision making, which I did not find in strict adherence to formulas.

Fortunately, I soon had an opportunity to attend a full-day workshop led by Dr. J. E. Sparks, the author of Write for Power (1982), which had the reputation of being another of those rigid formulas for writing essays. However, during the workshop Dr. Sparks never pushed a rigid formula like the ones that I had seen in other workshops. He discussed structures of text. He demonstrated how to move from general to specific ideas as an organization pattern, and he talked about sentence patterns. He discussed vocabulary, sentence variety, and specific details. His book contained examples of thirty-nine sentence patterns that he recommended we use while writing essays. Dr. Sparks encouraged sentence variety but did not offer a specific way to teach the patterns. I was intrigued by this idea of sentence patterns because my students' essays were littered with fragments and run-ons. More disturbing, my students did not recognize these errors, nor did they have any idea how to correct those errors once I pointed them out.

I began researching and wondered how to go about teaching the patterns to my students. Living in a small town in the early 1980s meant that I did not have Internet access at school or home. Nor did I have immediate access to a library stocked with educational materials. Nonetheless, I did stumble upon two textbooks that helped me. The first was one about sentence patterns developed by the University of Michigan. The second was Barron's *The Art of Styling Sentences.* Both of these texts gave me valuable grammatical explanations of various patterns and alerted me to standard English rules and possible pitfalls. But neither provided me with a clear methodology.

I had begun haphazardly teaching patterns to my students. In spite of my somewhat disjointed efforts, the students began constructing effective sentences. I noticed fewer fragments and run-on sentences in their work. Students began to recognize fragments and run-ons and attempted to correct them. My students had an air of confidence as they tackled assignments. I knew the patterns were a valuable tool, so I continued my search for methods of instruction. I wanted all of my students to succeed.

The next piece of the puzzle came to me during a one-hour presentation by Herb Hrebic, one of the developers of the *Stack the Deck* writing program. During that hour, I came to understand that if I wanted students to become authors, I needed to teach with a positive attitude and build on students' skills rather than nitpick at their faults. I loved Hrebric's upbeat, kindhearted approach to teaching composition.

I continued to scramble for ideas to synthesize the information as it came to me. During Hrebic's presentation, he demonstrated sentence combining, a technique I had never used. Immediately, I saw how this technique could support sentence patterns, which led me to William Strong.

Strong's work on sentence combinations gave me a piece that was missing in the sentence pattern work that I had been doing with my students. I began developing combinations that matched the patterns to provide students additional support as they learned to write the sentences independently. I cannot say that my students enjoyed working on sentence combinations, but I can say that working on the combinations helped my students to develop a better understanding of the patterns and how to manipulate sentence elements. It also became my strongest tool in teaching the mechanics of writing. Sentence combining helped students who still struggled to write an original sentence after studying the models. After working on combinations, they could return to the models and write original sentences.

Over the years I continued to collect and refine ideas that would help the students learn sentence patterns. This book is a collection of those ideas and materials. I have been using most of these activities for twenty to thirty years, so in some cases I am not sure of the origin of the activity. I have made every effort to find the original sources. Over the years I have made numerous changes to the activities, and I find that I still change the activities as classrooms and student needs change.

I often have thought that only a fool would attempt to write a book about writing or how to teach writing; so yes, I am a fool. Writing such a book is an invitation to argument, to fault-finding, to accusations. Syntax sticklers will find errors. Good writing, style, voice—I challenge my readers to define any of these. If they do manage to define voice or style, I challenge them to find ten people who will agree on one definition of these elements. I do feel that writing rests on the back of grammar, but even those rules are nebulous. For example, I consulted three respected resources concerning the rules for punctuating sentences with conjunctive adverbs, and I came away with three distinct sets of rules.

With each pattern, my students learned punctuation rules, or as I preferred to teach it—punctuation courtesies. Lacking a classroom textbook, I researched the mechanics for each pattern and made decisions about correct usage. I researched some of the giants of writing—Strunk and White, Graves, Zinsser, and others. I scanned textbooks and manuals of style. I often found disagreements concerning usage of commas, semicolons, and colons.

The requirements of our high school programs also influenced my decisions. I wanted my students' transition to high school to be as effortless as possible. Hence, when my resources disagreed on rules, I turned to the high school texts for guidance on standard written English and chose to teach the rule that the students most likely would be expected to use in high school.

I know that people will disagree with some of my decisions about grammar and punctuation. No doubt, my suggestions may even offend some. But language is not static, and rules do fall by the wayside or change dramatically with time. Sentence patterns, vocabulary, punctuation, spelling—all of these elements of language do change. If you doubt me, read a bit of Thomas Jefferson's second inaugural address, and notice the enormous differences in spelling, sentence structure, punctuation, and vocabulary:

> I repair, then, fellow-citizens, to the post you have assigned me. With experience enough in subordinate offices to have seen the difficulties of this the greatest of all. I have learnt to expect that it will rarely fall to the lot of imperfect man to retire from this station with the reputation and the favor which bring him into it. . . . The approbation implied by your suffrage is a great consolation to me for the past, and my future solicitude will be to retain the good opinion of those who have bestowed it in advance, to conciliate that of others by doing them all the good in my power, and to be instrumental to the happiness and freedom of all.

I am not a grammar goddess; I am not a maven of mechanics. But I am a teacher who has had success teaching sentence patterns to students. My goal is to share those techniques and ideas. This is a book of suggestions, not a rigid script. Good teachers will change my suggestions to fit their teaching style and the needs of their students. My goal is to share ideas with other teachers; my hope is that they will share their success stories and ideas with me.

OVERVIEW OF THE BOOK

Chapter 1 provides reasons and research to support the teaching of sentence patterns. It shows the link between grammar and writing and offers encouragement to break from traditional grammar lessons. Chapter 2 provides a range of activities that can be used to teach the parts of speech. The premise of the book is that all patterns grow from two basic patterns: noun-verb and noun-verb-noun. Hence, it is crucial that students develop a strong understanding of the concept of a noun and the concept of a verb before they begin studying the patterns.

Chapter 3 is the meat of the book and might seem overwhelming at first. I suggest that readers at first focus on the patterns for one grade level, which will make the task of teaching patterns manageable. This chapter provides directions and suggestions for teaching the patterns, including the teacher's role and the students' roles. Background Information sections concerning punctuation and grammar are provided for each pattern. Readers also will find Points for Student Analysis sections and helpful hints for teachers. The idea of teaching patterns is to show students models of the pattern and then provide them time to analyze the pattern prior to a teacher-led discussion. A reliable English textbook will be a valuable resource at this point.

Chapters 4 through 6 provide sentence combination exercises, games, and activities tied directly to each pattern. The opportunity to deconstruct and reconstruct sentences will be most helpful to teachers moving students through the tiers of response to intervention (RTI). If students find themselves struggling with a pattern, the activities in Chapters 4 through 6 can be used to provide additional help so that students understand the structures.

Chapters 7 and 8 explain the relationship between sentence patterns and writing paragraphs, essays, and narratives. One new pattern is analyzed and practiced on the first day of every week. The remaining days are writing workshop days that require students to use the patterns as they develop longer pieces of text. This book does not intend to teach all the ins and outs of a writing workshop, but it does address how to use the patterns in a workshop setting.

Acknowledgments

My former students are the single group of people who have given me the most help on this project. Administrators cited my students' consistently excellent test scores on mandatory state tests as proof of the power of sentence patterns. In twenty-five years of teaching, 99 percent of my students scored *meets and exceeds* on state writing tests. For me, the proof of success was evident in my students' enthusiasm for writing. They enjoyed writing for authentic audiences: contests, local organizations, family and friends, and student publications. The positive feedback from each audience provided my students with a sense of success that fueled their enthusiasm.

I also would like to acknowledge the numerous teachers who not only have attended my workshops on sentence patterns but also implemented and improved the strategies and techniques. I would like to give a special thanks to Laura Pruett, JoAnne Lambert, and Kim Henke of the Triad School District for allowing me to visit their classrooms and gather samples of student work. Thank you to the teachers at District 87 in Illinois who also shared samples of student work. Consistent requests from teachers for a book about the patterns finally spurred me to undertake this task.

PUBLISHER'S ACKNOWLEDGMENTS

Corwin wishes to acknowledge the following peer reviewers for their editorial insight and guidance.

Kim Austin
Third-Grade Teacher
C.C. Ring Elementary School
Jamestown, NY

Norma Barber
Language Arts Teacher
Ukiah School District
Ukitah, OR

Deb Bible
Literacy Teacher
Dundee Highlands
Hanover Park, IL

Jolene Dockstader
Seventh-Grade English Teacher
Jerome Middle School
Jerome, ID

Linda Louise Eisinger
Third/Fourth-Grade Teacher
West Elementary School
Jefferson City, MO

Wanda Mangum
GCPS Language Arts Instructional Coach
Curriculum and Instruction
     Department
Suwanee, GA

About the Author

 **Phyllis Hostmeyer** lives in Southern Illinois but is a language arts consultant for Educational Resources Group, Inc., (www.ergsc.com) of Charleston, South Carolina. A frequent speaker and presenter throughout Illinois, Phyllis also has worked as a language arts consultant throughout the country and abroad. She conducts a range of workshops on reading, writing, assessment, poetry, and other topics. But her favorite presentations revolve around the sentence patterns. In addition, Phyllis is a professional storyteller who turns fables and fairy tales into rap, jazz, and ballads. She also does Bible tellings and has traveled to Israel as part of an American Bible telling team. She uses her storytelling skills to bring life and learning to her educational workshops.

Introduction

Why Teach Sentence Patterns?

1

"**W**hat problems do you encounter when teaching writing to students?" For several years now, I have been collecting and categorizing answers to that question from thousands of teachers across the country. All of their answers can be gathered under four ideas. First, teachers consistently cite three student-related problems related to teaching writing: lack of motivation, lack of basic writing skills, and lack of content knowledge or information for writing topics. Teachers also cite their own lack of confidence concerning how to teach writing. Teachers seem to think of themselves as skilled readers, but most do not think of themselves as skilled writers.

When I completed my undergraduate degree, I took a host of methods classes. Not one of those classes dealt with methods of teaching writing. Teachers tell me that the same holds true for them. Thus, many teachers end up teaching writing the way that they were taught writing: worksheets, diagramming, and rewriting essays in ink after the teacher has corrected every possible error. Even though these teachers readily admit that they hated to write and have never felt successful as writers, they continue to use the very methods that left them bewildered and bored. Some tell me that they hated to diagram sentences. Others confess that they loved to diagram sentences, but admit that it taught them very little about writing. It did not give them the skills to create beautiful sentences. The teachers who liked diagramming are often the same ones who like to work puzzles, crosswords, or cryptograms. For them, diagramming was just one more puzzle to enjoy.

I have worked with hundreds of teachers who throw their hands in the air, shake their heads, and say, "We teach the grammar rules year after year, day in and day out. I have students who earn perfect scores on every worksheet we do, but they hand in essays riddled with errors. They just don't care." I think most students do care, but fixing obvious errors on a worksheet is a far cry from editing a paper. The skills do not transfer. If the worksheets and grammar drills are not working, then why continue to use them?

Teachers cite the pressures of high-stakes testing and the demands of the district as reasons for teaching grammar. I agree; we cannot thumb our nose at those demands. Teachers mention the importance of knowing grammar because it is a mark of an educated person. I agree with that too. But I do wonder what teachers mean when they say *grammar.* Does knowing grammar mean labeling every word in a sentence? Does it mean knowing all the parts of speech? Does it mean diagramming? Reciting rules about spelling, punctuation, and capitalization—is that grammar? When we demand good grammar, are we talking about speech, writing, or both? Are there differences in the grammar of speech and the grammar used in writing?

If current methods are not working, then why continue using those methods? I began teaching sentence patterns in the 1980s and found that my students enjoyed working on the patterns. More importantly, they developed writing and grammar skills together. "Good grammar and good writing are not twins, but they are usually found in the same places." (Provost, 2001, p. 44)

With the advent of the Common Core State Standards, the ability to write coherent essays and narratives will be crucial. Students will be required to "develop and strengthen writing as needed by planning, revising, editing, rewriting, or trying a new approach" (National Governors Association Center for Best Practices and Council of Chief State School Officers, 2010, CC.K-12.W.R.5. All rights reserved.). Knowing a range of patterns will give students the ability to revise sentences by adding or deleting information and by rearranging the elements of a sentence. The rules of standard written English are taught with each pattern so that students can edit their work.

Linguists cite eight major sentence patterns in the English language (Benjamin & Oliva, 2007). I think that can be simplified for our students by teaching two basic patterns: noun-verb (N-V) and noun-verb-noun (N-V-N). After all, noun–linking verb–noun is just a variation of noun-verb-noun. So I opted to focus on the two most concrete, most basic of the eight patterns. Once students can create those, they can then embed or add sentence elements to create a wide range of patterns. Let me demonstrate by embedding or adding sentence elements into one noun-verb sentence, "The dragon roared." (See Figure 1.1.)

Figure 1.1 Sample Enhanced N-V Sentences

Element to Be Embedded	Enhanced Noun-Verb Sentence
Noun-Verb Sentence	The dragon roared.
Question	*Did* the dragon roar?
Opening Adverb	*Ferociously*, the dragon roared.
Prepositional Phrase	*In the morning*, the dragon roared.
Compound/Coordinator	The dragon roared, *and the knight retreated.*
Appositive	The dragon, *one of the king's pets*, roared.
Opening Adverb Clause	*Because his dinner was late*, the dragon roared.
Closing Adverb Clause	The dragon roared *because his dinner was late.*

Verbs in a Series	The dragon roared, *growled, and hissed.*
Opening Adjective	*Angry,* the dragon roared.
Adjective Phrase	*Grumpy because of a hangnail,* the dragon roared.
Infinitive	*To frighten the tourists,* the dragon roared.
Present Participle	*Glaring at the knight,* the dragon roared.
Past Participle	*Frustrated,* the dragon roared.
Perfect Present Participle	*Having burnt his dinner again,* the dragon roared.
Restrictive Clause	The dragon *that lives next door* roared.
Nonrestrictive Clause	The dragon, *who normally loves company,* roared.
Compound; Semicolon	The dragon roared; *the knight whimpered.*
Conjunctive Adverb	The dragon roared. *Nevertheless, the knight approached his lair.*
Absolute	The dragon, *his claws slashing the air,* roared.
Opening Series	*Tired, cold, and hungry*—the dragon roared.

The same sentence elements can be embedded into a noun-verb-noun sentence, as shown in Figure 1.2.

Figure 1.2   Sample Enhanced N-V-N Sentences

Element to Be Embedded	Enhanced Noun-Verb-Noun Sentence
Noun-Verb-Noun Sentence	The astronaut repaired the Hubble.
Question	*Did* the astronaut repair the Hubble?
Opening Adverb	*Carefully,* the astronaut repaired the Hubble.
Prepositional Phrase	*On day three,* the astronaut repaired the Hubble.
Compound/Coordinator	The astronaut repaired the Hubble, *and mission control monitored the event.*
Appositive	The astronaut, *Dr. Megan McArthur,* repaired the Hubble.
Opening Adverb Clause	*Because the bolts had frozen,* the astronaut repaired the Hubble.
Closing Adverb Clause	The astronaut repaired the Hubble *because its bolts had frozen.*
Verbs in a Series	The astronaut repaired the Hubble, *collected data, and conducted a demonstration.*
Opening Adjective	*Confident,* the astronaut repaired the Hubble.
Adjective Phrase	*Nervous because of the fire,* the astronaut repaired the Hubble.
Infinitive	*To ensure clear photographs of the galaxy,* the astronaut repaired the Hubble.
Present Participle	*Struggling with the frozen bolts,* the astronaut repaired the Hubble.

(Continued)

(Continued)

Past Participle	*Worried,* the astronaut repaired the Hubble.
Perfect Present Participle	*Having diagnosed the problem,* the astronaut repaired the Hubble.
Restrictive Clause	The astronaut *that waved to me at lift off* repaired the Hubble.
Nonrestrictive Clause	The astronaut, *who was on her fifth mission,* repaired the Hubble.
Compound; Semicolon	The astronaut repaired the Hubble*; the other crew members assisted her.*
Conjunctive Adverb	The astronaut repaired the Hubble. *Therefore, NASA received clear pictures of the galaxy again.*
Absolute	The astronaut, *arms growing weary,* repaired the Hubble.
Opening Series	*Tired, cold, and hungry*—the astronaut repaired the Hubble.

All of the above sentences in the figures have either N-V or N-V-N at the core. Once students understand those two basic patterns, they can imitate any of the new patterns by writing a basic sentence and then embedding or adding sentence elements. This empowers students to create a range of sentences. In addition, fixing fragments and run-on sentences becomes a student responsibility. I can help them to spot a run-on, but the student must deconstruct the sentence to determine the source of the problem. By crossing out sentence elements such as prepositional phrases, modifiers, and conjunctions, students can strip a sentence down to the basic sentence structure. Often they find that they have several N-V and N-V-N structures left. They can reconstruct those elements by selecting appropriate conjunctions and punctuation. The next step is to embed any necessary modifiers.

As early as third grade, the Common Core demands that students be able to "use linking words and phrases (e.g., because, therefore, since, for example) to connect opinion and reasons" (National Governors Association Center for Best Practices and Council of Chief State School Officers, 2010, CC.3.W.1.c. All rights reserved.). These skills are taught very explicitly with Patterns 5 through 9, which focus on prepositions, coordinating conjunctions, and subordinators (see Chapter 3). Subsequent patterns demonstrate the use of adjective clauses and verbals. All of these patterns are critical to linking ideas and phrases in a well-constructed piece of text.

My students were never given a prescription that dictates the number of words per sentence, the number of sentences per paragraph, nor the number of paragraphs per essay or narrative. The sentence patterns give students the skills to create original sentences that express their ideas and knowledge. Students learn to write through imitation. They study an author's craft and techniques. Once they have reached a comfort level with the patterns, I encourage students to play. Combine patterns, move embedded elements to new positions, take risks, make decisions, let voice evolve. Be an author.

Teaching Parts of Speech 2

For the following smorgasbord of activities, students will need a basic understanding of nouns and verbs. If they understand that a noun is a name for a person, place, or thing. and that a verb is an action word, they can complete these activities. Older students might understand that abstract words, such as *teamwork, maturity,* or *responsibility* are also nouns, but that information is not crucial at this point. The idea behind these activities is that students will develop an understanding of the concept of nouns, verbs, and other sentence elements as they work. It has been my experience that most students can recite definitions and even recognize noun and verbs—skills at the lowest levels of Bloom's Taxonomy. The goal is to have students who can discuss and manipulate nouns and verbs to create the two basic sentence patterns noun-verb and noun-verb-noun.

ACTIVITIES FOR NOUNS AND VERBS

Some of the activities might seem ridiculously simple, but sometimes ridiculously simple is exactly what a student needs. These activities will build the foundation for the sentence patterns. I have found that once students can generate a bank of nouns and verbs and use that bank to create the two basic patterns, they will be able to create the remaining patterns with little difficulty. So do not rush; never assume knowledge. Make sure that students understand the nature of a noun, the nature of a verb, and how to use them to create ridiculously simple sentences that will soon blossom into more complex structures.

The ability to use specific nouns and verbs in effective sentence structures forms the basis for good writing. Harry Noden, author of *Image Grammar,* says that once students understand the power of nouns and verbs, they can transform their writing to vivid photography. "Their use of specific nouns and verbs breathes life into cold corpse images" (Noden, 1999, p. 26). It is not enough to tell students to use specific nouns and vivid verbs. We must teach the skills: build vocabulary, develop an eye for the weak word, develop an ear for rhythm, and revise willingly.

I have not separated the following activities into grade levels; rather, I prefer that teachers select activities appropriate to their class and their students' needs. Just as I hope no one would ever eat every item on a smorgasbord, I cannot see anyone using all of these activities in one classroom. I have provided a range of activities so that teachers working as teams can select activities for all grade levels as needed.

FLOODLIGHT/FLASHLIGHT

Materials

A floodlight, a flashlight, and a picture or print that has a great deal of detail. I have often used Edward Hicks's *The Peaceable Kingdom,* Rockwell's *Freedom from Want,* Seurat's *Sunday Afternoon on the Island of La Grande Jatte.* I have used advertisements that include numerous items. Portraits and still life prints do not work as well; the picture used in this activity must have lots of detail. I also have done this activity with PowerPoint slides, which is explained in the procedure section.

Procedure

Tell the students that you will put a picture on the bulletin board, and you will shine a floodlight on it. The students are to study the picture for a few minutes. They may look at any part that is illuminated by the floodlight, which means they should be able to see the entire picture. Each student is to remember one detail—just one detail. Or you can show the picture using PowerPoint or a document camera. Explain that the entire picture is illuminated.

Give the students a few minutes to study the picture. Then turn off the floodlight and take down the picture. Ask some students which detail they remember. For example, if I have used *The Peaceable Kingdom,* some students might remember the ox in the center of the picture. Others might remember the child who seems to float in air, the lion, or the group of people gathered in the background.

Tell the students that you will put the picture up again, but this time you will shine a flashlight on it. Have them to look only in the small area illuminated by the flashlight. Be sure to illuminate only one item. For example, if using *Peaceable Kingdom,* make sure that the only thing included in the light is the head of the ox. If you are using PowerPoint, black out everything in the picture except one item. With a document camera, simply cut a small hole in a piece of paper and lay it over the picture to reveal only one item. After students have a few moments to look at the picture, turn off the flashlight, take down the picture, and ask them what they remember. Everyone should remember the ox, since it was the only thing illuminated. Some might remember the eyes of the ox; others might focus more on the white stripe on the face. But everyone should remember only the ox or something about it. No one should mention the other animals, scenery, or people because they were not illuminated by the flashlight.

Explain that sometimes words are like floodlights and flashlights. If I say the word *tree* and ask everyone to visualize a tree, what would people see? Some might visualize a Christmas tree, some a giant oak, others a weeping willow. If I ask them to visualize a dog, some might see a Doberman, others a poodle, and others a lab. *Dog* is the floodlight word; *poodle* is a flashlight word. The poodle we see might be different colors or sizes, but it will have the distinctive markings of a poodle. Hence, *poodle* is a flashlight word. It controls the visualizations.

Explain that over the next few days, they will be working with nouns and verbs, and they should try to use flashlight words.

Too often we tell students that their writing should show, not tell, but we give students no hint on how to do that. Their writing is often vague and lacks supporting details. In other words, their writing lacks flashlight words and flashlight sentences. We will return to the idea of the floodlight and the flashlight throughout this book. The words *floodlight* and *flashlight* will part of the instructional vocabulary. The lights become a metaphor for teaching general and specific. It gives students a concrete image.

The floodlight/flashlight metaphor helps students as they read and write to see the difference between general ideas and specific support statements. By highlighting floodlight and flashlight sentences with different color markers, students can see a concrete example of structures of text. In addition, the Common Core State Standards (National Governors Association Center for Best Practices and Council of Chief State School Officers, 2010. All rights reserved.) require students to develop a piece of writing through the use of facts, explanations, and reasons. Students who rely on floodlight sentences will not have facts and explanations; rather, they will have general sentences that vaguely refer to ideas. This concept is demonstrated in Chapters 6 and 8 with student samples of strong flashlight sentences.

Examples

Floodlight Words	Toy	Store	Car	Flower	Chair
Flashlight Words	Hula hoop	Pharmacy	Corvette	Yellow rose	Recliner
Floodlight Sentence	The bat has many adaptations that help it to survive.				
Flashlight Sentence	The bat's large ears with ridges and folds help it to hear a wide range of sounds.				
Floodlight Sentence	In Colonial times, peddlers delivered goods to people.				
Flashlight Sentence	In Colonial times, peddlers delivered muslin, ribbons, pots, pans, and silverware to people.				

NOUN TOWN AND VERB SUBURB BULLETIN BOARD

Materials

- Large bulletin board
- A source for words, such as newspapers, magazines, or discarded books
- Glue and scissors
- Art and craft materials

Procedure

After reviewing the rules for brainstorming, put students into small groups to brainstorm a list of homes where people might live. A few ideas that I have seen students brainstorm: mansion, igloo, shack, cardboard box, houseboat, apartment, A-frame, army barracks, condo, jail cell, tipi, trailer, camper, yurt, tent—all flashlight words.

During brainstorming activities, I usually stop the students after a few minutes and ask them to circle their three most unusual ideas. "Find the three words your group has written that you think no one else in the room has listed." Each group quickly shares these words with the class. Throughout the room, one can hear, "Oh, yeah. We should have thought of that one." Once everyone has shared, the students complete a few more minutes of brainstorming, but those few moments of sharing have sparked new ideas and enthusiasm. Students begin to understand the value of teamwork.

When we finish brainstorming, the students count how many words they have listed. Each team circles the one word that they think is unique to their group. Often a group might have a small sampling of words, but they have a word that no one in the class has listed. No need for any group to feel that they lost a competition based on numbers; they are all winners for creativity. Next, students select one of the words, and they each create one of the lodgings they have brainstormed, perhaps during art class. Cover a large bulletin board with these paper lodgings. Label one side of the board Noun Town and the other side Verb Suburb. Some teachers have used other labels: Noun Neighborhood, Noun Nation, or Verb Village.

Draw streets to connect all of the houses. Students will pave the streets of Noun Town with nouns and the streets of Verb Suburb with verbs. How do they pave the streets? I have used a variety of methods. We have cut words from headlines and magazines and simply glued them to the streets. We have brainstormed words and written them on assigned streets. Some students have been given the option of adding pictures.

Also, this is a good time to reserve two streets in each section of town for the next challenge. Once students have a strong understanding of nouns and verbs, they will create Adjective Avenue in Noun Town and Adverb Alley in Verb Suburb. Preposition Park also can be added to one side of town or on another board. Once these displays are completed, students have strong visuals for five parts of speech. They also have access to word banks that can be used when they begin writing the sentence patterns.

I provide very little instruction during the street-paving activity, but I circulate the room nonstop and encourage groups to come up with specific nouns. Why add the floodlight word *dog* when the flashlight words *poodle* or *retriever* are more specific? Why not add *pharmacy* or *grocery* rather than the floodlight word *store*? Also look for groups that have selected words that are not nouns. Rather than stop their enthusiastic research, simply take the word from them and add it to a chart labeled Not Nouns. If they have been gluing words, peel off the word and stick it on chart paper. If they have been writing words, cross through the word and write it on the Not Nouns chart. Later, discuss the Not Nouns chart and help students to determine why these words do not qualify as nouns. The power of that group discussion helps students to develop an understanding of the nature or the concept of a noun. I could stop and tell them why certain words are not nouns, but that is learning that seldom sticks. A Chinese proverb says, "Tell me and I forget. Show me and I remember. Involve me and I understand."

Follow the same street paving procedure and Not Verbs chart analysis for Verb Suburb. Since the noun-verb sentence pattern is one of two basic patterns that stand at the core of all the patterns, I want to slow down these lessons. I want to give students an opportunity to "linger over learning" (Sprenger, 2005). Once they have a solid foundation in the concept of nouns and verbs and have built word banks, future lessons will move along efficiently with students working in independent teams and as independent individuals.

Once Noun Town and Verb Suburb are completed, I challenge students to design tests that they could use to determine if a word is a noun or a verb. It might seem counterintuitive to do this after they have created the bulletin boards, but I have found that they need the bank of words before them as they try to design the tests. Explain that scientists have tests to determine if a rock is igneous or metamorphic. They cleave a rock or study its luster. They add substances to see how the rock responds. Could we design similar tests for words? Could we add things to the words? Split the words into parts? Study the structures? It often takes classes an entire period to design the tests. I could have provided the information in a few minutes, but I think that their engagement in the activity enables them to retain and use the information. Research by Bruning, Schraw, and Ronning (1999) shows that students retain more material if they create a context for learning.

Students have found the following to be good tests to determine if a word is a noun.

Test 1. Put the word into a prepositional phrase: in the *morning,* at the *store,* under the *desk,* near the *sidewalk.* If phrase makes sense or sounds right, the last word is probably a noun.

Test 2. Try putting the word *the* in front of a word: the *poodle,* the *computer,* the *pretty.* If the word sounds good or complete behind the word *the,* it is probably a noun; hence, *pretty* is probably not a noun since *the pretty* sounds incomplete.

Test 3. Look for the suffix; sometimes suffixes have shown up in Noun Town often enough that students determined they must be the sign of a noun: *ment, ism, age, or.*

As the students work with the words, they realize that no test is foolproof, but designing and trying the tests does provide an opportunity for students to talk about the form and nature of a noun.

For an extensive list of affixes and roots listed by part of speech, visit http://academic.cuesta.edu/acasupp/as/506.HTM.

Students also have designed tests for verbs. Almost immediately, they realize that verbs make good words for a game of charades. They also realize that verbs have an *ing* form.

Older students might prefer one of these variations of Noun Town and Verb Suburb.

- Cut out the words *NOUNS* and *VERBS* and staple the letters to a bulletin board. Use one piece of poster paper for each letter so that the completed words are quite large. Assign each group to one letter that they will cover with nouns or verbs.
- Have teams create noun and verb posters with a variety of technology: Word Art in PowerPoint, Glogster, Poster Printing Blog, KidPix, or any number of technology tools can be used to create attractive posters. Whatever the students' level of expertise with technology, you can find a tech tool for your classroom.
- Create enormous classroom mobiles from the words *NOUN* and *VERB*. Each team is given one large letter to cover on both sides with noun or verbs. Hang these from the ceiling. I did not like this activity as well because it was difficult for the students to use the finished mobiles as a word bank when they began writing sentence patterns. The mobiles were often too far away, and they moved, making it difficult for the students to zero in on nouns and verbs.
- In *Teaching Grammar: What Really Works*, Benjamin and Berger (2010) create Verb Villages inhabited by irregular verbs. They identify seven groups of irregular verbs based on patterns.

CREATING NOUN BANKS

Materials

Charts for brainstorming nouns

Procedure

Prepare the chart ahead of time. I make a simple chart in Microsoft Word like the one in Figure 2.1. Fill in several blank headings with generic terms (floodlight words). Students will brainstorm specific nouns (flashlight words) that fit under the generic headings. I find it easiest to do this activity if students have access to computers and a spreadsheet or a word processing program. It is easier that way for students to add lines to the chart. The software also can alphabetize lists of words, making it easier for students to work with the word bank when they begin practicing all of the sentence patterns.

Encourage students to brainstorm for specific nouns to fit under the generic headings. Encourage students to visualize. Ask: "When I say the word *occupations*, what pictures pop into your mind?" Hopefully, they visualize specific occupations, such as farmer, rock star, pharmacist, Avon Lady, astronaut, and banker. They should think of people associated with each category. Under Politics, students could add *governor, senator, lobbyist, mayor,* or *campaign manager.* Under Technology, students might list *computer, data processor, programmer, Twitter,* and so on.

Figure 2.1 Chart for Brainstorming Nouns

Football	Politics	Entertainment	School
Technology	**Dance**	**Relatives**	**Occupations**

This noun bank will become a valuable tool as students practice the twenty-four sentence patterns introduced in Chapter 3. I have vivid memories of coming home as a child with this assignment: Write ten declarative sentences. Every sentence I managed to put on paper began *The boy, The girl, My mom,* or *My sister.* I knew other words—*astronaut, banker, pharmacist*—but those words were not part of my daily vocabulary, so I simply did not think of using them in a sentence while I struggled with homework. I used the words that were part of my daily schema and created a lot of dreadfully dull sentences. Having a noun bank to use would have given me better options.

Students who have a noun bank for reference can generate interesting sentences rapidly. The noun bank eliminates the whine, "I don't know what to write." One of the biggest blockades that students face when trying to write is lack of content knowledge. The noun bank provides content. Tell students, "Select a noun and visualize what that noun is doing. The picture you see will give you the vivid verb needed to write a sentence. So if you select the word *pharmacist,* visualize what she is doing and write that sentence." Visualization provides vivid verbs. The pharmacist counts pills. The pharmacist prints labels. The pharmacist struggles with the doctor's chicken-scratch handwriting. The pharmacist calls the doctor's office for more information. The pharmacist explains dosages. Anyone who has visited a pharmacist can visualize these actions and create the sentences.

One word of caution: Do not let students fall into the trap of using a ten-dollar word when the ten-cent version will do. The goal of building noun and verb banks is to have specific nouns and vivid verbs at their fingertips. Show the students how to use words that allow the reader to visualize. Writers must make decisions. Consider the following sentences:

- *The dog growled.* Ask students to visualize the dog. Some might see a poodle, others a German shepherd or a collie. The noun *dog* is general, or a floodlight word, and allows readers to visualize anything from their background knowledge.
- *The German shepherd growled.* Now everyone should be seeing a similar dog because *German shepherd* is a flashlight word. While the coloring and size of the dog might vary, the breed is consistent. The writer has controlled the readers' visualizations.
- *The Canis lupus familiaris growled.* Okay, this is just silly. The ten-dollar word is obscure and interferes with a reader's comprehension. But students often think that large words, no matter how obscure, are the equivalent of good writing.

You can model this exercise with verbs as well.

- *My grandma walked.* This sentence is grammatically correct, but the weak verb *walked* allows for numerous visualizations.
- *My grandma shuffled.* The verb *shuffled* provides a great deal of inferential information about Grandma and creates a more exact picture in every reader's mind.
- *My grandma perambulated.* The obscure word *perambulate* adds a level of complexity to the sentence and does not bring any benefits. The obscure word interferes with comprehension and creates no visuals.

Additional sets of sentences for this activity are listed below.

- *My sister asked. My sister begged. My sister supplicated.*
- *The ghost howled. The goblin howled. The supernatural being howled.*
- *They tricked me. They swindled me. They cozened me.*

THE LADY WALKED

Materials

Several noun-verb sentences such as the following:

- The lady walked.
- The man rushed.

- The child cried.
- The dog barked.
- The child spoke.
- The car stopped.
- The weather threatened.
- The animal ran.
- The woman smiled.
- The flowers grew.
- The man fell.

Procedure

Display a sentence from the suggested list. Ask students to take a minute to visualize the sentence. For example, for "The lady walked," students should visualize a lady walking. Ask some students to share what they see. Ask them to be specific. I have had students tell me that they saw a model on a runway, their grandma in the grocery store, or a teacher walking down the hall.

Next I say: "I gave all of you the exact same sentence and the same task. I asked you to visualize. But you are all seeing something different. I think you all did the assignment wrong. What happened?"

The students waste no time in telling me that they did exactly what I asked of them. They visualized a lady walking, but I didn't tell them enough about the lady. That is why everyone saw a different lady. Everyone has different experiences or background knowledge.

Then I issue this challenge: Rewrite the sentence in a way that will control the readers' visualizations. Rewrite it so that everyone in this room visualizes the same lady. The rewrite can only use three words, and one of the words must be *the*.

Let the students struggle. Often they want to fix the sentence by embedding an adjective. The *tall* lady walked. The *old* lady walked. Remind them—only three words in the new sentence, and one word must be *the*. Eventually someone will respond with a sentence that uses a specific noun: The cheerleader walked. The nurse walked. The astronaut walked.

At this point I might stop for a quick discussion of gender. *Cheerleader, nurse, astronaut*—none of those words are gender specific for female, but I allow them since a lady can be a cheerleader, nurse, or astronaut. I actually encourage these words. If the sentence were embedded in a longer piece of writing, the reader would have sufficient information to gather that the nurse, the cheerleader, or the astronaut is female. We discuss one of the sentences: *The cheerleader walked.* The students realize that no one is seeing a model, a grandmother, or a nurse at this point. We might be seeing differences in cheerleaders: different uniforms, different physical features such as hair color or height, but we all see a cheerleader.

Next, I ask the students about the word *walked.* How did the cheerleader walk? Remember, I want one strong verb, not a wimpy verb with an adverb attached. They realize that the verb also creates specific visualizations. The cheerleader *pranced.* The cheerleader *limped.* The sentences are strikingly different. Students begin to understand that the power of the verb creates visualizations and inferences. We can infer that the cheerleader is injured if she is limping.

Now we return to "The lady walked." Students work in small teams to generate new sentences. They have generated a wide range of replacement sentences.

- The cheerleader skipped.
- The coach stomped.
- The queen stumbled.
- The astronaut tottered.
- The model sashayed.
- The nurse sprinted.
- The nun strolled.
- The skater staggered.

Finally, have them select one of the sentences and ask them to visualize again. For example, if we all visualize "The nurse sprinted," students find that they visualize much more than just a woman dressed in white. Many students note that they see an emergency room and a great deal of commotion. Others see an accident scene. The power of specific nouns and vivid verbs becomes apparent. By using specific words, the author can help the reader to make inferences, draw conclusions, and create detailed visualizations. The reader can infer that a crisis is looming because the nurse sprints. Using their schema, readers can visualize settings that might demand a nurse to be sprinting. All of this can be accomplished by using specific nouns and verbs.

The Common Core State Standards (National Governors Association Center for Best Practices and Council of Chief State School Officers, 2010, all rights reserved) require that students conduct close readings of texts. Paying close attention to an author's choice of words is one skill needed in close reading. Students become aware of the nuances and connotations that a skilled writer can deliver through word choice. Writers make decisions that affect the message they want to deliver.

Using generic or floodlight nouns and verbs gives readers permission to visualize anything they want. The author can direct the readers' inferences and visualizations by using specific nouns and verbs or flashlight words.

SENTENCE SLAM

Materials

Posters with intransitive verbs splashed about randomly. I write the verbs with large markers in different colors and have them running in all directions. I use past tense verbs to avoid issues with subject-verb agreement during the game, but creating posters with a mixture of singular and plural verb forms increases the difficulty level. The suggested intransitive verbs in Figure 2.2 would be enough for four or five posters.

Figure 2.2   Verbs and Nouns for Sentence Slam

Verbs for Poster			
jogged	shouted	burned	rested
balked	bawled	burped	boasted
dieted	retired	crashed	spat
cheated	called	danced	twirled
left	disappeared	fainted	flinched
boiled	worried	fell	walked
glittered	twinkled	hissed	limped
lied	ran	jumped	cried
flew	galloped	loped	hurried
meditated	murmured	nodded	posed
growled	snarled	purred	cackled
giggled	wiggled	shouted	awoke
returned	screamed	sneered	sat
smiled	waved	stared	laughed

Nouns for 3 × 5 Cards			
astronaut	pharmacist	Santa Claus	ballerina
snake	governor	mechanic	truck driver
pitcher	accountant	author	poet
swimmer	gymnast	emcee	judge
banker	barber	cyclist	referee
umpire	librarian	rancher	biologist
chemist	marine	pilot	blacksmith
programmer	ringmaster	water	computer
clouds	chef	senator	principal

You also will need 3 × 5 cards with one specific noun on each card. Having the nouns on the cards keeps the game moving at a lively pace. Any specific noun will work, but I have often used the nouns in Figure 2.2.

Procedure

Display one poster of verbs, and make sure it is anchored securely to a wall. Students will form teams of four. Team A stands in a line to the right of the poster; Team B lines up to the left. Preview the verbs and provide definitions or examples as needed. The first player for Team A will race against the first player for Team B. Explain that you will call out one noun. The first person to slap a verb and say a simple noun-verb sentence will be given one point.

For example, call out the noun *swimmer.* The Team A player slaps the verb *giggled* and says, "The swimmer giggled." The Team B player slaps the verb *worried* and says, "The swimmer worried." The point will be awarded to the player that says the complete sentence first. They must say the complete noun-verb sentence, not just the verb. These two players for Team A and Team B move to the back of the line, and whoever is second in each line comes to compete. The first team to reach five points wins.

General Rules

1. No one may argue about which team was first to say the sentence.

2. Verbs cannot be used more than once in a game.

3. The sentence can be silly but must make sense.

Rule 3 can lead to interesting discussions, especially if you call out a noun that is not a person or occupation. Students see that words such as *computer* or *cloud* actually can pair up with almost any of the verbs to create a metaphor, personification, or imagery. The computer *hissed.* The computer *flinched.* I ask students to explain a situation where a computer might actually flinch. If they can explain that the sentence could be a personification in a piece of text about someone pounding on the keyboard, I award them the point.

I also like to have the final sentences written on a board or on a projection system. After calling out the word, I hand the noun card to a student sitting at a computer. This student types in the noun and then adds the verb once a team has created a winning sentence. This allows students to see basic noun-verb sentences as well as hearing them. It also keeps track of which verbs have been used. This game reaches all learning styles: kinesthetic, auditory, and visual.

Sentence Slam might seem silly, but the game is highly effective to teach students the core elements of sentences: nouns and verbs. I have asked students in hundreds of schools for the definition of a sentence, and they all respond something like this: "A sentence is a group of words with at least one subject and verb put together to make a complete thought." But when I show them a simple two word sentence such as "Birds fly" and ask them if it is a sentence, many students are unsure. They think a sentence should be longer. Some students point to the fact that it has a capital and a period, so it must be a sentence. They do not understand the concepts; they have merely memorized a definition. Memorizing the definition of a sentence is not enough. Students must manipulate nouns and verbs to create sentences in their most basic structure of noun-verb.

In his excellent book *Mechanically Inclined,* Jeff Anderson (2005) provides complete instructions for a similar activity called Two-Word Sentence Smack Down. This activity helps students to deconstruct sentences and find the basic noun-verb pattern.

RELAY RACE

Materials

One piece of paper per team and pens or pencils for each student

Procedure

Students form teams of five or six students per team. It does not matter if some teams have five members and other have six since students will work individually within the team. I like to have the teams sitting at tables or in rows so that no one has to move and the teams can work quietly and efficiently.

Each team needs one piece of paper, which should be labeled with a team number. When I say, "Go," the teams will begin writing specific nouns, one person at a time. Player 1 will write one noun and pass the paper to the next player. That player will write one noun and pass the paper to the next player. The paper continues to circulate from player to player, each writing one noun every time, until I call "Stop."

General Rules

1. No talking is allowed; the game is played in silence.

2. You must write something every time the paper is in your possession. You can cross out a misspelled word and correct it, or you can write a new noun. You cannot do both.

3. You cannot leave your seat.

4. Your team will receive one point for every word that is a noun.

5. Words must be spelled correctly to earn a point.

6. When I call "Stop," you may finish writing your word but all other pencils must be laid down.

The rules are simple and the game moves quickly. I don't let this game drag on very long. I like to use it as a filler at the end of a class period or as a break from drudgery.

After the game ends, I collect the papers. Students must listen as the list from each team is read. It is the students' responsibility to listen for words that are not nouns or for words that repeat. I check the spelling. The team with the most points wins the game. Sometimes to add to the fun, I tell students that I will give five bonus points to one team. The bonus points are awarded to the team that writes a specific noun that most impresses me. Each team should circle one noun after I call stop. Select the one noun that you think will most impress me. I give the bonus points to the team with the most specific, most creative, most exciting noun. All decisions are final!

Obviously, this game can be played for any part of speech that you want to review.

NOUN–VERB STORIES

Materials

Writing materials

Procedure

Allow the students to work in pairs or groups of three. Model how to write a story that uses only noun-verb sentences.

Sample stories for modeling:

- Dad slept. Scruffy growled. The burglar crawled. Scruffy attacked. The burglar howled. Dad awoke. Sirens wailed. The police arrived.
- The leaves fell. Dad raked. The piles grew. The skies darkened. The wind blew. The leaves swirled. The leaves danced. The piles disappeared. Dad groaned.
- The snow fell. The wind blew. The drifts grew. The phone rang. "School cancelled." The students cheered.

Ask students what they observe about these stories. They should notice that the stories are short and that all sentences follow the noun-verb pattern.

Point out that the stories also have the necessary elements of story: characters, setting, plot with rising action, a problem and a solution.

Brainstorm some ideas or topics for simple stories:

- A cooking or baking disaster
- A flat tire
- Arriving late for an event
- Caught in a rain storm
- Catching a foul ball
- Spilling or dropping something

Let the students try to create a short story of no fewer than five and no more than fifteen noun-verb sentences. Circulate to each group to make sure they are on target and using only the noun-verb pattern.

This activity looks easy on the surface, but actually it is quite difficult. It requires skills, abilities, and knowledge: visualization, organization, vocabulary, creativity, and an understanding of story structure. I usually reserve this activity for junior high students; I think it could be difficult and frustrating for younger students.

Keep these stories so that students can add to the sentences as they learn the next three parts of speech: adjectives, adverbs, and prepositional phrases.

GRAPHIC ORGANIZER SENTENCES

Materials

A graphic organizer with a few sentences for modeling

Procedure

Create the simple graphic organizer like the one shown in Table 2.1 and challenge students to create noun-verb sentences. Sometimes, I use this as an assessment after the students have completed several of the previous activities. If I am using it as an assessment, I have students working individually after I have modeled. It could be used also as a brainstorming tool with students working in small groups or pairs. If I use it for brainstorming, I have the students to select one person from each group to write while everyone else provides ideas. I also tell them to be creative about spelling, since the idea is to generate as many sentences as possible in a short time. If they worry about spelling, they do not generate as many sentences. But I do want them to use capitals and ending punctuation.

Table 2.1

Noun	Verb
The shortstop	tripped.
The quarterback	practiced.
The hippo	slumbered.
The butter	melted.
The detective	searched.
The magazine	ripped.
The hamburger	sizzled.

For a variation of graphic organizer sentences, give students a topic that they have recently studied in a content area class or in art, music, or PE. Let the students work in groups to brainstorm noun-verb sentences related to that topic. For example, perhaps your fourth-grade students have studied the muscular system in science (see Table 2.2). How many noun-verb sentences can they generate related to the muscular system?

Table 2.2

Noun	Verb
Tissues	work.
The heart	pumps.
Muscles	move.
Muscles	shorten.
Muscles	contract.
Muscles	relax.
Muscles	strain.
Muscles	tear.
Muscles	heal.

Again, this might seem like a ridiculously simple activity. But in the few minutes it takes students to brainstorm these sentences, they have reviewed some basic scientific concepts and have reinforced the idea of a noun-verb sentence.

SLAP—CLAP—SNAP—SNAP

Procedure

Students stand in a circle; I've found that groups of seven or eight work well for this activity. First students must get into the rhythm of the game. Students slap hands on their thighs, clap their hands, and then snap first with the right hand and then the left hand. Have the students do these motions together: slap—clap—snap—snap. Do this a few times to make sure that all students have the rhythm. Then the fun begins.

Students begin to call out nouns and verbs to create sentences. One word is called every time they snap the fingers on their right hand. Player 1 calls out a noun on the first snap. Keeping that noun in mind, Player 2 must call out a verb on the next snap of the right hand. That verb will create a noun-verb sentence. Anyone who cannot call out a word is eliminated. Nouns and verbs cannot be repeated. A game might sound like this:

slap—clap—*dogs*—snap/slap—clap—*growl*—snap

slap—clap—*cars*—snap/slap—clap—*race*—snap

slap—clap—*parents*—snap/slap—clap—*frown*—snap

slap—clap—*the computers*—snap/slap—clap—*crashed*—snap

Students will drop out quickly because it requires great concentration to come up with words and keep the rhythm of the slap—clap—snap—snap moving. Some students have discovered that if they call out an inanimate noun, the next person's task is difficult.

slap—clap—*the rock*—snap/slap—clap—*????*—snap

It is more difficult to come up with a verb for *rock* than it is for a noun such as *dog, farmer,* or *rock star.* Rocks don't do much. The rock *weathered.* The rock *eroded.* The rock *fell.* The rock *crumbled.* But it is difficult to think of that in a fast-paced game.

Again this is a game that I use when students need a break or to fill in a few moments at the end of a class period. It is also the game that students want to play frequently.

Variation: Sometimes I use this game to teach forms of irregular verbs, which I discuss with students when we begin studying the noun-verb-noun sentence pattern.

I agree with my favorite author, Amy Benjamin, who recommends that you "drill your students on the preferred forms of irregular verbs. Why? Because patterns are learned though repetition" (Benjamin & Berger, 2010, p. 32). To help students internalize the irregular verb forms, I return to the slap—clap—snap—snap game. Students gather in a circle and begin the rhythm: slap their thighs—clap hands—snap right—snap left. Once the rhythm is established, the teacher calls out the base form of an irregular verb on the slap. The students then call out the progressive form on the clap, the past form on the first snap, the past participle form on the second snap (see Table 2.3).

Table 2.3

SLAP—Base (Teacher Provides This Word)	CLAP—Progressive	SNAP—Past	SNAP—Participle
bite	biting	bit	bitten
bleed	bleeding	bled	bled
bring	bringing	brought	brought
drive	driving	drove	driven
see	seeing	saw	seen

I prefer to be the one to call out the base verb so that I can keep the game moving. I want all of the students to chant the forms of the verb in order to reinforce the forms. Lists of irregular verbs can be found easily in any textbook or through a simple Internet search.

I HAVE/WHO HAS

Materials

A deck of cards, prepared as described below

Procedure

I originally read about this game in an Idea Exchange for English Teachers. (Kutiper, 1983). My students loved playing I have/who has, but in all honesty, I am not certain if it helped any of them to internalize the verb forms. You will need to create a deck of cards, one card for every student in the class. Each card will have this template: I have _____. Who has_____? Fill in the blanks with a verb form. It is imperative that the cards come full circle. Here is an example of what a short game might sound like as students read their cards.

Student 1: I have *begin*. Who has the present participle of *raise*?

Student 2: I have *raising*. Who has the past form of *sit*?

Student 3: I have *sat*. Who has the base form of *found?*

Student 4: I have *find*. Who has the base form of *began?*

Student 1: I have *begin*. And this is where the game ends.

If each student has read a card, then probably no one has made a mistake. But if someone has not read, then a mistake has been made at some point. For example, if Student 2 asks for the past form of *sit*, someone might answer, "I have *sitting*." If no one catches the error, the game will continue but several cardholders will not get to read aloud.

To encourage listening skills, I instructed the students that they cannot speak out when a mistake is made nor can they call out the verb that is needed. The game must keep moving. Inevitably, someone would make a mistake and the body language of the students who caught it gives away the error. The game is especially difficult if you include similar irregular verbs such as *rise* and *raise, lie* and *lay*, and any of the forms of *be*.

ADDING JEWELRY TO NOUN-VERB SENTENCES

Teachers often ask me, "How many days should I teach nouns and verbs to the students before moving on to other parts of speech?" I have a difficult time answering that question because I think that assessment must drive instruction. I have had eighth-grade classes that needed to work with the noun-verb activities for a full two weeks. I have had third-grade students who needed no more than three days to develop a strong grasp of the concepts. Do not use every activity; choose the activities that will resonate with your students and prepare them to move on to more complex structures. Do not drive the activities into the ground either. Teachers are professionals. They know how to assess students and how to determine the needs and strengths of their students. I have no intention of providing a teaching script. Teachers do not need scripts to teach; teaching is an art. My goal is not to provide a step-by-step procedure to teachers. Rather, I hope to honor teachers by allowing them to make sound pedagogical decisions.

When I first began teaching the sentence patterns, I made mistakes, and you can learn from my mistakes. I decided that once students understood the noun-verb pattern, I would move them immediately on to the noun-verb-noun pattern. It seemed like a logical next step. After all, I was only asking students to add one more word to a now firmly entrenched pattern. I envisioned one quick lesson that would dazzle my students; they would then create noun-verb-noun sentences with no effort. From there I would move on to the other parts of speech. Wow, did I miss the boat on that one.

Instead of brilliant moments of writing, my classroom was filled with the weeping and gnashing of teeth. I have learned that it was easier to teach students about adjectives, adverbs, and prepositional phrases before moving on to the second basic pattern. I would suggest keeping the students immersed in the noun-verb pattern while you teach adjectives, adverbs, and prepositions, before moving on to the next pattern.

A SMORGASBORD OF ACTIVITIES FOR ADJECTIVES

For those looking for an amazing, utterly fascinating, stupendous, functional, and substantial Web site that provides lists of the parts of speech, please visit www.momswhothink.com/reading/list-of-adjectives.html. The MomsWho Think.com site has extensive lists of words alphabetized and categorized by nouns, verbs, preposition, adjectives, adverbs, pronouns, and rhyming words. It can provide students with usable content as they work their way through the twenty-four patterns.

I have two authors that I like to introduce to the students when we are learning the parts of speech: Ruth Heller and Brian P. Cleary. Both authors have written books that focus on specific parts of speech. In *Hairy, Scary, Ordinary: What Is an Adjective?* Cleary (2000) dances through the pages providing adjectives for nouns common to a student's life. Prosmitsky's illustrations add a hilarious visual for every adjective. Heller (1989), the author and illustrator of *Many Luscious Lollipops*, provides delightful information on the types of adjectives: predicate adjectives, demonstratives, articles, and proper adjectives. Both authors have published books on other parts of speech too.

Before we move on to studying adjectives and adverbs, let me offer one final word of caution. I want students to focus on specific nouns and vivid verbs when they write. I do not want students creating fluffy, overblown, verbose, overinflated, grandiose pieces of text by using lengthy, overdrawn, cumbersome, endless strings of adjectives. (Irritating isn't it?) "Kicking things off with adjectives is a little like starting a kids' birthday party with the broccoli course. Because as far as not getting respect goes, adjectives leave Rodney Dangerfield in the dust" (Yagoda, 2007, p. 15).

ADJECTIVE AVENUE

Materials

If you recall, I suggested that when you create Noun Town, it would be a good time to reserve an area for Adjective Avenue. You will need a source of adjectives as well, so that students can pave Adjective Avenue the same way they paved the streets of Noun Town.

Procedure

I return to some of the noun-verb sentences we have created and add adjectives to these. I share these new sentences with the class and ask them if each sentence is still the noun-verb pattern.

Samples of noun-verb sentences with adjectives:

- The clumsy queen stumbled.
- The queasy astronaut tottered.
- The grubby detective searched.
- The glossy magazine ripped.
- The ancient computer crashed.

Most students tell me that these sentences are not noun-verb sentences because an extra word has been added. I explain that these are indeed noun-verb sentences. A sentence by its nature has two parts: the noun part and the verb part. As long as those two parts are present and working together to create sense, we have a sentence. But we can add numerous other elements to each part of a sentence and still have the basic noun-verb pattern at the core. My goal is to broaden students' concept of a sentence.

In the examples provided, I have added one word to the noun part of the sentence. The word that has been added is an adjective. I tell students that an adjective is like a piece of jewelry. We do not need that sparkly necklace to create an outfit, but sometimes it adds a bit of punch to a humdrum wardrobe.

An adjective is a word that describes a noun. Adjectives tell us what kind, which one, or how many. I have students look at the sentences again and determine what type of information each adjective has provided.

- The clumsy queen stumbled. What kind of queen? A clumsy queen.
- The queasy astronaut tottered. What kind of an astronaut? A queasy astronaut.
- The grubby detective searched. What kind of detective? A grubby detective.
- The glossy magazine ripped. Which magazine ripped? The glossy magazine.
- The ancient computer crashed. Which computer crashed? The ancient computer.

The students quickly see that a fine line of distinction exists between what kind and which one. An adjective can often answer both questions. *Queasy astronaut* might tell us which astronaut as well as what kind of astronaut.

I have one more thing that I want students to understand about adjectives: They need to be anchored to a noun. The adjective is found most commonly in front of the noun it describes, but later we will learn ways to manipulate the adjective. We will look at the idea of adjectives being anchored to nouns when we study the noun-verb-noun pattern. I want students to see that anchoring the adjective to a different noun changes the meaning of the sentence.

Before I have the students pave Adjective Avenue, I might do a relay race on adjectives. Students already are familiar with the activity, so it goes quickly. We can use the adjectives from the relay race to pave Adjective Avenue. And I have the students write the adjectives on a paper cut in the shape of an anchor.

ADJECTIVE BOXES

Materials

Create a chart with twenty-six boxes and a letter of the alphabet for each box.

Procedure

Students work in teams to generate adjectives for every letter of the alphabet. You might want to assign a topic to the graphic organizer. For example, if one wanted to write a story about a day at a baseball game, what are some adjectives that might be used? Other possible topics include a surprise birthday party, a day at the beach, or a trip to your favorite restaurant. Ideas are limitless.

Variation: You can give students a list of nouns from Noun Town, or any other noun bank they have created, and have them write an adjective in front of each noun.

EXTENDED STORIES

Materials

Remember the stories that the students wrote using only noun-verb sentences? The students will need them. And if you have created Adjective Avenue or completed a graphic organizer for adjectives, allow students to access those as well.

Procedure

Students should embed two or three adjectives in their short stories. Do not allow them to add an adjective to every sentence.

- Dad slept. Scruffy growled. The chunky burglar crawled. Scruffy attacked. The burglar howled. Dad awoke. Sirens wailed. The fearless police arrived.
- The vibrant leaves fell. Dad raked. The piles grew. The skies darkened. The crisp wind blew. The leaves swirled. The leaves danced. The piles disappeared. Dad groaned.
- The snow fell. The powerful wind blew. The icy drifts grew. The phone rang. "School cancelled." Joyous students cheered.

APPETIZING ADJECTIVES

Materials

A variety of menus from a range of restaurants. I especially like to find menus online from upscale restaurants because they provide the best vocabulary words.

Procedure

Students work in groups to study menus and create a list of adjectives that make the dishes sound scrumptious. At this point I do not discern between adjectives and participles that work as adjectives. I want students to understand the function of an adjective: a word that works to describe a noun. Students then use these adjectives to rewrite the school menu so that it sounds like the menu of an elegant restaurant. This makes a wonderful book to present to the cafeteria staff.

Table 2.4 provides a sampling of some of the interesting adjectives students have found while studying menus. What a fun way to build vocabulary.

Table 2.4

ambrosial	appealing	aromatic	baked
bite-size	buttery	broasted	caramelized
chilled	dazzling	decadent	delectable
drizzled	dulcet	encrusted	exquisite
flaky	heaping	heavenly	honey-glazed
intense	lavish	lip-smacking	luscious
mouthwatering	palatable	piquant	pungent
sautéed	savory	silky	simmered
smothered	sprinkled	succulent	tantalizing
tempting	velvety	zesty	zingy

Obviously, some vocabulary work is needed before students can begin writing with these words. For many of the words, I supply a student-friendly definition. I also have assigned one word to each student whose task is to find a picture of a food having that characteristic, post the picture, the word, and a definition. After a time, I take down the words, leaving only the pictures and the definitions, which I have numbered. Students then try to supply the vocabulary word for each picture. For some of the words, I bring food to class: ambrosial salad loaded with pineapples, marshmallows, and mandarin oranges; succulent peaches; dulcet puddings; or pungent horseradish dip. Students who want may sample the food and describe what they tasted.

Once students have a grasp of the words, they rewrite the school lunch menu. The new lunch menu might look like this:

- Delectable hamburgers on fresh-baked buns with a secret piquant sauce
- Tantalizing green salad drizzled with an ambrosial ranch dressing
- Silky cold milk

Variation: I have had students ask if they could rewrite the menu to sound like items on the television program *Fear Factor.* As much as I resist this activity, I often lose and let the students have fun with the *Fear Factor* menu.

DEGREES OF ADJECTIVES

Materials

Sets of adjectives that are synonyms

Procedure

I want students to be selective when they use adjectives in a sentence, not just to throw in an adjective willy-nilly. They must understand that words create images and carry a message. To get them to understand this, I have teams of students study a set of synonyms and rank order the words. Let's look at the following list of adjectives: cool, cold, chilly, nippy, brisk. The dictionary definition of each adjective is similar; they all describe cold weather. But clearly, the adjectives have different connotations or different shades of meanings. I have the students discuss the words and then rank them from the word that creates a visualization of least cold to the word meaning the coldest.

I also want students to understand that they might disagree on the ranking of the words because we have different experiences and background knowledge. The value of the activity comes in the student discussions and the opportunity to think about and visualize each word. One student might rank the words this way: cool, chilly, nippy, cold, brisk. Another student might rank them: cool, chilly, nippy, brisk, cold. Either ranking could be correct. My concern would lie with the student who insists that cool expresses the coldest temperature because that ranking would reflect a lack of comprehension.

I have used the adjectives in Table 2.5 for this activity. Students must rank the words by degrees: smallest to largest, degrees of temperature, degrees of emotion, and so on. This activity can be simplified by reducing the number of words in each set; give the students three words to rank instead of five. Watch for those tired adjectives that your students use repeatedly and use them to create sets of words for this activity.

Table 2.5

1.	frightened	startled	terrified	scared	afraid
2.	nervous	skittish	unstrung	anxious	jittery
3.	happy	joyous	content	ecstatic	elated
4.	sad	downcast	blue	miserable	crestfallen
5.	tired	fatigued	exhausted	worn out	weary
6.	silly	foolhardy	ridiculous	inane	ludicrous
7.	big	huge	gigantic	large	enormous
8.	sweet	pleasant	good-natured	kind	lovable
9.	bad	wicked	mischievous	evil	naughty
10.	little	tiny	petite	itsy-bitsy	wee
11.	friendly	pleasant	cordial	chummy	outgoing
12.	wet	soaked	drenched	damp	soggy
13.	messy	cluttered	untidy	littered	jumbled
14.	dirty	grimy	soiled	grubby	filthy
15.	angry	irritated	riled	furious	boiling
16.	upset	crabby	flustered	annoyed	troubled

This activity also can be used with other parts of speech, but I tend to use it most often with adjectives because I want students to be judicious in their use of adjectives. I want them to think about the adjectives they use and not simply pad their writing. The adjective is often unnecessary because a specific noun and a vivid verb have already created the image.

By sixth grade the Common Core State Standards (National Governors Association Center for Best Practices and Council of Chief State School Officers, 2010, all rights reserved) require students to determine connotations of words. This activity directly supports that requirement.

CC.6.L.5.c Vocabulary Acquisition and Use: Distinguish among the connotations (associations) of words with similar denotations (definitions) (e.g., stingy, scrimping, economical, unwasteful, thrifty).

A SMORGASBORD OF ACTIVITIES FOR ADVERBS

Stephen King provides some brilliant words of caution about adverbs:

. . . they're like dandelions. If you have one on your lawn, it looks pretty and unique. If you fail to root it out, however, you find five the next day . . . fifty the day after that . . . and then, my brothers and sisters, your lawn is totally, completely, and profligately covered with dandelions. By then you see them for the weeds they really are, but by then it's— *GASP!!*—too late." (King, 2000, p. 118)

ADVERB ALLEY

After a day or two of working with adjectives and finishing Adjective Avenue, we complete Adverb Alley in Verb Suburb.

Materials

A source of adverbs to pave Adverb Alley

Procedure

I return to the same noun-verb sentences with embedded adjectives and show them again with embedded adverbs.

- Yesterday the clumsy queen stumbled.
- The queasy astronaut tottered quietly.
- The grubby detective searched deliberately.
- The glossy magazine ripped noisily.
- Suddenly, the ancient computer crashed.

Again I ask the students, "Are these noun-verb sentences?" Some students realize that they still follow the noun-verb pattern but that another word has been added. Some students still think that these sentences have way too many words to be the noun-verb pattern.

To help the students, I sometimes color code the sentences. The noun part of the sentence is highlighted in red; the verb part of the sentence is highlighted in green. This helps students to see that the pattern is still noun-verb, but that I have added additional jewelry. This time I have added an adverb.

Many of the students are quick to note that sometimes the adverb is added to the noun part, other times to the verb part. I am thrilled when they recognize the placement of adverbs because it is one of the first things I want them to understand about adverbs. Adverbs bounce.

Adjectives must be anchored to a noun, but adverbs often can bounce around in a sentence. So we begin playing with the sentence. I ask someone to read the first sentence to me but to put the adverb in a different location.

1.   Yesterday the clumsy queen stumbled.

2.   The clumsy queen stumbled yesterday.

3.   The clumsy queen yesterday stumbled.

We listen to the sentences a few times. I want students to listen closely to determine if each sentence has a pleasant rhythm. Most students can hear that the last sentence is awkward. Placing the adverb between the noun and the verb has interrupted the rhythm of the words. This is an important revision skill that I want the students to understand. Revision is not just about making a piece of text correct; it is also about making the text better. Revision requires the author to make decisions about word choice and placement of words. Simply moving one word in a sentence can make the difference between writing that flows and writing that clunks.

QUESTION THE ADVERB

Materials

*   Sentences containing adverbs
*   Adverb suffix list (*wise, ly, ward*)

Procedure

I teach the students that adverbs are usually easy to find in a sentence. They already know one trick. If they suspect a word might be an adverb, try bouncing it to another part of the sentence. If it can bounce easily without altering the meaning of the sentence, it might be an adverb. Another way to spot adverbs is to look at the suffix. Many adverbs end in the following suffixes:

*   *wise* (edgewise, clockwise, sidewise)
*   *ly* (happily, slowly, cheerfully)
*   *ward* (backward, heavenward, eastward)

Caution students to look beyond just the suffix since words like *backward* and *eastward* can function as adjectives as well. They need to look at the sentence and determine what job the word is doing if they want to know the part of speech.

Adverbs work with verbs, adverbs, or other adjectives. They answer the questions how, when, where, how often, how long, and how much. Return to the sample sentences and ask, "When did the queen stumble?" The answer to that is an adverb: yesterday.

BRAINSTORM BY CATEGORY

Materials

The graphic organizer shown below

Procedure

Adverbs provide the following information: manner, place, time, frequency, degree, or certainty. Let the students work in small groups to brainstorm adverbs according to categories. I simplify the activity by narrowing it to four broad categories.

Manner How Something Is Done	Place Where Something Is Done	Time When Something Is Done	Frequency How Often Something Is Done
noisily	here	yesterday	daily
gently	indoors	today	regularly
quietly	home	suddenly	often

BRAINSTORM BY ACTIVITY

Materials

A list of grade-appropriate verbs with questions

Procedure

Since the adverb works to give additional information about a verb, I list a simple verb and challenge the class to supply three to five adverbs that could describe the verb. I normally do this as a whole-class activity because I do not want to spend a great deal of time on adverbs.

- Tell me how someone might eat: greedily, sloppily, hungrily.
- Tell me how someone might talk: angrily, boastfully, excitedly.
- Tell me how someone might dance: happily, crazily, gracefully.
- Tell me how someone might walk: painfully, triumphantly, cautiously.

This is also a perfect time to discuss whether the adverb is necessary. Use the Which Is Stronger Activity to determine whether a sentence needs an adverb.

WHICH IS STRONGER

Materials

Sets of sentence pairs. One sentence will have an adverb; the other will have a vivid verb.

Procedure

The second part of the Brainstorm by Category activity is to look at the adverb-verb combinations and discuss better alternatives. I tell students, "Please look at the following sets of sentences and decide which one you prefer." Common Core State Standard LR5 (National Governors Association Center for Best Practices and Council of Chief State School Officers, 2010, all rights reserved) requires students to "demonstrate an understanding of word relationships and nuances in word meanings."

- The hikers ate the beef stew greedily.
- The hikers wolfed down the beef stew.
- The sprinter walked off the track painfully.
- The sprinter hobbled off the track.
- The quarterback talked boastfully about beating the crosstown rivals.
- The quarterback boasted about beating the crosstown rivals.

During the course of the year, I jot down sentences from student work that use unnecessary adverbs. These sentences provide material for mini-lessons during writing workshop. With the student author's permission, I share the adverb-weary sentence with the class and ask for alternatives. This quick mini-lesson provides the author with a wealth of new ideas and teaches students an important revision skill. All revision comes down to four skills: add, delete, change, or rearrange information. Students can see that substituting a vivid verb for the weak adverb-verb combination results in stronger sentences.

A SMORGASBORD OF ACTIVITIES FOR PREPOSITIONS

My students always seemed to enjoy learning about prepositions. Learning these tiny words was fun and easy. Also, once students understood prepositional phrases, it became easy for them to deconstruct sentences. By crossing out every prepositional phrase, students could quickly strip a sentence down to the base to reveal a fragment or a run-on. Novice writers often pile up prepositional phrases one behind the other. The "prep phrase"—as my students liked to call it—can destroy the rhythm of a sentence because it allows the writer to use weaker verbs. But a well-placed phrase can allow a piece of writing to ring with clarity and rhythm.

PREPOSITION PARK

Materials

- Construction paper birds in a range of colors
- Materials for creating a bulletin board tree

Procedure

I draw one or two simple birds with their wings outstretched and create pages of them on the copier. Write one preposition on each bird.

For a complete list of prepositions, use a search engine to find any one of dozens of sites. But again, my favorite site for these types of lists is MomsWhoThink.com (www.momswhothink.com/reading/list-of-prepositions. html), which I mentioned earlier for finding lists of adjectives.

Create a large tree on a bulletin board. You can create the tree in a variety of ways. The simplest is to just cut a tree trunk and several branches from brown paper. But I have often stapled dry tree limbs to a bulletin board and created the trunk of the tree from bark. (Be sure to spray all of this with bug spray before bringing it into your classroom; please learn from my mistakes.)

I give each student a paper bird that has a preposition written on it. I keep one bird for myself. I then say, "My bird flew. What type of sentence is that, students?" By now they should all recognize a simple noun-verb sentence.

I say, "My red bird flew." They tell me it is still a noun-verb sentence.

I say "Yesterday my red bird flew." Growing weary, the students respond, "It is still a noun-verb sentence with jewelry."

Next I say, "Yesterday my red bird flew over the tree." And I staple the red bird onto the tree. Some students will say that they think it is still noun-verb; others repeat the sentence to themselves wondering if a sentence with that many words can still be noun-verb.

Explain that they are all holding a bird that has a preposition written on it. Add the words Preposition Park to the bulletin board. And then repeat the sentence, "Yesterday my red bird flew over the tree." (Sometimes I drop the adjective because it is obvious that the bird is red.) At this point, I spend no time teaching anything about the form or the function of a preposition or the prepositional phrase, but challenge the students, "Who can bring a bird to Preposition Park and say a noun-verb sentence that contains a prepositional phrase?" I have never had a class that could not do this, even though I have not yet taught them anything about prepositions.

One by one the students approach with a bird, staple it to the tree, and provide a sentence.

- My bird flew under the tree.
- My bird sat in the tree.

- My bird flew into the tree.
- My bird flew around the tree.
- My bird climbed down the tree.
- My bird walked to the tree.

As each student staples a bird to the tree and says the sentence, ask the class to echo the prepositional phrase. As they hear prepositional phrases over and over, they begin to absorb the form of a prepositional phrase.

PREPOSITIONAL PLATES

Materials

- Paper plates
- Markers
- Construction paper in several colors
- A list of prepositional phrases that function as adverbs

Procedure

Ask students to draw a silly face on paper plates you have provided. The sillier the face, the better. The face can frown, smile, look surprised or angry; any type of face is fine.

Draw several large tongues on a sheet of paper. The tongue must be large enough that you can write a prepositional phrase on it. Copy the tongues onto red or pink construction paper. One sheet of paper should yield about sixteen tongues.

Write an adverb phrase onto each tongue. Some suggested adverb phrases are shown in Table 2.6.

Table 2.6

after lunch	along with my brother	alongside of the curb
amid the chaos	around the corner	at eleven o'clock
because of the storms	before school	beneath the table
beside a large bouquet	beyond the horizon	by noon
considering our height	despite a broken toe	during English class
except for my sister	for seven years	in the evenings
in addition to a bonus	in place of homework	in spite of a downpour
inside our house	instead of clam chowder	like a rocket
near the alley	next to the trash can	on the airplane
on behalf of my friend	on top of the table	prior to our vacation
regarding your bonus	since dinner	throughout the school

Tape the tongue to the plate. I usually make a small slit in the mouth, slip the tongue through, and tape it on the back side. Next, cut several strips of construction paper in a range of colors. Attach five or six strips of paper to the top of the plate to create hair for the face.

Each student should have a plate with hair and a large tongue with a prepositional phrase written on it. Have a few students to read the tongues. Ask students what they hear. They should realize that each tongue has a prepositional phrase. Explain the form of a prepositional phrase: It begins with a preposition, ends with a noun or pronoun, might have adjectives and adverbs between, but will never have a verb. Explain that the prepositional phrase functions as an adverb by telling when, where, why, or how something happened.

Each student writes a sentence on one strip of hair. The sentence should sensibly follow the prepositional phrase. Have some students read the tongue and read the hair so that other students can hear a sentence that begins with a prepositional phrase. Then students should trade plates and write a sentence on the hair of a new plate. Keep trading plates until every piece of hair has a different sentence. All of the plates can be stapled to a bulletin board to make an interesting display.

This activity can be used with any of the patterns discussed in the next chapter. The tongues could have had a subordinate clause, an adverb, a participle, or an infinitive. Students would then write those sentences on the hair.

SING THE PREPOSITIONS

Materials

A list of prepositions

Procedure

At one point in my teaching career, I thought it would help my students to memorize a list of prepositions. I question the wisdom of that now, but at least I made the memorization work fun. We sang lists of prepositions to the tune of *Yellow Rose of Texas*, and did quizzes of ten prepositions per day. Almost any tune will work. I returned the quiz papers to the students every day so they could add ten more prepositions. By the end of the week, each student knew fifty prepositions. Recently, I was grocery shopping and behind me I heard, "As—about—ahead—around—along—against—above—among" to the tune of *Yellow Rose*. I knew immediately that I would turn around to see a former student.

I question the efficacy of memorizing that list because I have since learned that the prepositions *of, to,* and *in* are the second, fifth, and sixth most commonly used words in the English language. Add the prepositions *for, on, with, at, from,* and *by,* and we have the nine prepositions that account for 92.6 percent of all prepositions used (Schuster, 2003). But I have had numerous students tell me that knowing the prepositions helped them to eliminate run-ons. If a sentence seemed to sprawl across several lines, they could cross through the prepositional phrases and the noun-verb structures would remain standing. If they had more than one noun-verb structure, they knew they needed to check for conjunctions or semicolons to prevent a run-on.

FILL IN THE BLANK

Materials

Fill in the blank sentences

Procedure

This activity honors students' acquired knowledge. Provide one of the following sentences and allow groups to fill in the blank with as many words as possible. They will generate a fairly complete list of prepositional phrases. See Schuster (2003) for a similar activity.

- The picture _____ my sister made me laugh.
- The UFO flew _____ the clouds.
- The shed _____ the street burned down.

PENNY HUNT

Materials

Pennies

Procedure

Teachers spend a great deal of their own money purchasing classroom materials, so it is great to find a lesson that costs only pennies. Hide a few pennies around the room. As children find the pennies, they can keep them if they can write a sentence with a prepositional phrase explaining where they found it.

- I found a penny under my desk.
- My penny was hiding behind an eraser.
- I found a penny on top of the bookshelves.
- This penny hid inside the dictionary.
- I found this penny next to the pencil sharpener.

PREPOSITION FLIP BOOKS

These flip books can be used to help students see the difference between a prepositional phrase that functions as an adverb and one that functions as an adjective.

Materials

- Several sheets of paper folded lengthwise
- Stapler
- Sentence chart like the one below
- Colored paper for covers

Procedure

Give students a chart like one of the samples in Table 2.7. Fill in the first two or three lines to model the types of sentences the students should produce. The chart can be made any size needed. Ten sentences is a good number. If all of the verbs are written in past tense, there will be no problem with subject-verb agreement when students begin to flip the pages of the books. One word of caution: Some verbs may result in off-color sentences when students flip the pages of their books.

Table 2.7

Sentences with prepositional phrases that function as adverbs			
Phrase	**Noun**	**Verb**	**Noun**
In the morning	the truckers	loaded	the trucks.
After dinner	the ballerinas	practiced	pirouettes.
Because of the rain	the mayor	canceled	the parade.
In spite of a broken toe	the surgeon	performed	the appendectomy.
Sentences with prepositional phrases that function as adjectives			
Noun	**Phrase**	**Verb**	**Noun**
The pharmacist	behind the counter	measured	the medicine.
The movie star	with a bald head	sang	the ballad.
The ballerina	in a pink tutu	danced	*Swan Lake*.
The truck driver	in a plaid shirt	honked	the horn.

Once students have completed the chart and have ten acceptable sentences, they will be ready to create a flip book. If the students have ten sentences, the book will need ten pages. Add a bright colored cover and staple the book together. Cut the book into three sections, but be careful not to cut all the way to the top. Students next write one sentence on each page of the book.

Then they can flip the pages and create silly sentences because sentence elements will recombine. For example, if the sentences of the adjective book are flipped, the following sentences could be created:

- In spite of a broken toe, the mayor performed pirouettes.
- In the morning the ballerinas cancelled the appendectomy.

Using the adverb book, the following sentences could be created:

- The ballerina with a bald head danced the ballad.
- The truck driver in a pink tutu measured the horn.

By manipulating the sentence elements, students can see and hear that adjective phrases must be anchored to a noun because the adjective phrase describes the noun.

EXTENDED STORIES

Remember the short stories that consisted of nothing but noun-verb sentences? We revisited these stories to add adjectives. Now it is time to add a few prepositional phrases.

Procedure

I caution students to add no more than three prepositional phrases to the story. If they add a prepositional phrase to every sentence, it will sound awkward and formulaic. I also encourage them to add at least one prepositional phrase to the opening of the sentence—the noun part of the sentence.

- Dad slept on the couch. Scruffy growled. The chunky burglar crawled through a window. Scruffy attacked. The burglar howled. Dad awoke. In the distance sirens wailed. The fearless police arrived.
- The vibrant leaves fell. Dad raked for hours. The piles grew. The skies darkened. The cool wind blew. The leaves swirled. Like ballerinas the leaves danced. The piles disappeared in the wind. Dad groaned.
- The snow fell throughout the night. The powerful wind blew. The icy drifts grew into mountains. The phone rang. "School cancelled." Throughout the town joyous students cheered.

Students begin to see the power of adding a few pieces of jewelry, but the specific nouns and vivid verbs still carry the story. By adding at least one prepositional phrase to the opening, students can hear how that addition breaks up the monotony of every sentence beginning with the same word.

EXTRAS

This section contains information that will help students to analyze the craft of writing. Also, this information will be repeated throughout the year. The concept of form versus function can be difficult for students. I introduce it at this point and return to it often as we work with the sentence patterns. Form and function are part of the instructional vocabulary. It is not necessary for every student to master this concept before moving on to new patterns. Understanding of form and function and the facility with irregular verbs will improve throughout the year.

Form Versus Function

By this time, the students have worked extensively with five parts of speech: noun, verb, adjective, adverb, and preposition. I want students to understand the difference between the form of a word and the function of a word. I explain to them that I have one form: I am six feet tall; unfortunately, I probably never will weigh less than I currently do. My hair color is going slowly from blonde to gray. But all in all, I have this one body—this one form.

I do, however, have many different functions. When I am in the classroom with students, I function as a teacher. When I am performing in front of an audience, I function as a storyteller. Some days I function as a wife, a mother, a daughter, a cousin, or a neighbor. No matter which job or function I undertake, I still have this one form. It is my function that changes.

Words are similar. A word might not change its form, but it can function in several roles. Sometimes a word might change its form slightly to take on a new function. For example, the word *parachute* is a noun. By slightly changing the form and adding the letter *d*—*parachuted*—the word can function as a verb.

Together we look at these words and students tell me the form of each word, meaning the way the word is usually used. (For more on form and function, see Benjamin & Oliva, 2007.)

Word	Form
Cat	Noun
Brave	Adjective
Free	Adjective
House	Noun
Foot	Noun

Then we look at some sentences and determine the function of each word.

- *My baby brother took a bite of the cat food.* The form of *cat* is a noun, but *cat* functions as an adjective because it tells us what kind of food. Linguists refer to this as an adjectival.
- *I live in the land of the free and the brave.* The form for *free* and *brave* is adjective, but the words function as nouns because they are the objects of the preposition. Linguists would refer to these as nominals.
- *The new museum in Greenville will house antique tractors.* The form of *house* is noun, but *house* functions as the verb, telling us what the museum will do.
- *I will foot the bill for this dinner with my friends.* The form of *foot* is noun, but *foot* functions as a verb, telling us what I will do.

This is a very simple explanation of form and function, but numerous books and hours of research have been dedicated to the linguistics of form and function. The point of looking at form and function is not to drill students or turn them into linguists. I do not expect them to label every part of speech in a sentence and determine form and function. However, I do find great value in

TEACHING PARTS OF SPEECH

students understanding and recognizing parts of speech. Being able to talk about parts of speech gives us a common vocabulary, but I question the importance of spending precious class time labeling every word in a sentence. I want students to understand form and function of words in order to encourage a sense of play. I want them to experiment with the words to create images and phrases that reach the audience.

I have several authors that I love to use to demonstrate this sense of play or facility with words: Jane Yolen, Pat Polacco, Mem Fox, and Cynthia Rylant to name a few. But one of my favorite authors for showing students how to have fun with words is Libba Moore Gray. Read aloud the following sentence from *My Mama Had a Dancing Heart* and ask students to visualize the beauty and listen to the rhythm of this sentence: "And when the winter snows came softly down shawling the earth, out we'd go and do a body-flat arms-moving-up-and-down snow-angel hello winter ballet" (Gray, 1995, p. 19).

A close reading of that one sentence reveals numerous decisions made by Gray. She began a sentence with the word *and*. I shudder to think how many times in elementary and high school I was told, "Never begin a sentence with the words *and, but,* or *because.*" I never understood why; all I heard was the word *don't*, which severely limited my willingness to experiment with words. Gray places the adverb *softly* between came and down, rather than saying the more common "came down softly." She creates adjectivals by joining words with hyphens. And she plays with form and function. The form of the word *shawl* is noun; she adds an *ing* suffix to change the form and enable the word to function as a verb. She creates a beautiful metaphor: the image of earth wearing a shawl of snow.

Immerse the children in quality literature. Marinate them in beautiful language. Study one author, such as Libba Moore Gray, then have them write sentences that imitate her playful nature. Children learn to write by imitating other writers. Trust them to study the craft of writing and to create beautiful sentences by playing with the form and function of words.

Derivational Affixes

In *Engaging Grammar: Practical Advice for Real Classrooms,* Amy Benjamin offers this explanation of derivational affixes: "Simply stated, they are the prefixes and suffixes that morph a word into another word class (part of speech) or, in some cases, change the meaning." (Benjamin & Oliva, 2007, p. 31)

I have long railed against those dreadful spelling books that require students to complete pages and pages of exercises ad nauseam in order to spell twenty words for the Friday afternoon test. I prefer a range of other activities that provide "just-in-time" learning. Once students understood form and function, give them a graphic organizer like the one in Table 2.8 and ask them to play with the form of a word. Provide one word in each row; the students fill in the empty slots by playing with derivational affixes. I have completed all four slots in this example; however, the students would see only one word per row. Sometimes students had difficulty finding a word for each form, but they delighted in manipulating affixes to create new words such as *applelicious* or *quibblously*.

Table 2.8

Noun	Verb	Adjective	Adverb
mechanic	mechanize	mechanical	mechanically
graph	graphing/graphed	graphic	graphically
book	booking/booked	bookish/booklike	bookishly
apple	applefy	applelicious	appleliciously
quibbler	quibble	quibblous	quibblously

Allowing students to create neologisms might seem foolish to those who have been teaching language arts from a prescriptive stance. By prescriptive, I mean a heavy emphasis on the rules of writing—rules that often begin with the word *don't*. Don't split infinitives. Don't end sentences with prepositions. Don't repeat words. As a student, I never understood any of those rules and found myself afraid to write for fear I might be breaking some nebulous rule. And yet, as I would read, I was certain that many of my favorite authors were breaking the rules, were creating hilarious new words, were omitting commas and semicolons. I want students to understand what Katie Wood Ray tells us in her book *Wondrous Words*, "Language is beautiful, alive, wondrous, and studying the craft of it in use will remind you of this again and again" (Ray, 1999, p. 24).

COMPARING NOUN-VERB TO NOUN-VERB-NOUN

Before beginning to teach the twenty-four patterns, I have students compare the two basic patterns. I want them to have a grasp of the differences and the similarities. This understanding will be the tool to helping students take on the responsibility of revising and editing their own writing.

ASKING WHOM OR WHAT

Materials

A variety of sentences that are noun-verb and some that are noun-verbnoun

Procedure

Show students a list of sentences such as the one in Table 2.9 and ask them to compare the two lists and make note of any similarities or differences.

Table 2.9

The boys played.	The boys played basketball.
My neighbors waved.	Today my neighbors visited their grandma.
The physicist wondered.	The physicist pondered the question.
The aroma wafted through the air.	The fire alarm sounded a warning.
The cat purred.	The cat cleaned its fur.
The race cars rumbled around the track.	The racers revved the engines.
The computer crashed.	The hurricane pounded the coastline.

If the students have been working extensively with noun-verb sentences and adding jewelry, they should be able to quickly identify the sentences in the first column as noun-verb. Once they have noticed that, add the label Noun-Verb Sentences to that column. Let them struggle for a bit with the column on the right. Hopefully, they will recognize that the sentences in the second column do not end in a verb or a prepositional phrase the way those in the first column do.

Explain that the sentences in the second column represent the second pattern, noun-verb-noun, because they use a transitive verb. A quick way to determine if a sentence follows the noun-verb-noun pattern is to ask the question whom or what after the verb. The boys played what? Basketball. The neighbors visited whom? Their grandma. If the word that answers whom or what is a noun, the verb probably is transitive and the sentence probably follows the noun-verb-noun pattern. Label the column on the right Noun-Verb-Noun Sentences.

Many teachers prefer to teach this pattern as subject-predicate-direct object, but I prefer to teach it as noun-verb-noun. Adding abstract terms such as *direct object* simply adds an unneeded layer of difficulty for the students. My goal is to have students write strong, grammatically correct sentences, and I have never felt that knowing labels such as *direct object* offered a great deal of help in doing that. However, I am not creating a scripted set of lessons for teachers. Educators are professionals who must make decisions about instructional vocabulary in their schools and their districts. Teachers who prefer to teach it as subject-predicate-direct object can make that decision.

Students can write strong sentences without attaching a label to every word. I believe that the idea of memorizing rules and terms inhibits a student's creativity and passion for writing. Creative writers "demonstrate exceptional command of the syntactic resources of the language, yet they rarely can name the constructions they use. And the point is that as writers, *they don't need to.*" (Weaver, 1996). I can drive my car, but I could not locate the catalytic converter, voltage regulator, or the distributor. (I'm not completely sure my old car even has any of those things.) But I can drive the car quite capably. Students can and do write sentences with appositives, direct objects, and parenthetical expressions without naming them. And now I will step down from that soapbox and move on to the next lesson.

VERB POEMS

Materials

A noun bank and writing materials

Procedure

Once students have completed a noun bank (such as the chart of nouns or Noun Town), I have each student select one specific noun that they would like to use to create a verb poem. Selecting a person or an occupation rather than an inanimate object usually makes this activity easier. Use the verb poems in Figure 2.3 to model the task.

Figure 2.3 Sample Verb Poems

The Letter Carrier	**The Paleontologist**
Brings mail	Studies fossils
Reads postcards	Reconstructs history
Carries packages	Digs
Drives a little bitty truck	Dates rocks
Waves and smiles	Writes books
Sorts letters	Travels
Sells stamps	Names dinosaurs
Weighs packages	Visits museums
Walks	Identifies bones
Pets dogs	
The Farmer	**The Hair Stylist**
Plows fields	Cuts hair
Plants seeds	Straightens hair
Harvests crops	Gives perms
Drives tractors	Dyes, bleaches, and highlights
Milks cows	Curls and fluffs
Feeds pigs, sheep, ducks, and goats	Teases and sprays
Rests	Braids, weaves, and styles

The completed poems include noun-verb and noun-verb-noun sentence patterns. This activity gives the students an opportunity to manipulate vivid verbs and create a poem that encourages visualization.

Several teachers have told me that they had their students use digital cameras to take pictures of school employees. The students then wrote verb poems about the librarian, school secretaries, janitors, cooks, aides, bus drivers, volunteers, and playground monitors. The students created posters with the pictures and poems as gifts to the various faculty and staff members in the building. Not only is it a proper tribute to important people in the building, it also helps students to realize how hard people work because they believe in the value of education.

CLEARING UP CONFUSION

Materials

A range of sentences such as those below

Procedure

Show students the following sentences and have them determine which follow the noun-verb-noun pattern.

1. The horse jumped over the fence.

2. The horse jumped the fence.

3. The boys raced home.

4. We swam with the dolphins.

5. The soup tasted good.

6. My sister is a pilot.

7. My parents looked after their grandchildren.

In spite of extensive work with the noun-verb pattern, many students will select the first sentence as noun-verb-noun if you have recently taught them the trick of asking who or what after the verb. It is a novelty bump that creates an understandable confusion. The horse jumped what? The fence. We need to stop and ask students about the word *over*. Help them to see that *over the fence* is a prepositional phrase. Since it tells us where the horse jumped, it is an adverb phrase. I mentioned earlier that I used to teach noun-verb and then move immediately to noun-verb-noun. Many of my students found it nearly impossible to understand the structure of sentences such as "The horse jumped over the fence." Fence is very clearly a noun, so they reasoned that the structure should be noun-verb-noun. Once I introduced adjectives, adverbs, and prepositional phrases with noun-verb pattern before teaching noun-verb-noun, students quickly could see the difference in the two patterns.

The third sentence, "The boys raced home." can cause confusion because *home* is a noun. But does it accurately answer the what question? The boys raced what? Home? No, the word *home* tells us where the boys raced and so it functions as an adverb. Granted, it is not an adverb that can bounce, but it does tell us where the boys raced so it functions as an adverb.

The fifth sentence also can create confusion. The soup tasted what? Good. It sounds so logical that it is entirely reasonable to believe that sentence is noun-verb-noun. But is *good* a noun? No it is an adjective. I usually give the students a brief lesson on linking verbs and move on.

I explain that the sixth sentence is indeed a noun-verb-noun and it has a special verb called a linking verb. Again, pick your battles. Classroom time is so precious that I simply have not felt justified in spending extensive time on defining the difference between linking verbs and regular verbs. I understand that this will anger purists and grammarians, but I also know that my students were successful authors who used linking verbs correctly without having to spend hours of class time labeling them. I will address these special verbs when we begin writing all of the patterns.

The final sentence on the list is the most confusing for the students: "My parents looked after their grandchildren." The confusion comes about because *after* functions as a particle. Many linguists will refer to the verb *looked after* as a compound verb or a phrasal verb. (And I have had people argue intelligently that *jumped over* in the first sentence is also a phrasal verb, which makes *fence* a direct object. I disagree because *over* is unnecessary, as the second sentence demonstrates.) Again, I do not want to belabor the point. I want students to understand that some sentences will contain these types of verbs. Sometimes the verb is transitive; sometimes it is intransitive. My parents looked after whom? Their grandchildren.

Other examples of sentences that contain particles:

- My grocery bill *added up* to $47.53.
- I *asked around* about the new restaurant, but no one had any information.
- Bob *speeded up* the motor on our blender.
- The students *acted up* during the movie.
- I *set out* to win the race but lost on the last lap.
- The leaders *hammered out* an agreement to ensure peace in their countries.
- I hope this *clears up* any confusion.

Sentence Patterns by Grade Level

3

This chapter contains a list of the sentence patterns to be taught and models of each pattern by grade. For each pattern I have provided background information for the teacher that provides an explanation of the pattern and some tips or hints that can be used to help students understand it. I also have included Points for Student Analysis section. These are lists of observations that the students should be able to make during their small group discussions of each pattern after they have heard and read the five models. Students might make more observations than I have listed, but they also might miss an important detail. The Points for Student Analysis list will help teachers who need to provide additional instruction or explanation of the pattern. Never assume that students can do a thorough analysis without help. In addition, a reliable English book will provide a much-needed resource for teachers.

In the models, I have italicized the new sentence element for each pattern. For example, when students look at Pattern 7, which places an appositive behind a noun, the appositive is italicized. This helps students to focus on the new element. When I share the five models with the students, I use PowerPoint or a document camera and color code the sentence elements. The basic pattern (N-V or N-V-N) will be one color and the new element in a different color.

See Figure 3.1 for an overview of the sentence patterns and appropriate grade levels.

Figure 3.1 The Sentence Patterns

Grades	Pattern
3–8	Pattern 1: Specific Noun–Vivid Verb
3–8	Pattern 2: Noun-Verb-Noun

3–8	Pattern 3: Interrogative Sentences
3–8	Pattern 4: Open With an Adverb
3–8	Pattern 5: Open With a Prepositional Phrase
3–8	Pattern 6: Compound Sentence With a Coordinating Conjunction
3–8	Pattern 7: An Appositive Behind a Noun
3–8	Pattern 8: Open With an Adverb Clause
3–8	Pattern 9: Close With an Adverb Clause
3–8	Pattern 10: Parallel Items in a Series
3–8	Pattern 11: Parallel Verbs or Verb Phrases in a Series
3–8	Pattern 12: Open With an Adjective or an Adjective Phrase
3–8	Pattern 13: Open With a Present Participle
4–8	Pattern 14: Open With a Past Participle
6–8	Pattern 15: Open With a Present Perfect Participle
6–8	Pattern 16: Open With an Infinitive Phrase
6–8	Pattern 17: Restrictive Adjective Clauses
6–8	Pattern 18: Nonrestrictive Adjective Clauses
6–8	Pattern 19: Compound Sentence With a Semicolon
7–8	Pattern 20: Compound Sentence With an Elliptical Expression
7–8	Pattern 21: Opening With an Absolute
7–8	Pattern 22: Adjectives Moved Behind a Noun
7–8	Pattern 23: Open With a Parallel Structure
7–8	Pattern 24: Using Conjunctive Adverbs to Connect Two Sentences

Once my students developed an understanding of the two sentence patterns, N-V and N-V-N, I began teaching all of the patterns. I chose to teach one pattern per week. This offers them an opportunity to linger over the learning. My students knew that the first day of the week was always dedicated to sentence pattern work. This routine ensured time on task. Students knew that on the first day of the week, they were to come into the classroom, sit in their groups, and turn their attention to the five sentences on display. Each student also had an individual copy of the sentences available. I placed these in their work folders or home drive of their computer every Friday. My students knew that they would be required to analyze the patterns and then write five sentences in their group and five individually. If they did not complete their ten sentences during the class period, they would have to finish it as homework. This knowledge, and the fact that my students enjoyed sentence pattern day, meant that they settled down to the work quickly.

In Chapters 7 and 8, I share writing workshop activities for the remaining days of the week.

As early as third grade, the Common Core State Standards require that students "use linking words and phrases (e.g., because, therefore, since, for example) to connect opinion and reasons" (National Governors Association Center for Best Practices and Council of Chief State School Officers, 2010, CC.3.W.1.c. All rights reserved.). The sentence patterns clearly address this skill since students will work with coordinating conjunctions, subordinators, and prepositional phrases.

STEPS FOR TEACHING THE PATTERNS

Step 1: Read the title of the pattern and then read the five sentences aloud. Use rhythm and intonation to help students understand the pattern. Deal with any vocabulary issues. (two to three minutes)

Step 2: Students next work in teams of three to write a list of observations. What do these five examples have in common? What do you notice about the sentences that will help you when you begin creating your own sentences? Do you notice any consistent patterns of punctuation? Do you notice any inconsistencies in punctuation? Focus on the part in italics; how does the italicized part function in the sentence? Is the italicized part essential? What happens if we eliminate that section? (five minutes)

Step 3: Lead a whole-class discussion of the students' observations. Call on a team that will provide one observation. Make a list of student observations. If necessary, ask questions to make sure they have a complete understanding of the pattern. If the teams have missed an important element about the pattern, provide instruction. (five to seven minutes)

Step 4: Working in teams of three, the students then work to create five sentences that imitate the pattern. The teams have some strict rules to follow while they work.
  o Everyone in the team works on the same sentence at the same time.
  o Everyone in the team writes the sentences produced by the team. Do not expect one student to do all of the writing as others watch; everyone writes the full sentence.
  o Check each other's work to make sure spelling, punctuation, and structure is correct.
  o The following verbs will not be allowed on sentence pattern day: *is, are, was, were, am, be, been, being, seem, seems, get, got, appear, appears, appeared, became, become, go, goes, went.*
  o Every sentence must use vivid verbs and specific nouns.
  o Names of classmates are not be used in the patterns.
  o If proper names are used, it should be someone that everyone likely will know, such as celebrities, world leaders, sports greats, historical figures, and fictional characters.
  o Use your word banks as you work.
  o Once you feel confident that everyone on your team has written a perfect sentence, begin writing another.
  o Once everyone on your team has five sentences that you feel are perfect, your team disbands and everyone writes five sentences individually.

Step 5: Hand in the final sentences. Since the analysis of the five sentences can be completed in fifteen minutes, the students have thirty minutes (in a forty-five-minute block) to write ten sentences that imitate the pattern. Most of my students could complete the work by the end of the class period and hand it in prior to leaving for their next class. At the end of the class period, every student should have fifteen sentences that follow one pattern: five model sentences, five team sentences, and five individual sentences.

Step 6: When the sentences are returned the following day, students place them in a three-ring binder for future reference. Since I never taught in a school that had an English textbook, this binder became our textbook. Students referred to it when they worked on writing assignments. The binders helped them with revision and editing.

THE TEACHER'S ROLE

While the students create sentences that imitate the pattern, the teacher circulates the room to check work and offer assistance as needed. As I circulated the room, I looked for groups that functioned efficiently as well as groups that did not. Remember, as a team they are creating five identical sentences. Each student in the team should be writing the exact same sentence as the other team members. Let's imagine we have a team working on Pattern 10, parallel items in a series.

Team Member 1: Women on the Aran Islands use a honeycomb stitch, a cable stitch, and a basket weave to knit traditional Irish fisherman sweaters.

Team Member 2: Women on the Aran Islands use a honeycomb stitch, a cable stitch, and a basket weave to knit traditional Irish fisherman sweaters.

Team Member 3: Women on the aran Islands using a honeycomb stitch a cable stitch and a basket weave to knit a traditional irish fisherman sweater.

The third team member has obvious problems: missing capitalization, missing punctuation, incorrect verb form. If this team has moved on to writing their next sentence, I need to stop them and determine why. The team needs to understand that they have the following responsibilities.

- Work as a team to create five sentences that imitate the pattern.
- Check each other's work before moving on to the next sentence.
- Listen to one another as ideas are contributed.

I want to know why they are working on a new sentence when one member has numerous errors in the first sentence but the other two have perfect sentences. Is the third team member refusing to cooperate? Are the members not checking each other's work? Why is this team not functioning? They must understand their responsibilities and reach a solution before I let them continue writing.

As I circulate the room, I also check student work for accuracy. I check all three members of the team. I carry a rubber stamp with me and stamp every perfect sentence. (Yes, a marker would work just as well, but even my junior high students seemed to get a kick out of the silly stamps I used: rabbits, stars, and phrases such as "Way to Go.") The students receive instant gratification for their work, and I have sentences that I do not need to review when I am correcting homework. If the sentence has been rubber stamped, I know it is correct. Plus knowing that they have written effective, accurate sentences, the students are motivated to stick with the task and finish the work.

When I find sentences with errors, I stop and do some immediate instruction. Let's imagine that all three members of a team have written the following Pattern 5, open with a prepositional phrase:

- During the French Revolution, stone solitaire was invented by an imprisoned nobleman.

Point out that this sentence uses a form of *be*—*was*—and is in the passive voice. I give the students a chance to correct it. If they struggle, I will show them how to recognize passive voice and how to bring *imprisoned nobleman* to the front of the sentence: During the French Revolution, an imprisoned nobleman invented stone solitaire. The goal is for students to demonstrate a command of the conventions of standard English capitalization, punctuation, and spelling when writing (National Governors Association Center for Best Practices and Council of Chief State School Officers, 2010, CC.K-12.L.R.2. All rights reserved.).

Many teachers who use the patterns have asked me why I refuse to let students use forms of *be* while creating the patterns. They want the students to at least be able to use a form of *be* as an auxiliary. I have found that the students actually enjoy the challenge of avoiding the forbidden verbs, which I have posted on the wall. If they avoid the weak verbs, they will not fall into passive voice. In addition, when students are required to use vivid verbs, they learn how to use the valuable reading and writing strategy of visualization. When students begin creating sentences, I tell them to pull a specific noun from their word banks and visualize an associated activity. A vivid verb will pop into their heads, and the sentence practically writes itself. This awareness of specific nouns and vivid verbs serves students well when they begin writing lengthier text.

I shudder when I think of the writing advice that I heard repeatedly as a student: "Make your writing interesting. Use good vocabulary. Avoid wordiness. Use voice in your writing." And the most ironic piece of advice, "Show them, don't tell them." Yet I never had anyone who could actually show me how to show them. These vague pieces of advice meant nothing to me as a student, and I marveled at the students who did produce that elusive A+ story or essay. I knew that I was hearing greatness, but I had no clue how to create it myself. If someone had just demonstrated the power of specific nouns and vivid verbs, I would have had one foot on the path to showing rather than telling.

The ability to recognize and avoid weak verbs also serves students well when they begin creating lengthier text. Writing demands decision making. Students who can create a range of patterns and who can use specific nouns and vivid verbs also can make intelligent decisions about their writing. They know when a form of *be* is the perfect word for the sentence or when the text demands specificity. Writing must be taught at the sentence level if students are to create strong paragraphs, essays, and narratives.

At the end of the class period, students who have written ten sentences put their papers into the homework box for their grade. I looked forward to grading these papers because it was one of my easiest jobs as a teacher. Grabbing a stack of papers, I skimmed down the work and bypassed anything with a rubber stamp; those sentences had already been checked in class. For many students, I needed to read only two unmarked sentences to determine a grade. I had a simple system for scoring. Students lost 5 points for a spelling error and 5 points for a punctuation error—providing it was a punctuation rule that had already been taught. They lost 10 points if one of the forbidden verbs appeared and 10 points if the sentence did not follow the pattern. In over twenty-five years of teaching, I think I never had any student with a score lower than a B on sentence patterns. I think students succeeded because the patterns were rolled out in logical steps: teacher modeling, group work, and then individual work.

Those good marks every week on sentence patterns created a positive atmosphere in my classroom. Seeing those marks made students realize that they could be authors. I will never forget the student who stared in disbelief at his score of 95, an A. I felt a sense of pride and excitement for this student right up to the moment he turned to me and said, "Gosh, Mrs. H., I ain't never had no A's in English—never." Okay, his grammar and speech still needed work, but the point is this: This young man viewed himself as a winner and a capable writer and he was willing to do the work to improve.

We are not born with motivation. It follows success and action. I hate going to the gym, but if I just put on my exercise clothes and go, I feel motivated once I am there. Motivation follows action. And at the end of the workout, when I see myself dripping in sweat, when I feel my heart pumping, when I feel my muscles stretched and limber, I feel a sense of success. That feeling makes me decide to put it all into action again. It is the same for my students. When they see a good grade, when they hear effective sentences, when they see text that they have created, they feel successful and motivated.

I have all of the students begin with Pattern 1, even though they have written numerous sentences while studying nouns and verbs. The students earn good grades on this pattern, they learn the procedure for pattern work, and they develop team bonds and a comfort level with their writing teams. This early success helps as they progress to more difficult patterns.

Remember the four problems teachers cited in Chapter 1? Lack of motivation, basic writing skills, and content knowledge or information for writing topics, as well as teachers' lack of confidence concerning how to teach writing. Teaching the patterns can eliminate those problems. The consistent good grades and deliberate pacing gives students motivation and the skills they need to create effective sentences. Using the word banks provides content for the students as they work on the patterns. In addition, the students develop automaticity with sentence construction. This ability to generate sentences rapidly boosts confidence as well. If the patterns are taught one per week, the skills develop with time. Fragments and run-on sentences disappear because students develop writing skills. And I hope that the information I provide with each pattern gives teachers sufficient background knowledge so that they feel confident to teach writing.

Remember, when returning the patterns, make sure the students keep those patterns in a three-ring binder. This binder will be invaluable to students as they revise and work on longer assignments.

PATTERN 1: SPECIFIC NOUN–VIVID VERB

Background Information

Students should be able to write this pattern quickly because they have been studying nouns, verbs, and the noun-verb pattern extensively. Many students will want to add "jewelry" to these sentences, but I encourage them to keep the sentences as simple as possible. If students do add an occasional adjective or prepositional phrase, I don't mind as long as the basic pattern is noun-verb.

Points for Student Analysis

- Every sentence begins with an article or a possessive pronoun.
- Each sentence contains a specific noun and a vivid verb.
- The sentences contain only three or four words.
- Sentences that contain more than three words have possessive nouns, adjectives, or a noun that functions as an adjective.

Grade 3 Models

1. A volcano exploded.

2. The burning lava flowed.

3. The islanders escaped.

4. The earth's crust cracked.

5. The sky darkened.

Grade 4 Models

1. The alligator swam.

2. The crocodile hunted.

3. The nurse whistled.

4. A television blared.

5. My cell phone rang.

Grade 5 Models

1. The fog lifted.

2. The plants wilted.

3. My muscles ached.

4. The citizens protested.

5. Our car stalled.

Grade 6 Models

1. The infection spread.

2. The bloom opened.

3. The sponge dripped.

4. My headache pounded.

5. Our car swerved.

Grade 7 Models

1. The radio blared.

2. The balloon burst.

3. Her grades slipped.

4. His pet turtle disappeared.

5. My cake flopped.

Grade 8 Models

1. The water evaporated.

2. The computer crashed.

3. Her diamonds sparkled.

4. His racecar flipped.

5. My wristwatch beeped.

PATTERN 2: NOUN-VERB-NOUN

Background Information

This pattern also should go quickly for the students if sufficient groundwork has been completed on the concept of nouns and verbs. Allow students to use their noun banks as they work on the sentences. Remember, the noun that follows the verb will answer the question whom or what. Again, I encourage the students to limit the amount of jewelry that they add to the sentences they compose.

Points for Student Analysis

- Every sentence begins with an article or a possessive pronoun.
- The sentences are short; they contain few words.

- Each sentence contains a specific noun and a vivid verb followed by a noun.
- The noun (direct object) behind the verb answers the question whom or what.
- Sentences might contain prepositional phrases, possessive nouns, possessive pronouns, adjectives, an occasional adverb, or a noun that functions as an adjective.

Grade 3 Models

1. The spider spun a lacy web.
2. Mammals feed their babies.
3. The snake shed its skin.
4. The snake flicked its tongue.
5. Most snakes lay eggs.

Grade 4 Models

1. The children picked blackberries.
2. My grandfather plays checkers every day.
3. The shepherd herded the flock.
4. The humidity frizzed my hair.
5. The extreme temperatures baked the earth.

Grade 5 Models

1. The roots absorbed the rain.
2. Benjamin Franklin invented eyeglasses.
3. The explorers searched the peninsula.
4. The archaeologist discovered a mummy.
5. Ethan Allen led the Green Mountain Boys.

Grade 6 Models

1. The president vetoed the bill.
2. The squid shot a cloud of ink.
3. The dentist filled my bottom molars.
4. The glacier scoured the land.
5. My sister's poodle wears pink bows.

Grade 7 Models

1. The tow truck hauled my car.

2. Our butcher made deer sausage.

3. A wasp stung the third baseman.

4. The coyote chased the rabbit.

5. Degas painted ballerinas.

Grade 8 Models

1. The car crusher devoured the junkers.

2. Our secretary typed the newsletter.

3. A bumblebee stung my sister.

4. The waiter dropped a tray of dishes.

5. Van Gogh painted sunflowers.

PATTERN 3: INTERROGATIVE SENTENCES

Background Information

Students hear interrogative sentences daily. When I created these sentences, I opted to begin each sentence with one of the following words: *who, whose, which, when, where, how.* I did not use *can, do, will, have, has,* or *had;* too often those words are followed by the ubiquitous *you,* which I try to eradicate from student writing. Also, I have found that students find it easier to craft interrogative sentences with vivid verbs if they use they use *who, what, when, where, why,* and *how.* If they use specific nouns, the task also becomes much easier. I encourage students to write questions that use the content they are currently studying in another class. The interrogative sentence often pulls the verb in front of the noun; at the very least it often pulls an auxiliary word such as *do* or *can* in front of the subject noun.

Points for Student Analysis

- Every sentence begins with one of the following question words: *who, whose, which, when, where, how.*
- Every sentence ends with a question mark.
- Every sentence has a specific noun and a vivid verb.

Grade 3 Models

1. Why do rain forest trees have shallow roots?

2. How many acres does the South America rain forest cover?

3. Why do so many types of trees grow in the rain forest?

4. What do orangutans eat?

5. Which mammal can fly?

Grade 4 Models

1. How can people help to stop air pollution?

2. Which minerals does a body need for strong bones?

3. How many inches make up a foot?

4. Where did the tornado touch down?

5. When did the hurricane strike the Carolinas?

Grade 5 Models

1. Who can find the metaphor in this poem?

2. What animals besides fish live in water?

3. What year did the drought create the Great Dust Bowl?

4. How long can a harbor seal stay underwater?

5. Where did the tornado touch down?

Grade 6 Models

1. Which strait separates Alaska from Asia?

2. Who can name Socrates' most famous student?

3. Why did the state condemn Socrates to death?

4. When did Hannibal cross the Alps to invade Italy?

5. Where did the Romans build the first underground aqueduct?

Grade 7 Models

1. What caused that oak tree to die so suddenly?

2. When did the USS Monitor sink?

3. How many soldiers died during the Civil War?

4. Who wants a second slice of ice cream cake?

5. Where did the archaeologist find the jade jewelry?

Grade 8 Models

1. What steps do good writers follow to produce work?

2. When will this boring English class end?

3. How many paintings did Picasso produce during his Blue Period?

4. Who drives the red Corvette?

5. Where have all the flowers gone?

PATTERN 4: OPEN WITH AN ADVERB

Background Information

At some point most of us probably memorized a definition something like this: "An adverb is a word that modifies an adjective, a verb, or another adverb." But quite often an adverb seems to modify an entire clause or sentence (Weaver, 1996). During writing conferences and mini-lessons, I encourage students to look closely at any sentence that has an *ly* adverb. Often that adverb can be eliminated simply by using a stronger verb. For example, let's look at the first Grade 3 sentence: "Slowly, the Conestoga wagons creaked along the Oregon Trail." If the wagons creaked along, one could infer that they were moving slowly, so the adverb is redundant. Teaching this pattern might seem counterproductive; however, the adverb does serve a purpose for an author. Students must be taught that part of writing is making decisions about the words they select and the sentences they construct. They need to recognize and understand the function of an adverb in order to make intelligent decisions about its use as they develop writing maturity.

Adverbs that introduce a sentence are usually followed by a comma, especially if a slight pause is needed (University of Chicago Press, 2003). Based on that, I use a comma after adverbs that end in *ly*; I omit the comma if the adverb does not end in *ly*.

Do not bog yourself down trying to decide if words like *today* or phrases like *last Thursday* are nouns or adverbs. If the word opens the sentence and functions like an adverb, then it is an adverb in this pattern.

Points for Student Analysis

- Every sentence begins with an adverb.
- If we take off the adverb, we still have a complete sentence.
- The sentence following the adverb can be N-V or N-V-N.
- When the initial adverb ends in *ly*, it is followed by a comma.
- When the initial adverb does not end in *ly*, the comma is omitted.
- The adverb provides the following information: when, where, how, how often, or how much.

Grade 3 Models

1. *Slowly*, the Conestoga wagons creaked along the Oregon Trail.

2. *Frequently*, the pioneers faced fatigue and hunger.

3. *Often* fires broke out in the wagons.

4. *Daily*, the pioneers hunted for food.

5. *Tragically*, cholera spread through the camps.

Grade 4 Models

1. *Interestingly,* the wind vane pointed to the north.

2. *Silently,* the temperature climbed to 100 degrees.

3. *Unexpectedly,* the weather changed from hot to cool.

4. *Soon* black clouds rolled through the sky.

5. *Suddenly,* rain poured down on us.

Grade 5 Models

1. *Boldly,* Magellan approached King Charles to request money for his voyage.

2. *Ruthlessly,* Magellan stopped a mutiny in 1519.

3. *Finally,* the three vessels reached the Pacific Ocean.

4. *Later* Magellan sailed to the Philippines.

5. *Eventually,* the *Trinidad* tried to cross the Pacific again.

Grade 6 Models

1. *Quickly,* the students listed all the factors of 100.

2. *Unfortunately,* the United States does not use the metric system for all measurements.

3. *Today* the track team ran around the perimeter of the baseball field.

4. *Suddenly,* the computer froze.

5. *Yesterday* the school served waffles for breakfast.

Grade 7 Models

1. *Luckily,* the Wright Brothers' parents encouraged their love of science.

2. *Quickly,* the helicopter lifted from the hospital pad.

3. *Silently,* the cardiologist repaired the damage to the man's heart.

4. *Unselfishly,* women gave their wedding rings to support the war.

5. *Yesterday* my grandpa finished knitting a new sweater.

Grade 8 Models

1. *Noisily,* the mosquitoes buzzed around our heads.

2. *Quickly,* the beautician shaved my head.

3. *Stealthily,* the mouse nibbled on the cheese.

4. *Ferociously,* the bull charged the matador.

5. *Yesterday* my grandmother polished her Harley.

PATTERN 5: OPEN WITH A PREPOSITIONAL PHRASE

Background Information

All of the prepositional phrases in this pattern will be adverb phrases that tell when, where, why, or how something happened. Adjective phrases follow nouns. Since these phrases open the sentence, they cannot follow a noun; hence, they will be adverb phrases. You will need to decide how to punctuate these sentences. Some grammar books insist that any prepositional phrase at the beginning of a sentence must be set off with a comma. Others suggest that the comma is needed only when the phrase is long or when omitting the comma would cause confusion. When my students write narratives or essays, I teach them that the use of prepositional phrases should be limited. Use the phrase if it serves a purpose—provides needed information, a strong visualization, or rhythm to the sentence.

Prepositional phrases do not have verbs. Since some prepositions can function as subordinating conjunctions as well, this can create some confusion. Look at the following examples:

- *Because of the storm,* the school cancelled the picnic. (It is a prepositional phrase.)
- *Because the storm roared through town,* the school cancelled the picnic. (*Roared* is a verb, making this a subordinate clause; therefore, this sentence is not Pattern 5.)
- *After lunch* Dad takes a long nap. (It is a prepositional phrase.)
- *After he eats lunch,* Dad takes a long nap. (*Eats* is a verb, making this a subordinate clause; therefore this sentence is not Pattern 5.)

Points for Student Analysis

- Every sentence in this pattern begins with a prepositional phrase.
- Prepositional phrases never have verbs.
- If we lop off the prepositional phrase, the remaining words form either a N-V or a N-V-N sentence.
- Some phrases are followed by commas; others are not. Long phrases usually have a comma.
- Commas are used if the author wants the reader to pause after the prepositional phrase.

Grade 3 Models

1. *In 1607* people settled Jamestown.

2. *During the first year,* disease killed many colonists.

3. *Instead of growing crops,* the settlers quarreled.

4. *Because of their foolishness,* many settlers starved the first winter.

5. *In the spring,* John Smith bought corn from the Indians.

Grade 4 Models

1. *In the morning,* the committee met to discuss the new park.

2. *By noon* the members decided to build a memorial for the veterans.

3. *Before the next meeting,* an artist had completed a drawing of the memorial.

4. *During the summer,* the city held a competition for people to name the new park.

5. *At the next meeting,* the mayor will announce the winner.

Grade 5 Models

1. *During math class* the students named the types of triangles.

2. *In spite of the rain storm,* the track team ran around the town square four times.

3. *In St. Paul, Minnesota,* the railroad tracks run parallel to the river.

4. *For thousands of years,* doctors have studied how our bodies work.

5. *During its lifetime,* an alligator can lose 3000 teeth.

Grade 6 Models

1. *During the basketball game,* our center sprained her ankle.

2. *After lunch* my dad likes to take a long nap.

3. *In the future* many cars will run on alternate fuel sources.

4. *Because of the tornado warning,* the city cancelled the parade.

5. *Instead of tomato bisque,* the restaurant served clam chowder.

Grade 7 Models

1. *During the Civil War,* a few privateers harassed Union merchant ships.

2. *On June 19, 1864,* the USS *Kearsarge* put an end to CSS *Alabama's* raiding.

3. *Between 1861 and 1864,* Confederate blockade runners made many trips to Bermuda.

4. *During this time* many blockade runners earned vast amounts of money.

5. *Because of improvements in Union blockades,* many Confederate runners found themselves captured.

Grade 8 Models

1. *During the day* the robber hid in a dingy basement apartment.

2. *In the morning* the blackbirds stole the berries from the bushes.

3. *Between 1900 and 1902,* Picasso made three trips to Paris.

4. *During this time* Picasso painted with shades of blue.

5. *By the end of the day,* the Wright Brothers' plane completed a journey of 852 feet.

PATTERN 6: COMPOUND SENTENCE WITH A COORDINATING CONJUNCTION

Background Information

Pattern 6 is two simple sentences joined together with a coordinating conjunction: *so, and, but, or, nor, for, yet.* My students used to call these the "SABONFY" words; an acronym using the first letter of each conjunction. I chose to teach the students that they will need a comma in a compound sentence that uses a coordinating conjunction. But as they develop writing maturity, they can make a decision to eliminate the comma if it interrupts the rhythm of the sentence. They will begin to notice that many authors drop the comma in this pattern.

I provide students with a list of the coordinating conjunctions (see Table 3.1) before asking them to analyze the model sentences. Some students have a difficult time deciding when to use *and* and when to use *but.* Allow the discussion; students must decide what they are trying to convey and which word better expresses their meaning. At the third-grade level, I introduced only two conjunctions: *but* and *and.* At each level I introduced more coordinators. Students need to understand the relationship expressed by the conjunction.

Table 3.1	
So	Shows a consequence or cause and effect: The shoppers wanted easy access to coupons, so our company created an app.
And	Provides additional information or continues a thought: The app will provide coupons for all of the major department stores, and it also provides discounts at many restaurants.
But	Shows a contrast or opposition: Several newspapers criticized Lincoln's Gettysburg Address, but today we honor it as an American classic.
Or	Provides an alternative or another opinion: We can spend the day cleaning the garage, or we can drive to the beach for a picnic.
Nor	Continues a negative statement: The robber showed no remorse for stealing the car, nor did he offer a reason for the theft.
For	Provides a reason why something did or did not happen, or a synonym of *because*: I did not eat the chocolate cake, for I still need to lose twenty pounds.
Yet	Implies that something is true or will happen in spite of obstacles: Our point guard sprained her wrist, yet she scored ten points in the championship game.

Points for Student Analysis

- Every sentence has a SABONFY—a coordinating conjunction.
- Every sentence has a comma before the coordinating conjunction.
- There is a complete sentence on each side of the coordinating conjunction.
- The complete sentences can be N-V or N-V-N.
- The two sentences are related: additional information, contrast, or cause and effect.

Grade 3 Models

1. Abraham Lincoln grew up in a log cabin, *but* by 1862 he lived in the White House.

2. Thomas Jefferson built Monticello, *and* he planted 1,000 peach trees there.

3. Benjamin Franklin invented the Pennsylvania fireplace, *but* today we call it the Franklin stove.

4. Martha and George Washington married in 1759, *and* he adopted her children.

5. My family visited the White House, *and* we saw a picture of George Washington.

Grade 4 Models

1. The veins carry blood to the heart, *but* the arteries carry blood away.

2. The heart belongs to the circulatory system, *and* the lungs belong to the respiratory system.

3. The humidity rose, *so* my hair frizzed up.

4. Plants produce oxygen, *and* humans produce carbon dioxide.

5. An anemometer measures wind speed, *and* a barometer measures atmospheric pressure.

Grade 5 Models

1. My sister sprained her ankle, *but* my brother broke his foot.

2. The football player tore a ligament in his leg, *so* he could not finish the season.

3. My dad said we could go to the theater, *or* we could rent a movie and stay home.

4. The students loved to write sentences, *and* the teachers enjoyed grading them.

5. My family planned on going to the Fourth of July parade, *but* the heavy rains kept us at home.

Grade 6 Models

1. Archeologists use tree ring dating, and they use carbon-14 testing to determine the age of artifacts.

2. Several archeologists had discovered the ancient Mayan city Palanque, but extensive research did not begin until 1957.

3. Small rain forest creatures have many predators, so they have many ways to defend themselves.

4. The bats in our neighborhood eat hundreds of insects, yet the mosquitoes thrive.

5. Do you want to wash the dishes, or do you want to carry out the trash?

Grade 7 Models

1. In the 1500s, sons routinely entered their fathers' professions, but Galileo's father wanted a more prestigious profession for his son.

2. Galileo usually wrote in Italian, but he also wrote in Latin so that people in Europe could read about his discoveries.

3. With his telescope, Galileo could see the mountains on the moon, and he could see the four moons of Jupiter.

4. Galileo took an interest in how things move, and this curiosity led to important discoveries in physics.

5. Galileo's eyesight declined in later years, so several students stayed in his home to read to him and write his letters.

Grade 8 Models

1. The right tackle must stop the quarterback, or we will lose the game.

2. Cassandra had the gift of prophecy, but no one believed her.

3. In 1993 Michael Jordan retired from basketball, for he dreamed of beginning a career in professional baseball.

4. Taft and Roosevelt split the Republican vote, so Woodrow Wilson won the presidential election.

5. William Howard Taft served as the 27th president of the United States, and he later served as the 10th chief justice of the United States.

PATTERN 7: AN APPOSITIVE BEHIND A NOUN

Background Information

This pattern can be difficult to master. I have not taught it to students younger than fifth grade, but I know teachers who have. Therefore, I have included the pattern for Grades 3 and 4. I trust teacher expertise to decide whether to present this pattern. If you feel that this pattern is too difficult for your students, skip it and move on to the next pattern. Every pattern is based on a N-V or N-V-N, so it is easy to change or modify the teaching sequence.

Appositives are difficult because the form of an appositive is noun, but it functions like an adjective. The appositive renames or classifies the noun preceding it. It might help to think of the appositive as a synonym of the noun that it follows. The appositive does not describe a noun the way an adjective might. Notice the difference in the following sentences:

1. My brother, tanned and muscular, won six medals at the competition.

2. My brother, captain of the swim team, won six medals at the competition.

3. The rabbit, like many animals, eats dung pellets for nutrition.

The first sentence uses a participle and an adjective to describe the brother; since it does not have a noun between the commas it is not an appositive. The words *tanned* and *muscular* are set off by commas because they are free adjectival modifiers—in other words, *tanned and muscular* is interesting information but not necessary. I tell the students to think of the commas as little handles that can be used to lift the phrase from the sentence and throw it away.

The second sentence renames the brother. *Captain* is a noun, so the phrase *captain of the swim team* functions as an appositive.

The third sentence places a prepositional phrase behind the subject. It is not an appositive.

Appositives can follow any noun. To make it easier for the younger grades, I always place the appositive behind the subject; in the upper grades, the appositive may appear behind a variety of nouns. In the lower grades I also keep the appositives short. And I try to avoid extra adjectives or prepositional phrases within the appositive.

Some of my students find it easier to write a complete sentence, and then embed the appositive.

Points for Student Analysis

- The appositive always comes behind a noun.
- The appositive is set off with commas.
- The first word of the appositive is often a noun.
- The first word of the appositive might be an article or possessive pronoun followed by a noun.
- The first word of the appositive might be an adjective followed by a noun.
- The noun in the appositive might be followed by a prepositional phrase.
- The appositive could be lifted out of the sentence and the remaining words would be a N-V or a N-V-N sentence.
- There must be a noun in an appositive.
- The appositive renames the noun it follows.

Grade 3 Models

1. My brother, *a pilot*, flies planes out of the St. Louis airport.

2. My dog, *a German shepherd*, likes to chase cats.

3. John Glenn, *a famous astronaut*, visited our school.

4. Our principal, *Mrs. Smith*, rides a bicycle to work.

5. Albert Pujols, *my favorite baseball player*, played for the Cardinals.

Grade 4 Models

1. My favorite driver, *Jeff Gordon*, has won the Brickyard 400 four times.

2. The Great Skua, *a seabird*, steals food from smaller birds.

3. George Washington, *our first president*, worked as a surveyor.

4. Jupiter, *the largest planet in our solar system*, completes a rotation in less than ten hours.

5. Alligators, *swamp animals*, like to hide in the water.

Grade 5 Models

1. John Paul Jones, *an American naval hero*, raided the British warships.

2. Patrick Henry, a *great speaker*, described the colonists' fears.

3. Champlain, *the founder of Quebec*, discovered the Ottawa River.

4. Lafayette, *a friend of George Washington*, served at Valley Forge.

5. Abigail Adams, *the second first lady*, had many strong opinions.

Grade 6 Models

1. The Nile, *the longest river in the world*, flows from Lake Victoria to the Mediterranean Sea.

2. The Nile enters the Mediterranean Sea by a delta in Egypt, *a country in northeastern Africa*.

3. Scholars could decipher hieroglyphics after discovering the Rosetta Stone, *a black basalt slab found in 1799*.

4. The Sumerians invented cuneiform, *a style of writing using wedge-shaped strokes*.

5. The pyramids of Egypt, *one of the Seven Wonders of the Ancient World*, served as tombs for the pharaohs.

Grade 7 Models

1. Raphael Semmes, *captain of the CSS Alabama*, challenged the *Kearsarge* to a ship-to-ship battle.

2. Robert Smalls, *a slave*, piloted the CSS *Planter* in the Civil War.

3. The British Navy designed a set of visual communication signals, *semaphore*.

4. Sailors cleaned the decks with holystones, *pieces of soft sandstone.*

5. Many Civil War sailors died from malaria, *a mosquito-transmitted disease.*

Grade 8 Models

1. Claude Monet, *a French Impressionist,* painted outdoor scenes.

2. Mary Lincoln gave Frederick Douglas a special gift, *her husband's walking cane.*

3. *Tyrannosaurus rex, a carnivore,* lived during the Mesozoic era.

4. Alvin Ailey, *an American choreographer,* created the masterpiece dance performance called *Revelations.*

5. Picasso depicts the horrors of war in *Guernica, one of his most famous paintings.*

PATTERN 8: OPEN WITH AN ADVERB CLAUSE

Background Information

Every sentence in this pattern will begin with a subordinator, a word used to join two sentences. Since some of the subordinators also can function as prepositions, students might confuse the two patterns. Students need to understand the difference between a clause and a prepositional phrase. An adverb clause will contain a verb; a prepositional phrase will not. Students who can use subordinators can meet the requirements of the Common Core standard to use appropriate and varied transitions to create cohesion and clarify the relationships among ideas and concepts (National Governors Association Center for Best Practices and Council of Chief State School Officers, 2010, CC.8.W.2.c. All rights reserved.).

- *Before dinner* we washed our hands. (Pattern 5)
- *Before we ate dinner,* we washed our hands. (Pattern 8)
- *Because of the rain,* the principal cancelled the school picnic. (Pattern 5)
- *Because the rain flooded the playground,* the principal cancelled the school picnic. (Pattern 8)

The most common subordinators are shown in Table 3.2.

Table 3.2

Time	Place	Condition	Compare/Contrast	Cause/Effect
After* As* As soon as Before* Since* Until When Whenever While	Wherever Where	As if As though Although Even if If Though Unless Whether	Although Even though Though While Whereas	As* Because In order that Since So that
*Can also function as a preposition				

Select the subordinators that you want to teach and create a list to give to your students before you have them analyze Pattern 8.

Here is a lesson on naming the clause:

I ask students, "What is my name?"

They usually respond, "Mrs. H."

I ask, "What is another one of my names?"

They respond, "Mrs. Hostmeyer."

I continue this dialogue, asking them for my names. They realize that I am called Phyllis, Phyl, sis, Aunt Phyllis, and so on.

Then I explain that the clauses we will be working with also have several names. They are called subordinate clauses because they begin with a subordinator. I ask students if the clauses in italics can be bounced to the back of the sentence. Since they can bounce, we can call them adverb clauses. I ask them if the clause in italics is a complete sentence. Because it is not a complete sentence, we can call it a dependent clause. It depends on the words after the comma to make it complete. The clauses in Patterns 8 and 9 have multiple names: subordinate clause, adverb clause, dependent clause.

Points for Student Analysis

- Every sentence begins with a word from the subordinator list.
- The words in italics do not make a complete sentence.
- The words in italics are followed by a comma.
- If the words in italics are taken away, a complete sentence remains.
- The remaining sentence can be N-V or N-V-N.
- The sentence (clause) after the comma sometimes starts with a pronoun that refers to a noun in the subordinate clause. The pronoun and the

noun must agree in number and gender. For example, *When settlers moved to California*, they killed sea lions for blubber. *They* refers to settlers. Since *settlers* is plural, the pronoun must also be plural.

- The subordinate clause tells us how, when, where, or why something happened. The two clauses have a relationship.

Grade 3 Models

1. *Because the river flooded*, many people moved.

2. *When settlers moved to California*, they killed sea lions for blubber.

3. *Although laws now protect sea lions*, they still face extinction.

4. *Because litter can hurt ocean animals*, people should use trash cans.

5. *When people visit beaches*, they should not litter.

Grade 4 Models

1. *Because a virus infected my computer*, I could not finish my homework.

2. *When I had strep throat*, the doctor prescribed a medicine to kill the bacteria.

3. *Before the chef cooks dinner*, she must wash her hands to eliminate germs.

4. *After she studied my symptoms*, the doctor decided I did not have any serious diseases.

5. *Whenever I have a bad cold*, I drink lots of juice to help my immune system make me better.

Grade 5 Models

1. *When my sister spots a bargain*, she whips out her charge card.

2. *Because cheetahs face extinction*, hunters cannot kill them for their fur.

3. *After my dad fed the plants some Miracle Gro*, they sprouted many new leaves.

4. *As soon as Grandma arrives*, we will eat.

5. *After Jackson Haines added a toe pick to skates*, skaters developed new types of jumps.

Grade 6 Models

1. *Because the pitcher threw with great velocity*, the batters all struck out.

2. *When the race car driver entered the curve*, he reduced his acceleration.

3. *Although the technician worked on my computer all morning*, it still does not work.

4. *After he ascended to the throne,* Hadrian hired architects to design the Pantheon.

5. *As soon as the rain stops,* the ground crew will remove the tarp from the field.

Grade 7 Models

1. *When subway trains pull into a station,* their doors stay open for several minutes.

2. *Because passengers drop crumbs, pizza crusts, and food,* pigeons looking for a quick lunch walk onto the trains.

3. *Since the pigeons don't like riding on the trains,* they scurry off at the next stop.

4. *Although the pigeons clean up much of the spilled food,* they leave behind a bigger mess on the floors.

5. *As the trains pull out of the stations,* they make a strange high-pitched noise.

Grade 8 Models

1. *Because Renoir painted many oils of clowns,* people often recognize his work.

2. *After Thetis dipped Achilles in the River Styx,* arrows could not pierce his skin.

3. *Since Arachne wove a perfect tapestry,* the jealous Athena turned her into a spider.

4. *Even though people referred to Brahms as one of the three great Bs,* he felt inferior to Beethoven and Bach.

5. *Although the Beatles began singing in 1957,* they did not gain popularity until they hired Ringo Starr.

PATTERN 9: CLOSE WITH AN ADVERB CLAUSE

Background Information

This pattern is usually quite easy for the students since it is simply a reverse of Pattern 8.

Points for Student Analysis

- These sentences also have subordinators, but they are placed in the middle of the sentence.

- These sentences do not have commas before the subordinator.
- The two clauses have a relationship.
- The two clauses can change positions; therefore, the clause with the subordinator is an adverb clause.

Grade 3 Models

1. Queen Elizabeth II knighted Edmund Hillary *after he climbed Mount Everest.*

2. The archeologists found artifacts *when they dug near the mesa.*

3. The hiker broke her leg *when she tumbled into the canyon.*

4. Players wear protective gear *when they play football.*

5. Wildflowers grew in the valley *after the spring rains fell.*

Grade 4 Models

1. The advertisers placed a jeep on top of a mesa *because they wanted to make the vehicle look powerful.*

2. My sister sunburned her face *when she skied on the mountains.*

3. The water felt icy *because the melting glacier fed the lake.*

4. Hundreds of years ago, many people lived near the Mississippi Delta *since the rich soil grew many crops.*

5. Our bunny-ears cactus lives outside through the winter *even though we live in a cold climate.*

Grade 5 Models

1. During English class the students had an interesting conversation *after they had read* Witch of Blackbird Pond.

2. The pirates buried treasures on this island *so that no one could steal the jewels.*

3. The rescue teams flew to Japan *as soon as they heard about the disaster.*

4. The baseball player tried to argue *when the umpire called the second strike.*

5. Our school recycles paper *because we care about the earth.*

Grade 6 Models

1. My brother and his family lived with us *until the hurricane left Florida.*

2. Grandma bought a cat *after she found a mouse in her pantry.*

3. Salamanders shed their skin *as they grow.*

4. Our German shepherd barks *whenever the UPS driver delivers a package.*

5. My sister's friends flew to the kitchen *when Mom called out, "Pizza's ready."*

Grade 7 Models

1. In 1804 Sir George Cayley designed the first successful model glider *after he studied birds' flight patterns.*

2. Strong-armed men dropped the castle's portcullis *if invaders tried to break into the castle.*

3. Thousands of men left their homes in the late 1800s *because they hoped to discover gold in the Yukon.*

4. Jack London wrote about his experiences *after he returned from his Klondike adventure.*

5. The North-West Mounted Police stopped all travelers near the British Columbia border *in order to make sure the travelers carried one year's worth of food and supplies.*

Grade 8 Models

1. Greco-Roman wrestlers cannot trip each other *because they must apply all holds above the waist.*

2. My nephew camped at Glacier National Park *when he vacationed in Montana.*

3. The space shuttle will launch tomorrow *unless the weather turns nasty.*

4. My dad barbecued some garden burgers *so that my vegetarian sister could have a sandwich too.*

5. Spectators clambered from their seats *when the marathon runners entered the arena.*

PATTERN 10: PARALLEL ITEMS IN A SERIES

Background Information

Calling these sentences with parallel structures might create some confusion. Pattern 10 requires students to write sentences that have elements in a series. However, when elements appear in a series, each element must be parallel in form and function. As students become adept at the patterns, they learn the power of using parallel sentence patterns in lengthier pieces of text.

Some grammar books demand that a comma be used after all nouns that appear before the connecting word (usually *and*). Other grammar books suggest that the comma before the connector can be eliminated. I chose to have students always use the comma in order to prevent confusion. For example, without the comma the following sentence can be confusing. We planted red, yellow, blue and white flowers. If the comma is used after blue, it is clear that four colors of flowers have been planted. Without the comma, one could question if some of the flowers are blue and white striped.

Again, for the younger students I chose to teach the items in a series as parallel subjects. For middle grade students, items in a series might be in subjects or direct objects. For the junior high students, the sentences might have parallel objects of a preposition or parallel prepositional phrases. Parallel structure of verbals is addressed in subsequent patterns.

I chose to teach parallel structure because it can be a powerful tool for authors. Once students understand how to create a parallel structure, they can use that skill to eliminate short choppy sentences in their work. "Parallelism is often used for emphasis, for impact: to make a point, to shock, to fire the imagination, to inspire, to rouse to action" (Weaver, 2007).

At this point students might begin to merge patterns. For example, they might include an appositive after the serial subjects or after a direct object. This is not mandatory, even if an appositive appears in the models. Keep the focus on the one new skill of the pattern. But as students internalize the patterns and skills, structures from prior patterns will appear.

Caution the students to maintain parallel structure. This is usually easy enough to do when the parallel structure appears in the subject or direct object. Maintaining this parallelism becomes more challenging as sentences grow in complexity and form. See the following models:

1. The dancers jumped over the barrels, onto chairs, and off of the stage.

2. The dancers jumped over the barrels, onto chairs, and run like crazy.

The first sample is parallel because all of the items in the series are prepositional phrases. The second example lacks parallel structure because *run like crazy* is not a prepositional phrase.

Three items in a series is not mandatory for this pattern. Students will begin to notice professional authors may use five or six items in a series. Three is simply a manageable number for students as they are learning the pattern. In addition, many standardized tests tend to use the magical three items in a series when testing for punctuation and parallel structure of grammatical elements.

Points for Student Analysis

- The sentences have sets of three or more.
- The words or phrases in the sets are separated by commas.
- The words in the series are identical in form: three nouns, three phrases, three verbs.
- Do not mix forms in the series.
- The verb also must be a plural form if the subject is a series.

Grade 3 Models: Parallel Subjects

1. *Alligators, crocodiles, and gharials* grow their entire lives.

2. *Sharks, humpback whales, and manatees* face extinction.

3. *Penguins, caribou, and polar bears* live in the Arctic.

4. *Snakes, lizards, and turtles* belong to the reptile family.

5. *Yaks, llamas, and goats* can climb to the tops of huge mountains.

Grade 4 Models: Parallel Subjects

1. *Volcanoes, earthquakes, and erosion* create new landforms.

2. *Scruffy, Victor, and PJ,* my pet dogs, chased rabbits yesterday.

3. *Apples, oranges, and pears* fill the bowl on the table.

4. *Blogs, texting, and Facebook* keep me connected with my friends.

5. *Thunder, lightning, and fierce winds* frighten my little sister.

Grade 5 Models: Parallel Subjects and Direct Objects

1. *America, Fiji, and Chile* have the same color flags. (parallel subjects)

2. *Pelicans, vultures, and wolves* feed their babies partially digested food. (parallel subjects)

3. At the skateboard park we practiced *kickflips, nosegrinds, and ollies.* (parallel direct objects following the verb *practiced*)

4. Our family roots for *the Cubs, the White Sox, and the Grizzlies.* (parallel direct objects following the verb *roots for*)

5. We photographed *the White House, the Washington Monument, and the Lincoln Memorial.* (parallel direct objects following the verb *photographed*)

Grade 6 Models: Parallel Subjects and Direct Objects

1. *Whales, sharks, and porpoises* live in the ocean. (parallel subjects)

2. *Centaurs, Harpies, and Gorgons* add terror and excitement to Greek myths. (parallel subjects)

3. Deer antlers provide *calcium, phosphorus, protein, and fat* for a porcupine's meal. (parallel direct objects following *provide*)

4. At Cahokia Mounds the archeologists found *a copper snake, pottery birds, and sandstone tablets.* (parallel direct objects following *found*)

5. Thomas Jefferson invented *the swivel chair, the spherical sundial, the moldboard plow, and the cipher wheel.* (parallel direct objects following *invented*)

Grade 7 Models: Parallel Structure in a Series

1. *Tony Braxton, Monica, and Mary Blige* sing powerful ballads. (parallel subjects)

2. *Alastair Reynolds, Andrew Drilon, and Fritz Leiber* write science fiction novels about alien invaders. (parallel subjects)

3. The Edmonton Street Performers Festival attracts *jugglers, dancers, mimics, and musicians.* (parallel direct objects following *attracts*)

4. Lincoln's funeral train passed *through Baltimore, Cleveland, and Chicago* before it arrived in Springfield. (parallel objects of a preposition)

5. The trail ride wound *through the forest, across Coleman Creek, and over Star Hill.* (parallel prepositional phrases)

Grade 8 Models: Parallel Structure in a Series

1. *Lucy Walker, Annie Peck Smith, and Meta Brevoort,* three brave women, each climbed the Matterhorn during their lives. (parallel subjects)

2. *Jousting tournaments, melees, and sword fights* entertained the king's court during medieval festivities. (parallel subjects)

3. For Christmas my sister received *an MP3 player, a computer, and a new coat.* (parallel direct objects following *received*)

4. Last night we found half-price sales *at the drug store, the grocery store, and a flower shop.* (parallel objects of a preposition)

5. During vacation our family traveled *through the Black Mountains, into Death Valley, and across the Panamint Range.* (parallel prepositional phrases)

PATTERN 11: PARALLEL VERB PHRASES IN A SERIES

Background Information

Consistency of tense is the major concern when teaching parallel verbs in a series. Many students have a tendency to lose focus when writing longer sentences. Hence, the final verb often shifts tense. Samples of inconsistent verb tense:

- Aretha sang, danced, and entertains the audience five nights a week during her tour of the Midwest.
- The governor stayed in the auditorium, talked with the reporters, and shakes hands with the voters.
- Clouds formed, thunder rumbled, and the rain pours.
- The skydivers jump, flip, and landed in the open field.

Points for Student Analysis

- All of the sentences are N-V or N-V-N.
- The sentences have three or more verbs separated by commas.
- The verbs are consistent in tense.
- The verbs agree in number with the subject.
- Some of the verbs have direct objects; some are followed by prepositional phrases.

Grade 3 Models

1. Rabbits *hop, scurry, and hide.*

2. The basketball players *ran, shot, and scored.*

3. The clown *juggled, tumbled, and laughed.*

4. The expensive lamp *wobbled, fell, and broke.*

5. Every night my uncle *washes, rinses, and dries* the dishes.

Grade 4 Models

1. The cheerleaders *jumped, hollered, and cheered* for the team.

2. My grandma *gardens, travels, and plays* cards.

3. The boat *rocked, dipped, and sank* during the storm.

4. The pot on the stove *simmered, bubbled, and boiled over.*

5. After dusk the mosquitoes *swarmed, buzzed, and bit.*

Grade 5 Models

1. The beetles *chewed* the leaves, *nibbled* the roots, and *killed* my favorite plant.

2. The umpire *adjusted* his mask, *watched* the pitch, and *called* the strike.

3. The guard *picked up* her dribble, *eyed* the basket, and *sank* the three-point shot.

4. My new shoes *squeaked* with each step, *hurt* my feet, and then *fell apart* in the rain.

5. The mouse *approached* the trap, *looked* at the cheese, then *scampered* to safety.

Grade 6 Models

1. Pirates *chased* the merchant vessels, *captured* the crew, and *looted* the treasure chests.

2. The pirate *stole* the treasure chest, *buried* it on the island, and *drew* a map.

3. On Halloween the children *paint* their faces, *don* their costumes, and *run* from door to door.

4. President Lincoln *opened* the paper, *put on* his spectacles, and *read* the Gettysburg Address to the crowd.

5. The jester *danced* a jig, *juggled* apples, and *told* silly jokes.

Grade 7 Models

1. Maada, a proud and spirited princess, *dug* a tunnel, *crawled* under the tepee, and *escaped* into the woods.

2. The candidate *lost* in sixteen primaries, *trailed* in Wisconsin, but still *campaigned* in the western states.

3. The chef *selected* fresh vegetables, *sliced* them, and *fixed* a stir fry.

4. During the hike the students *will cross* the swinging bridge, *scale* a hill, and finally *picnic* at the lake.

5. My Siamese cat *eats* his food, *cleans* his fur, then *curls up* to sleep.

Grade 8 Models

1. Fabio *drew* her to him, *whispered* in her ear, and *asked* for change for the soda machine.

2. Delta II *approached* Mars, *mapped* its surface, and *tracked* its cloud cover.

3. Pinochet *entered* the courtroom, *stared* at the reporters, and *spoke* in a weak voice.

4. Gandalf *visited* Bilbo, *sat* at the table, and *shared* a meal.

5. Gutenberg *arranged* the metal letters, *applied* the ink, then *pressed* them onto the paper.

PATTERN 12: OPEN WITH AN ADJECTIVE OR AN ADJECTIVE PHRASE

Background Information

Do not be fooled by this pattern; it is more difficult than one might think. Many assume it is simple to write because it pairs adjectives and nouns, a task students have done often. Students are familiar with adjectives, but in this pattern the adjective is used in a slightly different manner. The adjective still precedes the noun, but it is set off by a comma at the beginning of the sentence since it is a free modifier—one that is not essential to create meaning. The adjective does provide information that might be useful or interesting, but it is not essential.

This is another pattern that I have not taught lower than fifth grade, but I opted to create model sets for all grades for those teachers who do opt to teach it. If you feel this pattern would frustrate or confuse your students, omit it. Or perhaps you would like to model this pattern and try writing a few as a whole class. Another method is to brainstorm a bank of adjectives for students to use before they begin writing. This will assure that they have true adjectives and not participles.

Another way to help students is to provide posters or pictures. Give the students something concrete to use. For example, provide a picture of a young animal and ask students to brainstorm a few adjectives, such as *cute, wobbly, cuddly,* and *furry.* Next, use one of those words to begin a sentence: Wobbly, the calf tried to stand up. Curious, the calf looked at its mother.

The early grades will create sentences that open with a simple adjective or a pair of adjectives. By sixth grade the students will be creating sentences that use an adjective phrase. An opening adjective can be followed by a prepositional phrase.

This is not a pattern that students will use often, but it is a pattern that can create drama or emphasis in a longer piece of writing. Listen to the difference in the following sentences.

1. The dark murky water poured over the levee.

2. Dark and murky, the water poured over the levee.

The second sentence has an ominous tone lacking in the first. The emphasis is placed on the description of the water.

Another point that makes this pattern difficult is the confusion between adjectives and participles. I encourage the students to use true adjectives rather than participles because we will address participles in a later pattern. Participles are verbs that function as adjectives. If the word ends in an *ing* or *ed,* it is probably a participle. To help students with this pattern visit www.momswhothink .com/reading/list-of-adjectives.html and create a bank of adjectives. One word of caution: The list will contain participles since they function as adjectives.

Points for Student Analysis

- The first word in every sentence is an adjective.
- The adjective can be followed by a prepositional phrase.
- The adjective or adjective phrase is always followed by a comma.
- The adjective or adjective phrase describes the noun that follows it.
- The adjective or adjective phrase can be eliminated and the remaining words will still be a complete sentence.

Grade 3 Models

1. *Happy,* the children hugged their teacher.

2. *Wobbly,* the baby calf stood up.

3. *Hot,* the farmer took off his heavy jacket.

4. *Lonely,* my sister stared out the window.

5. *Sleepy,* the baby rocked in the cradle.

Grade 4 Models

1. *Bashful,* my sister hid behind Mom's legs.

2. *Clumsy,* the tour guide slipped on the trail.

3. *Nervous,* the gymnast stepped onto the platform.

4. *Agile,* the trapeze artist leaped from bar to bar.

5. *Chilly,* Grandma put on a sweater.

Grade 5 Models

1. *Ancient,* the oak tree swayed in the storm before crashing to the ground.

2. *Hysterical,* the crowds raced from the exploding volcano.

3. *Dark and murky,* the water flowed over the levees.

4. *Victorious,* the team hoisted the trophy into the air.

5. *Cold and hungry,* the young boy pulled the blanket around himself.

Grade 6 Models

1. *Aware of the danger,* the tour guide emphasized the importance of staying behind the safety rail.

2. *Impervious to pain,* the magician walked across the burning coals.

3. *Confident of her shooting,* the point guard launched the winning three-point shot.

4. *Elegant in her designer gown,* the actress walked the red carpet.

5. *Wise beyond her years,* the child dazzled the judges.

Grade 7 Models

1. *Quiet as the falling snow,* Mom tiptoed from the baby's room.

2. *Undetectable to the naked eye,* the new star circled the planet.

3. *Famous for his elegant desserts,* the chef created a seven-tier wedding cake.

4. *Worthy of praise,* the Olympic skater held the flag high above his head as he circled the track.

5. *Worn out from the field trip,* the teachers soaked their feet in a tub of hot water.

Grade 8 Models

1. *Nervous about her recital,* my sister took deep breaths to calm herself.

2. *Invisible because of a secret potion,* the spy copied the top secret defense plans.

3. *Woozy from the Teacup Ride,* my friend plopped down on the nearest bench.

4. *Lazy as a sloth,* my sister refuses to clean her room.

5. *Stiff from the long plane ride,* the passengers stretched as they stood up.

PATTERN 13: OPEN WITH A PRESENT PARTICIPLE

Background Information

This pattern uses a present participle—the *ing* form of the verb. I taught this pattern to a group of third graders as they were finishing a unit on the rain forest. Each group of students selected one animal that they had been studying: Morpho butterfly, monkeys, boa constrictor. Then I instructed the students to skim and scan through their books to look for interesting verbs related to their animal. They would then turn the verb into a participial phrase. For example, they might find a sentence that said, "Monkeys forage through the forest in search of food." The students would write the participial phrase, "Foraging through the forest." Once each group had found four or five participial phrases to describe their animal, they used those to create sentences. The subject of every sentence was the animal they had selected. For example: Foraging for food, the monkeys found berries. By doing this the students avoided dangling participles.

Students likely will need some instruction on how to prevent the dreaded DPs: dangling participles. If they understand form and function, this lesson becomes easy for them.

The form of a present participial phrase is always an *ing* word followed by modifiers and possibly a noun. The function of the participial phrase is always an adjective. When the students studied adjectives with the activities in Chapter 2, they learned that adjectives are anchored to nouns. Since present participial phrases function as adjectives, they must be anchored to the noun they describe.

1. Using her beak, the stork makes a clapping noise for the zookeeper.

2. The stork makes a clapping noise for the zookeeper, using her beak.

In the first sentence, the participle is anchored to the noun it describes; thus, it is clear that the stork is using her beak. The other sentence makes it sound as though the zookeeper is using the beak. Sentence 2 has a dangling participle.

1. Opening her huge mouth, the leopard seal threatens the photographer.

2. The leopard seal threatens the photographer, opening her huge mouth.

In the first sentence the reader correctly understands that the leopard seal is opening her huge mouth. The second sentence tells us that the photographer is opening her huge mouth. The participial phrase must be anchored to the noun it describes.

This will be the final pattern for Grade 3.

Points for Student Analysis

- Every sentence starts with an *ing* word.
- Other words follow the *ing* word:
- Sometimes the words are prepositional phrases.
- Sometimes they are nouns.
- A comma always follows the *ing* phrase.
- The *ing* phrase always describes the first noun behind the comma.
- The subject of the sentence is always doing the action of the *ing* phrase.
- If the *ing* phrase is removed, the remaining words form a N-V or a N-V-N sentence.

Grade 3 Models

1. *Foraging for food,* the monkeys found ripe bananas.

2. *Swinging from tree to tree,* the monkeys found ripe bananas.

3. *Having found some nuts and seeds,* the parrot uses his powerful beak to crack them open.

4. *Spotting its prey,* the jaguar leaps from the tree and pounces.

5. *Opening its jaws,* the emerald tree boa swallows the opossum in one gulp.

Grade 4 Models

1. *Eating twenty-eight hotdogs in three minutes,* the young boy won the contest.

2. *Hoping to find the perfect dress,* the girls walked from store to store.

3. *Wanting a helper in the lab,* the scientist built a robot to do simple tasks.

4. *Stretching to reach the top of the tree,* the giraffe munched on the tender leaves.

5. *Noticing the stale odor in the house,* my grandma lit several candles.

Grade 5 Models

1. *Blending in with its surroundings,* the praying mantis hides from predators.

2. *Using its long sticky tongue,* the echidna catches ants and termites.

3. *Herding her young into a burrow,* the warthog kept them safe from a nearby lion.

4. *Sinking its fangs into the body of its prey,* the horned viper killed the rodent.

5. *Squirting a cloud of brown ink into the water,* the cuttlefish confused its enemies.

Grade 6 Models

1. *Feeling only a slight vibration,* the crew of the *Titanic* did not realize they had struck a glacier.

2. *Realizing the extent of the damage,* the captain sent distress signals.

3. *Watching in horror,* people in the lifeboats watched the *Titanic* break apart and disappear into the ocean.

4. *Running an obstacle course of icebergs,* the *Carpathia* raced toward the sinking ship.

5. *Ignoring caution,* the *Carpathia* managed to save 705 people.

Grade 7 Models

1. *Hoping for a good fortune,* my sister took the largest Chinese fortune cookie.

2. *Rolling eighty-two feet to the south,* NASA's Spirit Rover stopped to examine a rock.

3. *Waking early,* the doctor sipped a cup of coffee before leaving for work.

4. *Looking for alternative fuel sources,* the researchers studied the feasibility of using hydrogen.

5. *Poring over their books,* the students looked for answers to the questions.

Grade 8 Models

1. *Gazing at the ballerinas,* Degas planned his next painting.

2. *Studying with Anne Sullivan,* Helen Keller quickly learned to read Braille.

3. *Experimenting with phonographs,* Edison invented the first talking motion picture.

4. *Working as a team,* the students produced a PowerPoint presentation for science class.

5. *Hunching over the quilt,* my grandmother looked for missed stitches.

PATTERN 14: OPEN WITH A PAST PARTICIPLE

Background Information

This pattern is similar to the previous pattern. This pattern is also identical to Pattern 12. Pattern 12 uses an adjective; Pattern 14 uses a past participle to open the sentence. At Grade 4, the models show a simple past participle. Models at other grade levels show a simple past participle as well as past participle phrases. The models for eighth grade use irregular and regular verbs. Students at any grade level can create sentences using regular or irregular verbs, but I have found that the regular verbs tend to be easier for the students to use.

To help the students as they begin writing sentences, provide them with a list of verbs and the verb forms such as the one in Table 3.3. Most English books will have such a list; an Internet search also will provide such lists. As students scan the column of past participle verbs, I tell them to stop on a verb and visualize. For example, as they read the verb *gazed*, they should stop and visualize who or what might be gazing. An artist might gaze at a sunset; a rider might gaze at a new motorcycle; a teenager might gaze at their favorite star; or a deer might gaze at its fawn. The ability to visualize helps students create interesting sentences.

Table 3.3

Regular Verb Forms			
Base Form	**Present Participle**	**Past**	**Past Participle**
Gaze	Gazing	Gazed	Gazed
Tire	Tiring	Tired	Tired
Surprise	Surprising	Surprised	Surprised
Irregular Verb Forms			
Base Form	**Present Participle**	**Past**	**Past Participle**
Catch	Catching	Caught	Caught
Drive	Driving	Driven	Driven
Find	Finding	Found	Found
See	Seeing	Saw	Seen
Tear	Tearing	Tore	Torn

Again, the students need to understand that participles function as adjectives, so they must be anchored to a noun.

1. Torn in two, my brother returned the dollar bill to the bank.

2. Torn in two, the dollar bill fell to the floor.

In the example above, the participle in the first sentence makes it sound as though *my brother* is torn in two. In the other sentence, the dollar bill is torn in two. The following models also use a past participle to open the sentence. In the first example, the scale model tractor is powered by gas. In the second example, the placement of the participle tells us that the farmers are powered by gas.

1. Powered by gas, the scale model tractor impressed the farmers.

2. Powered by gas, the farmers were impressed by the scale model tractors.

Do we even need to discuss the fact that the second sentence has a dangling participle and its implications clearly are not the author's intent?

Points for Student Analysis

- Every sentence starts with a past participle verb. (Students might say that every sentence begins with a word ending in *ed*.)
- Every sentence has a comma.
- The first word is a verb form.
- The introductory word or phrase functions as an adjective.
- The introductory word or phrase describes the first noun behind the comma.
- The introductory word or phrase can be deleted, and the words behind the comma still make a complete sentence.
- The sentence behind the comma can be N-V or N-V-N.

Grade 4 Models

1. *Defeated,* the runner cried tears of bitter desperation.

2. *Frightened,* the baby ran to his mother.

3. *Alarmed,* the puppy hid beneath the couch.

4. *Confused,* the student asked for help.

5. *Tired,* the racer struggled to finish the race.

Grade 5 Models

1. *Trained to survive,* astronauts solved difficult problems while in space.

2. *Exhausted after his spacewalk,* Alexi Leonov struggled to reenter the spacecraft.

3. *Rocked by a small explosion,* Apollo 13 lost oxygen, electricity, and water.

4. *Aided by Houston,* the astronauts on Apollo 13 worked four days to solve the problems.

5. *Relieved,* the country cheered when the crew returned.

Grade 6 Models

1. *Frightened by the earth tremors,* shoppers rushed from the open-air market.

2. *Shoved by someone,* the girl dropped the basket of figs and dates.

3. *Outlined in a blaze of red flame,* Mount Vesuvius spat giant plumes of smoke and ash.

4. *Trapped between the mountain and the sea,* the people could not escape.

5. *Huddled together in the dark cave,* the people of Herculaneum listened to the volcano erupting.

Grade 7 Models

1. *Hobbled by a sprained ankle,* our shortstop sat the bench during the game.

2. *Named best supporting actress for her performance in* Precious, Mo'Nique smiled for the cameras.

3. *Abandoned by the owners,* the house needed a coat of paint.

4. *Tattered and torn,* the dress hung on the girl.

5. *Powered by a gas engine,* the scale model tractor impressed the farmers.

Grade 8 Models

1. *Known as a landscape painter,* Monet gave a shimmering quality to his artwork.

2. *Caught red-handed,* my brother admitted he had taken the chocolate chip cookies.

3. *Startled by everyone's positive reaction,* Beethoven cried tears of joy.

4. *Priced at $200,000,* the shoes cost more than I could afford.

5. *Built in Kansas,* the world's first bulldozer could fill in over one mile of trench in a day.

PATTERN 15: OPEN WITH A PRESENT PERFECT PARTICIPLE

Background Information

This pattern also uses a participle form of a verb paired with the helping verb *having.* Present perfect tense states an action that began in the past but the action or the effect of the action is still happening. For example: "Having finished writing the book, the author celebrated." The book was written in the past, but it still exists (and perhaps the celebration continues too). The form is easy to recognize; every sentence begins with the word *having* followed by a participial phrase. The phrase functions as an adjective.

Points for Student Analysis

- Every sentence begins with the word *having*.
- Immediately following the word *having* is a past participle phrase.
- Every sentence has a comma after the opening phrase.
- The opening phrase functions as an adjective to describe the first noun behind the comma.
- The opening phrase can be deleted, and the remaining words make a complete sentence.
- The sentence behind the comma can be N-V or N-V-N.

Grade 6 Models

1. *Having burnt the roast,* my dad ordered pizzas for supper.

2. *Having listened to the testimony,* the jury left for their quarters.

3. *Having sprained his ankle,* the quarterback could not play.

4. *Having won the scholar bowl match,* the team celebrated at DQ.

5. *Having recited the pledge,* the class sat down to listen to morning announcements.

Grade 7 Models

1. *Having battled the punishing rapids,* the Sockeye salmon deposited 4,000 eggs on the floor of the Adams River.

2. *Having stocked his sled,* the musher began the long race to reach Fairbanks, Alaska.

3. *Having examined the dog team at the first checkpoint,* the veterinarian allowed them to continue the race.

4. *Having carved canoes from cedar trees,* the whale hunters chased whales as far as forty miles from the shore.

5. *Having explored the Pacific Ocean,* Captain James Cook sailed his ship to Vancouver Island.

Grade 8 Models

1. *Having served the kiburu soup,* the chef waited for the critic's reaction.

2. *Having broken the lamp,* the boys tried to hide the pieces behind the couch.

3. *Having endured months of summer heat,* the construction workers relished the cool autumn weather.

4. *Having sailed the Pacific Ocean*, Magellan landed in the Philippines.

5. *Having eaten a huge Thanksgiving meal*, my aunts sat down to watch football.

PATTERN 16: OPEN WITH AN INFINITIVE PHRASE

Background Information

The word *to* is the sign of the infinitive. Add it to a base verb to create a simple infinitive. To create an infinitive phrase, add jewelry (adjective, adverbs, prepositional phrases) or nouns. Infinitives can appear anywhere in a sentence because they can function as adjectives, adverbs, or nouns. In this pattern the infinitive is always used to open the sentence.

While this might appear to be a difficult pattern, it can be quite easy to create if students are given support and guidance. Begin by showing students the five model sentences and have them make note of what they observe. Before students try to create this pattern in their groups, spend some time brainstorming infinitive phrases. Remember, one problem writers face is lack of content knowledge, so provide the content for their brainstorming. For example, think about the fairy tale Little Red Riding Hood (Polette, 2012). Think about the various characters and ask yourself what each one wanted to do. That answer can be expressed as an infinitive phrase. (See Table 3.4.)

Table 3.4

Little Red Wanted	The Big Bad Wolf Wanted
To help her Grandma	To hide Grandma from sight
To stay safe from the wolf	To wear Grandma's nightgown
To reach Grandma's cottage	To trick Little Red
To chase the wolf away	To find a yummy meal

Now ask a question about each character's actions. That answer becomes the complete sentence behind the infinitive.

- To help Grandma, (What did Little Red do to help Grandma?).
- To help Grandma, Little Red brought her a basket of goodies.
- To stay safe from the wolf, (What did Little Red do to stay safe?).
- To stay safe from the wolf, Little Red stayed on the path to Grandma's house.
- To trick Little Red, (What did the wolf do to trick Little Red?).
- To trick Little Red, the Big Bad Wolf put on Grandma's cap and gown.

This exercise also can be completed by using text from science or social studies class. Perhaps students have read Biel's (1992) article about mother tigers and their cubs. (See Table 3.5.)

Table 3.5

Mother Tigers Want	What Did Mother Tigers Do?
To keep their cubs safe,	mother tigers stay with cubs for three years.
To keep their babies warm,	mother tigers cuddle their cubs.
To teach young tigers how to hunt,	mother tigers let them follow when they hunt.
Tiger Cubs Want	**What Do Tiger Cubs Do?**
To prepare for their first hunt,	tiger cubs chase each other.
To stay safe when their mother hunts,	tiger cubs must stay in their den away from predators.

Let's imagine that your students have just read Rickitt's (2003) article "Magic in Middle-Earth" about the making of the movie trilogy *Lord of the Rings.* Let students brainstorm ideas from the article.

What did special effects technicians and makeup artists have to do to create this movie? (See Table 3.6).

Table 3.6

What Technicians Wanted or Needed to Do	How They Did It
To create the huge battle scenes,	the technicians wrote a new computer program.
To create a data bank of 250 body moves,	cameramen recorded stunt men wearing special black jumpsuits.
To make the battles look real,	the computer programmers created a digital brain for each warrior.

When we provide content, the writing becomes a manageable task. As an added bonus, students are deepening their comprehension of the material they have read.

Another way to help is to have students use their word bank of verbs and visualize as they follow a set of steps. Perhaps a group selects these verbs from their bank: *avoid, brew* and, *learn.*

Step 1. Create the simple infinitives: *to avoid, to brew,* and *to learn.*

Step 2. Create an infinitive phrase: *to avoid the tag, to brew the perfect cup of coffee, to learn my vocabulary words.*

Step 3. Finish the sentence by visualizing someone doing the action of the infinitive:

- To avoid the tag, the runner slid under the catcher's mitt.
- To brew the perfect cup of coffee, the chef used a French press.
- To learn my vocabulary words, I wrote each one five times.

These sentences answer two questions: What did someone want to do? How did they do it?

One final point about infinitives. Perhaps as a student you were taught to never split an infinitive. I prefer not to teach negative rules, ones that start with the words *never* or *do not.* I prefer to teach students that an infinitive is created by following the word *to* with a verb. If the student can avoid splitting an infinitive, I would encourage that. So the rule I teach is, "Always try to keep the sign of the infinitive *to* anchored to the verb." Teaching "Never split an infinitive" as an iron-clad rule can create stilted writing. True, in languages such as Latin an infinitive is considered one word. Hence, it cannot be split. But why would we follow rules of Latin when speaking or writing in English? Take note of professional authors who often split infinitives. Continuing to teach this ancient rule means that students often end up writing weak or awkward sentences (Schuster, 2003).

Points for Student Analysis

- Every sentence begins with the word *to.*
- The *to* is followed by a base form verb.
- Sometimes that is followed by adjectives, adverbs, prepositional phrases, or nouns.
- The phrase is always set off by a comma.
- The first noun tells who or what is doing the infinitive phrase.

Grade 6 Models

1. *To evade the police,* the robber hid in a trash dumpster.

2. *To catch a glimpse of the deer,* the children moved closer to the edge of the forest.

3. *To understand the story,* my sister read it a second time.

4. *To surprise our parents,* my brother cooked supper before they returned from work.

5. *To celebrate,* the team ate pizzas.

Grade 7 Models

1. *To congratulate Earnhardt,* the crew lined up in front of Victory Lane.

2. *To assure a spot in the playoffs,* the Blues need to win three more games.

3. *To impress the king,* a miller bragged that his daughter could spin gold from straw.

4. *To prevent forest fires,* the rangers taught the campers how to put out campfires.

5. *To frighten the audience,* the storyteller told a ghost story.

Grade 8 Models

1. *To create suspense,* the author hid the face of the robber.

2. *To protect the waterway,* the U. S. Army built Fort Dearborn along the Chicago River.

3. *To brighten the kitchen,* we painted the walls and ceiling white.

4. *To reach the new world,* the Pilgrims set sail on the *Mayflower.*

5. *To communicate with Helen,* Anne Sullivan taught her sign language.

PATTERN 17: RESTRICTIVE ADJECTIVE CLAUSES

Background Information

We can say two things about this form of an adjective clause. First, they begin with a relative pronoun: who, whose, whom, which, or that. In addition, they have verbs. Since the clause follows a noun and tells us which one or what kind, the dependent clause functions as an adjective.

Pattern 17 models restrictive adjective clauses. In other words, the clause is an essential part of the sentence. If the clause is removed, we still have a complete sentence but the sentence lacks essential information. This is a difficult concept for the students to grasp because they must determine the intention of the author. Let's look at an example.

1. The principal threw a pizza party for the students.

2. The principal threw a pizza party for the students who had perfect attendance.

Does the above first sentence tell the reader which students received the pizza party? As we read that sentence, it seems that all of the students enjoyed pizza. The second sentence provides the essential information that lets us know exactly which students enjoyed pizza.

If the adjective clause is essential to the sentence, no commas are required. If the adjective clause follows a floodlight noun or a common noun, the clause might very well be essential to the sentence. In Pattern 18, the students will write sentences with nonrestrictive clauses that do require commas.

If the adjective clause comes behind a proper noun, it is usually a nonrestrictive or nonessential clause. In the following models the first sentence demonstrates a nonrestrictive adjective clause. The reader does not need the extra information to know who gave the new cars, so they do need commas. In the second sentence the adjective clause is restrictive. The clause is needed so commas are eliminated. Because there are many talk shows, the reader needs the information to know that Oprah gave the cars.

- We received new cars from Oprah, who hosts a daytime talk show. (We do not need any more information about Oprah, so use the commas.)

- We received new cars from the talk show that Oprah hosts. (We need the adjective clause to know which talk show gave cars. Since the clause is needed, the commas are not needed.)

I tell students to think of it this way: If you do not need the clause, add handles (commas) that can be used to pick up the clause and throw it away. If you do need the clause, do not add the throwaway handles. I had student volunteers create the following poster for my classroom:

Restrictive Clause = Required = No Commas

Nonrestrictive Clause = Not Required = Commas

Students also struggle with understanding which relative pronoun should be used to introduce an adjective clause. Zinsser provides this warning, "Anyone who tries to explain 'that' and 'which' in less than an hour is asking for trouble" (2001, p. 118). Use *who, whose,* or *whom* if the clause refers to a person. Use *which* if the clause refers to things or animals; a *which* clause always needs commas. Use *that* if the clause refers to things; a *that* clause never needs commas. And when all else fails, trust grammar check.

The Benjamin and Berger (2010) book *Teaching Grammar: What Really Works* provides several games that can be played to help students understand the concept of essential versus nonessential adjective clauses.

Points for Student Analysis

- All of the clauses start with *who, whose, whom, which,* or *that.*
- None of the clauses has any special punctuation.
- All of the clauses come behind a noun; they are anchored to a noun.
- All of the clauses follow a common noun.
- All of the clauses give information about the noun they follow.
- All of the clauses have verbs.
- The clauses can be removed and a complete sentence remains.
- Without the clause, the exact meaning of the remaining sentence might be hazy.

Grade 6 Models

1. The astronaut *who fixed the hatch* waved to the cameras.

2. The mountain climbers used a cam *that protects the lead climber from falling.*

3. The giraffe *that had a broken leg* stared at the curious crowd.

4. Samuel Adams organized a group of men *who dumped tea into Boston Harbor.*

5. The dress *that the First Lady wore to the ball* had a diamond belt.

Grade 7 Models

1. The mountains *that flanked the western shore of the river* created problems for the explorers.

2. In midwinter the people *who live in northern Scandinavia* see no daylight for a month.

3. Of every ten salmon *that begin the trip up the Fraser River System* only two survive to reproduce.

4. The states designed a coat of arms *that showed a ship, a plow, and sheaves of wheat.*

5. A sash *that belonged to General Richard Montgomery* hangs in the Smithsonian.

Grade 8 Models

1. Some people *who remained loyal to Britain* formed a Loyalist Calvary in 1775.

2. The gunboat *that divers recovered in 1935* had sunk at Valcour Island.

3. The watch *that fell into the swimming pool* never kept time again.

4. The CEO bought a new car for each employee *who had worked for him ten years.*

5. The girls *who bought new cell phones* could not find a signal.

PATTERN 18: NONRESTRICTIVE ADJECTIVE CLAUSES

Background Information

Most of the background information for this pattern can be garnered from that discussed under Pattern 17. This pattern also uses relative pronouns to introduce dependent adjective clauses. But these clauses are not essential to the sentence, so they are set off with commas. Students may think of commas as little handles that can be used to throw away the non-essential clause.

Points for Student Analysis

- Every sentence has a clause that starts with *who, whose, whom,* or *which.*
- The clause is always set off with commas.
- The clause often appears behind a proper noun.
- The clause can be eliminated and the remaining words create a complete sentence.

Grade 6 Models

1. The pharaoh Khufu, *who ruled Upper and Lower Egypt,* built the Great Pyramid to serve as his tomb.

2. The British archeologist Sir Petrie, *who worked extensively on the Great Pyramid,* never found the mummy of Khufu.

3. Eskimo tell the story of Sedna, *who causes terrible sea storms and rules the migration of whales, seals, walruses, and all fish.*

4. The Irish have a myth about Cú Chulainn, *who could change forms to fight evil.*

5. Ictinus designed the Parthenon, *which has fifty columns.*

Grade 7 Models

1. Admiral David Farragut, *who joined the Navy at the age of nine,* fought in the War of 1812.

2. Robert Smalls, *who earned his freedom in the Civil War,* later served as a U.S. congressman from South Carolina.

3. A Duke University research vessel discovered the USS Monitor, *which sank during a violent storm in 1862.*

4. Navy divers have attempted to recover large sections of the Monitor, *which the U.S. government listed on the National Register of Historic Places.*

5. The *Monitor* expedition team, *which recovered the ship's 235-ton turret,* included 120 Navy divers.

Grade 8 Models

1. Our art class studied the paintings of Seurat, *who developed a technique called pointillism.*

2. Pablo Picasso, *who invented cubism,* also painted tranquil neoclassical pieces.

3. Hank Aaron, *who played for the Braves,* beat Babe Ruth's home run record.

4. Rocky Marciano, *who boxed from 1947 to 1956,* won the heavyweight championship title six times.

5. My brother climbed Arapaho Peak, *which belongs to the front range of the Rocky Mountains.*

PATTERN 19: COMPOUND SENTENCE WITH A SEMICOLON

Background Information

Teaching Pattern 19 probably will bring the wrath of editors, authors, grammar gods, and mechanics mavens raining down on my head. Pattern 19 creates a compound sentence joined by a semicolon, a format that most editors reject. Most editors suggest that the author revise and write two simple sentences or perhaps consider a sentence with a subordinate clause.

For example, take the following sentences.

1. The mountain climber checked his watch; only one hour of sunlight remained.

2. When the mountain climber checked his watch, he realized only one hour of sunlight remained.

3. Checking his watch, the mountain climber realized only one hour of sunlight remained.

4. The mountain climber checked his watch. Only one hour of sunlight remained.

Each sentence is grammatically correct, but I think that the first one does the best job of creating the sense of urgency. Teaching students how to use a semicolon effectively honors their role as authors who make decisions as they write. Students who have reached this point in pattern study are used to making decisions. I feel that lessons like this emphasize the craft of writing over the rules of writing.

The semicolon functions as a "light period" (Schuster, 2003). In other words, if the author has written two sentences that are closely related, they can be joined by a semicolon. The semicolon allows the reader to pause briefly; the period requires a full stop. The difficulty comes in determining whether the two sentences are closely related. Does the author want the two sentences to have equal weight? Does the author want the reader to take note of the close relationship? Is the close relationship obvious without the use of a connecting word? If the answer to all of these questions is yes, then perhaps a semicolon is the correct punctuation mark to use.

Points for Student Analysis

- Every sentence has a semicolon.
- The semicolon has a complete sentence on both sides.
- The sentences on either side can be N-V or N-V-N.

- The two sentences express a close relationship, such as cause and effect, contrast, or needed additional information.
- Parallel structure, such as repeating a verb or a noun phrase in both sentences, helps to show how the sentences relate.

Grade 6 Models

1. Ben Franklin wanted to swim faster than anyone; he invented flippers for his hands and feet.

2. At the age of twenty-six, Franklin wrote *Poor Richard's Almanac;* people loved it.

3. Franklin invented a wood-burning stove; it kept homes warmer than a fireplace.

4. Franklin began America's first library; he also began America's first fire station and hospital.

5. One day he began doodling during a meeting; he had invented the magic square.

Grade 7 Models

1. Sherpas searched for the missing woman; they spotted her ankle sticking out of the snow.

2. The mountain climber checked his watch; only one hour of daylight remained.

3. Americans buy vast amounts of processed food; Americans suffer from obesity and diabetes.

4. Taste buds can detect six tastes; the sense of smell can detect thousands of aromas.

5. Harriet Tubman signaled for silence; the barking of the bloodhounds drew near.

Grade 8 Models

1. Zeus blasted a lightning bolt from the sky; Io had angered him.

2. Apollo played his lyre for the gods; Artemis ignored them to hunt for wild boars and bears.

3. In a fit of anger, Artemis killed Orion; grieving, she turned him into a constellation.

4. The *Iliad* relates the story of the Trojan War; the *Odyssey* relates the return journey of Odysseus.

5. Epimetheus had no gift for the humans; Prometheus gave the gift of stolen fire.

PATTERN 20: COMPOUND SENTENCE WITH AN ELLIPTICAL EXPRESSION

Background Information

This is another difficult pattern because it requires the use of a semicolon and an elliptical expression. It is a pattern that is used rarely, but one that can be effective if done properly. Again the two sentences that are merged with a semicolon must have a very close relationship. The sentences show a comparison or a contrast of two actions. The sentence behind the semicolon substitutes a comma for a word or words. If the omitted words were used, they would be the same as the words used in the first sentence. I tell students to think of these two sentences as a teeter-totter with perfect balance. The comma used in the second sentence carries the same weight as the words used in the first sentence. Using the comma eliminates redundancy.

To help students understand this pattern, in the models I have italicized the words in the first sentence that are eliminated in the second sentence. Try reading the second sentence by substituting the italicized words for the comma. The meaning becomes clear.

Points for Student Analysis

- Every sentence has a semicolon.
- The sentence in front of the semicolon is complete.
- The sentence behind the semicolon has a comma.
- The sentence behind the semicolon is missing words and cannot stand alone.

Grade 7 Models

1. Michelangelo *painted* the Sistine Chapel; Raphael, the Vatican.

2. Jason Marquis *pitched* for the Cardinals; Josh Beckett, for the Marlins.

3. Luke Donald *ranks number one in* golf; Caroline Wozniacki, in tennis.

4. The sixth graders *read Harry Potter;* the eighth graders, *Lord of the Rings.*

5. On Wednesday *the cafeteria served* pizza; on Thursday, tacos.

Grade 8 Models

1. Darby *played a musical number* by Bach; Joan, one by Mozart.

2. Eric the Red *explored* the coast of Greenland; Leif Ericson, the coast of Labrador.

3. Galileo *invented* the water thermometer; Fahrenheit, the mercury thermometer.

4. My mother *drinks* tea *for breakfast;* my father, coffee.

5. In science class *we use* laptops; in English class, iPad tablets.

PATTERN 21: OPENING WITH AN ABSOLUTE

Background Information

The absolute is a powerful structure that can add energy to writing. My students have found the absolute to be especially helpful when writing personal narratives or fiction. Students who are adept at visualizing will have an easier time creating absolutes.

The form of the absolute is a noun modified by a participial phrase (used in Patterns 13 to 15). Let's look at some models.

- *Tails curled around a branch,* the howler monkeys perched in the treetops.
- *Eyes darting,* the toucan searched for a meal of figs.
- *Wings fluttering,* the hummingbird hovered near the feeder.

I have found that the easiest way to teach this pattern is to show students a picture that has a great deal of action. Focus on the animal or person in the picture and select a body part to describe. Mention the body part and then follow that with a participial phrase. Or perhaps focus on a person and take note of something they might be holding. Mention that noun and follow it with a participial phrase. The trick to creating the absolute is to always begin with a noun. The students tend to fall into the trap of creating a participial phrase without the noun when they first learn this pattern. They write a participial phrase instead.

Once students become adept at writing this pattern, I encourage them to experiment with moving the absolute behind the noun that it describes. But they should remember to always anchor the absolute to the correct noun.

Points for Student Analysis

- Every sentence begins with a noun or a possessive pronoun followed by a noun.
- The noun is followed by a participial phrase.
- The phrase that opens the sentence is followed by a comma.
- The phrase can be removed and a complete sentence remains.
- The phrase describes the first noun after the comma.
- It is easy to visualize the phrase in front of the comma.

Grade 7 Models

1. *His back straight and chin raised,* General Washington impressed everyone as he rode his horse across his plantation.

2. *Muskets loaded,* the troops awaited the attack.

3. *His voice booming,* Henry Knox shouted orders to the officers in training.

4. *Hands bound by thick ropes,* the captured artillerymen shuffled toward the stockades.

5. *Hands trembling and heart pounding,* the young boy entered the battle.

Grade 8 Models

1. *Her hand resting upon the wheel,* Anne Hutchinson prepared to spin thread.

2. *Eyes lowered and head bowed,* the bride spoke her wedding vows.

3. *Finger pointed at the women,* the judge accused them of witchcraft.

4. *An arm outstretched, hand open,* Williams offered his friendship to the Narragansett chief.

5. *Hands clapping and toes tapping,* the colonists enjoyed the fiddler's songs.

PATTERN 22: ADJECTIVES MOVED BEHIND A NOUN

Background Information

One of my most vivid memories from grade school English class is teachers saying, "Use lots of adjectives to make your writing interesting." So I would proceed to describe that cold, soggy, sticky, drippy, enormous chocolate ice cream cone that dripped on my crisp, new, blue, pleated skirt. As Mark Twain might suggest, when you find an adjective, cross it out. For some time I taught my students that if they found themselves listing three adjectives, they had to cross out at least one of them, preferably two. Then I read Noden's *Image Grammar* (1999) and learned a trick used by professional writers. Rather than using a string of three adjectives, writers leave one adjective in place and shift the other two behind the noun.

The technique is particularly useful while creating personal narratives or fiction, but my students have found it serves them in informational writing as well.

Points for Student Analysis

- Each sentence is N-V or N-V-V.
- Each sentence has one or two adjectives or participles that function as adjectives placed behind a noun.
- The adjectives and participles behind the noun are set off with commas.

Grade 7 Models

1. My sister slipped a flower lei, *fragrant and colorful,* around my neck.

2. The star fruit, *ripe and yellow,* dangled just out of my reach.

3. The path, *steep and crooked,* zigzags down the side of a mountain.

4. The volcano, *ominous,* looms before me and blocks the setting sun.

5. The children danced in the waterfall, *cold and sparkling clear.*

Grade 8 Models

1. As I stepped off the airplane, I inhaled an unfamiliar scent, *acrid and sweet.*

2. The tourist joined in the celebrations on Tahir Square, *crowded and noisy.*

3. The pyramids, *mystical and immense,* pointed toward the sky.

4. The dirt alleys, *narrow and twisting,* ran past the ancient mausoleums.

5. The felucca's sails, *unfurled and patched,* caught the wind that took us down the Nile.

PATTERN 23: OPEN WITH A PARALLEL STRUCTURE

Background Information

In all my years of teaching, I have yet to meet a class that did not like Pattern 23. I caution the students that using this pattern more than once in an essay can weaken its effect. The pattern is unusual and does seem to catch a reader's attention. I do not want students to use a range of patterns just to achieve sentence variety. I want them to give careful thought to how the patterns can bring power to their words.

This pattern makes a perfect opening for mapping expository essays. Many of my students had been taught to begin expository essays with a dreadful formula. For example: "There are three rides that I like at Six Flags. First, I like the Screaming Eagle. Second, I like the Log Flume. Finally, I enjoy Thunder River." I repeatedly modeled how to use sentence patterns to transform those horrible mapping paragraphs into something interesting. The students quickly saw the power of Pattern 23. "Screaming Eagle, Log Flume, Thunder River—stand aside; I'm on my way to enjoy the rides at Six Flags."

Most of the sentences below do model a parallel structure in threes, but I have included models that use pairs as well.

The most difficult feature of this pattern is avoiding the words *these are* to begin the sentence behind the dash. Using such an empty construct diminishes the beauty of the sentence. Listen to the following sentences and notice the difference in the rhythm of each. The first sentence is the most fluid.

1. Howler monkeys, jaguars, anteaters—a menagerie of animals make their home in the Amazon Rain Forest.

2. Howler monkeys, jaguars, anteaters—these animals make their home in the Amazon Rain Forest.

3. Howler monkeys, jaguars, anteaters—these are the animals that make their home in the Amazon Rain Forest.

Points for Student Analysis

- Each sentence begins with a set of nouns.
- Sometimes an adjective is used with the nouns.
- A dash follows the opening list.
- A complete sentence follows the dash.
- The sentence talks about the items in the list.
- The sentence can be N-V or N-V-N.

Grade 7 Models

1. *Pico, Zanzibar, Admirality*—I have visited each of these islands in the past five years.

2. *Blue fin tuna, anglerfish, and dolphins*—the oil spill impacted each of these creatures.

3. *Horses, elk, and bison*—these animals roamed near the geysers in Yellowstone.

4. *Hang gliding and windsurfing*—my brother tried both of these sports while vacationing on the outer banks of North Carolina.

5. *John Lennon, Bob Dylan, and Elvis Presley*—each of these musicians has had a strong influence on other musicians.

Grade 8 Models

1. *Chocolate and motorcycles*—these bring a smile to our teacher's face.

2. *Monet, Degas, Renoir*—these Impressionist painters lived in France.

3. *Whitney, McCormick, and Deere*—each American inventor changed the face of agriculture.

4. *Denali, Glacier, and Yosemite*—my sister has visited each of these national parks.

5. *Rippling curtains of pink, patches of red, flashes of green*—the aurora borealis painted the night sky.

PATTERN 24: USING CONJUNCTIVE ADVERBS TO CONNECT TWO SENTENCES

Background Information

Pattern 24 is the only pattern that asks the students to write two sentences. The second sentence is introduced with a conjunctive adverb. Grammar books that I have consulted disagree on the proper way to punctuate a sentence that opens with a conjunctive adverb. Some grammarians insist that a comma must always follow a conjunctive adverb. Others suggest that the comma should be used only after the conjunctives that end in *ly*. Still others suggest that the author must decide if a pause is needed after the conjunctive adverb and punctuate accordingly. I instruct the students that they must read the sentence and decide if a comma will provide clarity to the sentence. I have provided a partial list of conjunctive adverbs in Table 3.7.

Table 3.7

Type of Relationship	Conjunctive Adverbs
Addition	Besides, finally, furthermore, moreover
Comparison	Also, likewise, similarly
Contrast	Even though, however, instead, nevertheless, otherwise, though
Cause and Effect	Therefore, hence, consequently, subsequently
Sequence	Afterward, eventually, meanwhile

At one time I taught students to treat this pattern as a compound structure, placing a semicolon at the end of the first sentence and a comma after the conjunctive adverb. But the students ended up with cumbersome sentences that were difficult to comprehend. I now agree with Schuster, who says, "Good writers do *not* use semicolons before conjunctive adverbs and other transitional expressions. They use periods" (2003, p. 176).

Points for Student Analysis

- Each sample is two complete sentences.
- The second sentence is always introduced by a conjunctive adverb followed by a comma.
- The conjunctive adverb shows a specific relationship between the two sentences.
- The sentences can follow any pattern.

Grade 7 Models

1. The *Lord of the Rings* films include huge battle scenes. *Therefore,* computer programs created over 20,000 warriors with digital brains.

2. Creating wizards, orcs, and hobbits took gallons of make-up. *Consequently,* some actors spent hours preparing for each scene.

3. Archeologists discovered dinosaur fossils in Saskatchewan. *Therefore,* many archeology students now work there as interns.

4. The climate of Saskatchewan changed drastically. *Hence,* archeologists find dinosaur bones preserved in excellent condition.

5. Archeologists unearthed a *T. rex* head and backbone in Eastend, Saskatchewan. *Subsequently,* they uncovered a shoulder bone and two leg bones.

Grade 8 Models

1. Van Gogh suffered from mental illness. *Nevertheless,* his still lifes and landscapes hang in the world's greatest museums.

2. Van Gogh worked many years as a preacher among the poor miners of Belgium. *Consequently,* many of his early works express the poverty he saw.

3. In 1886 Van Gogh moved to Paris. *Therefore,* the Impressionists influenced him.

4. Van Gogh studied the works of the Impressionists. *Hence,* he adopted the brilliant hues found in works by Pissarro and Seurat.

5. Van Gogh visited farms in Arles in the springtime. *Subsequently,* he painted a series of flowering orchards.

EMPOWERING STUDENTS

I conduct numerous language arts workshops throughout the country, but my favorite workshop to present is the one that introduces these twenty-four patterns. I think I find that workshop most satisfying because I have seen firsthand how the patterns empower students. When students learn how to write at the sentence level, the essays, narratives, and reports that they produce are stronger. The students understand how to express relationships between ideas. They have a good foundation in the mechanics of writing. Knowing the sentence patterns gives them a way to attack a larger task. I hope the patterns are as effective for you and your students as they have been for mine.

In the next chapter, I introduce sentence combination exercises. Creating combinations gives students another way to learn the patterns. It also begins to teach students how to revise early drafts.

Sentence Combining to Reinforce Skills

4

Sentence combining is an instructional approach that can be used for students who need reinforcement in creating the patterns. It provides a more concrete way of producing the patterns. Since the words and ideas are provided for the students, they can concentrate on the pattern without struggling for content. They must decide how to combine the "kernels" to produce the designated pattern. In the exercises I have created, I chose not to break every sentence down to its smallest kernel. This will make it a bit easier for students to determine the relationship between the ideas. In the first set of activities, I have provided two sentences—occasionally three—that students need to combine to create the target pattern. Students will begin to develop a range of important skills through this work.

- Understanding the relationship between ideas: time, condition, cause and effect, and so on
- Selecting an appropriate conjunction to reflect the relationship
- Changing nouns to pronouns appropriate in case and number
- Embedding modifiers in appropriate locations
- Manipulating verb forms to create participles or infinitives
- Manipulating verb forms to show an accurate tense

Sentence combining also provides students with an introduction to revision and editing, skills that they need when creating original work. By the fifth grade, the Common Core State Standards require students to combine sentences. They are required to "expand, combine, and reduce sentences for meaning, reader/listener interest, and style" (National Governors Association Center for Best Practices and Council of Chief State School Officers, 2010, CC.5.L.3.a. All rights reserved.).

I encourage the students to work slowly on the combination exercises. I want them to read the kernel sentences and then work on combinations orally.

When they hear a sentence that is coherent and cohesive, they write the sentence. Once the sentence is on paper, I ask students to read it aloud again to listen for the rhythm of the words. I want them to internalize the patterns. Only then do I have them reread the sentence to decide on punctuation.

My students enjoy using word processing programs to complete the combination exercises since they can click and drag sentence parts to create a sentence. I prefer that they work the combinations on paper because it slows down the process. Students spend more time experimenting orally with possible combinations. Slowing down the process helps students to hear the relationships among ideas.

The final step to sentence combination activities is a teacher-led discussion of the final combinations. Without this discussion, the activities are nothing more than busy work. The discussions focus on the decisions that authors make as they work. We also discuss placement of sentence elements to create clarity and rhythm. And finally, we discuss punctuation and mechanics.

My hope is that students who practice sentence combinations will develop automaticity with syntax. Then when they are working on lengthier texts, they can dedicate their cognitive energies to content and organization. Students who labor over how to structure a sentence and how to express relationships of ideas suffer when developing content (Strong, 1986). Sentence combination work creates an awareness of sentence elements and how to put those elements together to create a range of sentences.

The first sets of sentence combination exercises are linked to specific patterns. Many of these exercises cite a magazine, book, or journal. While the sentences are not copied from those materials, I used a range of magazines and books to provide content. I found that the content in the combinations often sparked curiosity in my students and they wanted to read more. I hope that your students will have that same reaction and that the bibliographic information will lead you to a source of reading material for your students.

The sets that are linked to specific patterns require a student to write numerous sentences of one pattern. For example, set one of Pattern 9 offers this cued combination:

- Mrs. Quimby stood back from the sink.
- She swished suds in the dishpan. (as)
- Combined: Mrs. Quimby stood back from the sink as she swished suds in the dishpan.

Cleary's original text reads quite differently:

"Ha-ha to all of you if you don't hurry up," said Mrs. Quimby, as she swished suds in the dishpan. She stood back from the sink so she would not spatter the white uniform she wore in the doctor's office where she worked as a receptionist. (Cleary, 1981, pp. 13–14)

Am I implying that Cleary could have written a better sentence? Absolutely not.

The combinations are exercises for students who might need additional help to understand how to blend sentence elements to create a range of patterns. When the students have completed a set, they will have four or five sentences that all follow the same pattern. Such repetition is not a sign of good writing, but the repetition of one pattern does provide reinforcement in the pattern. It is comparable to piano practice. A piano student might repeat scales several times to ingrain patterns and notes, to develop automaticity while playing. But in the final product, a musical piece, we would not expect to see a dull repetition of scales.

SENTENCE COMBINATIONS: PART 1

Each pattern is introduced with a tip, or a helpful hint, for the teacher to use while helping the students.

Pattern 6: Compound Sentence With a Coordinating Conjunction

Tip: Coordinating conjunctions: so, and, but, or, nor, for, yet

Once students have written a combined sentence, ask them to put a finger on the coordinating conjunction. Now check to make sure that they have a complete sentence on each side of the coordinating conjunction. Often they will have a complete sentence before the conjunction but not behind it. While that may be a grammatically correct sentence, it does not hit the target pattern.

In the later non-cued sets for Pattern 6, students will need to learn how to use the correct pronoun in place of the nouns in the second sentence. Example:

- Trainers use Arabians in children's therapy programs.
- *Trainers* use *Arabians* to work cattle.
- Combination: Trainers use Arabians in children's therapy programs, and *they* use *them* to work cattle.

Set 1: Cued Combination

Samples gathered from "Let's Get to Know One Another" by Danielle Poorman (2011).

The little girl wanted to pet the horse.

She felt afraid. (but)

She approached the horse slowly.

She held her hand flat near its nose. (and)

The horse bent its head down.

It sniffed her hand. (and)

The girl petted the horse slowly.

She talked in a soft voice. (and)

The horse nuzzled her hand.

The young girl felt like his special friend. (so)

Set 2: Cued Combination

Samples gathered from "So You Want to Work With Horses" by Lusted and Derby (2011).

An equine dentist grinds excess material from a horse's teeth.

It can chew its food properly. (so)

Some horses wear metal horseshoes.

Other horses need plastic shoes. (but)

A farrier nails on the metal shoes.

A horse podiatrist glues on the plastic shoes. (but)

Veterinarians can work with horses on a ranch.

They can work in an animal hospital. (or)

Horse owners need special equipment for their horses.

They shop at a special store called a tack shop. (so)

Set 3: Non-cued Combination—And, But, So

Samples gathered from "Horses Helping Others" by Natasha Yim (2011).

Erin Livingston wanted horses to help children with special needs.

She researched several programs.

She learned that some children cannot walk.

They can ride a horse.

Riding a horse makes these children use their leg muscles.

This helps to keep their legs strong.

The horses need many skills to help these special children.

Erin spends a lot time training the horses.

The horses teach children about trust.

They teach children about patience.

Set 4: Non-cued Combination—And, But, So

Samples gathered from "Arabian Horses—From the Family Tent to the 4-H Ring" by Susan Bavaria (2011).

The beautiful Arabian horses have large dark eyes.

Arabian horses have a graceful arched neck.

Bedouins treasured their Arabians.

The horses often slept in the family tent.

For thousands of years Arabians have lived closely with humans.

Arabians have a special ability to bond with humans.

Quarter horses and Thoroughbreds run short races.

The Arabian can run the 100-mile marathon race.

Trainers use Arabians in children's therapy programs.

Trainers use Arabians to work cattle.

Set 5: Non-cued Combination

Samples gathered from "Extreme Mustang Makeover" by Miller and Lusted (2011).

Every year the Bureau of Land Management rounds up thousands of wild mustangs.

People can adopt a mustang for $125.

The mustang needs a large pen, a high fence, and shelter.

The mustang also needs an owner with patience and a kind heart.

A mustang named Blue Phantom had lived her life in the wild.

Now Blue Phantom needed to learn how to wear a saddle and bridle.

The owner needed to gain Blue Phantom's respect.

Blue Phantom would never learn to wear a saddle.

Owners need a great deal of patience.

Gentling a horse can take several months.

Pattern 7: An Appositive Behind a Noun

Tip: Remember that the appositive must be set off with commas. In the first sets, the second sentence will have a group of italicized words that will be used as the appositive behind the subject of the first sentence. In later sets, students must determine which words will serve as the appositive and decide where to place it. But the appositive can always be pulled from the second sentence.

Example:

- Special effects technicians found a solution to creating the huge battle scenes.
- The solution to creating battle scenes was *computer technology.*
- Combination: Special effects technicians found a solution to creating the huge battle scenes, computer technology.

Set 1: Cued

The cheetah sprints at sixty miles an hour.

The cheetah is *an African cat.*

My puppy snuggled on my lap.

My puppy is named *Scamp.*

The camel had one hump.

The camel is *a Bactrian.*

My brother plays football.

My brother is *an eighth grader.*

The parrot used its beak to crack the nuts.

The parrot is *a macaw.*

Set 2: Cued

Samples taken from the August 2010 edition of *National Geographic Kids.*

Nonja takes pictures of visitors at the zoo.

Nonja is *an orangutan.*

The baby floated on its mother's tummy.

The baby is *a sea otter.*

Butch strapped on a winged jet pack.

Butch is *the spy dog.*

Kitty Galore finds the top-secret files.

Kitty Galore is *an evil feline.*

Diggs accidentally doused Catherine with water.

Diggs is *a German shepherd.*

Set 3: Non-cued

Samples gathered from "John Muir, Nature Boy" (Buckley, 2011).

John Muir fought to preserve wilderness areas in America.

John Muir was a famous environmentalist.

A special group works to teach children about nature.

This group is the Sierra Club.

Theodore Roosevelt camped with Muir.

Theodore Roosevelt was the twenty-sixth president of the United States.

John Muir and Stickeen explored glaciers in Alaska.

Stickeen is a little dog.

Taylor Glacier carved the earth as it slowly moved.

Taylor Glacier is an endless sheet of ice.

Set 4: Non-cued

Samples gathered from "Buttons Are Fasten-ating" by Mitzi C. Smith (2011).

Large copper buttons on their uniforms earned the New York Police an unusual nickname.

The police were nicknamed coppers.

Spies and smugglers used buttons to hide things.

The things they hid were secret messages and poison.

Duke Ellington thought shirts with buttons brought bad luck.

Duke Ellington was a jazz musician.

Young girls used to collect 999 buttons on a charm string.

The charm string is an old American tradition.

The 1,000th button on a young girl's charm string came with something special.

The special thing was a marriage proposal.

Set 5: Non-cued

Samples gathered from "Magic in Middle-Earth" by Richard Rickitt (2003).

J. R. R. Tolkien created a fantasy world of hobbits, ringwraiths, and wizards.

Tolkien is the author of *Lord of the Rings*.

Special effects technicians found a solution to creating the huge battle scenes.

The solution to creating battle scenes was computer technology.

Computers created the wargs and mumaks.

Wargs are wolflike creatures.

Mumaks are elephantlike animals.

Andy Serkis provided Gollum's voice.

Andy Serkis is an English actor.

Model makers made Helm's Dike with styrofoam and a special paint roller.

The special paint roller was called the Fred Flintstone.

Pattern 8: Open With an Adverb Clause

Tip: In the first sets, a subordinator is provided in parentheses for the students. In later sets, students must determine the correct subordinator and the correct pronouns. In many sentences, several of the subordinators can be used correctly. A guided discussion demonstrating the different choices will help students to develop a deeper understanding of the relationship the subordinator creates between the dependent and independent clauses. (See Table 3.2 in the previous chapter for a list of the most common subordinators.)

Cued example:

- (as) For centuries people traveled.
- They took their games to new places.
- For centuries, *as* people traveled, they took their games to new places.
- Non-cued example:
- The Seminoles began living in concrete housing.
- The Seminoles still constructed thatched chickees for the summer.
- Even after the Seminoles began living in concrete housing, *they* still constructed thatched chickees for the summer.

Set 1: Cued

Samples gathered from "Animals at Play" by Jennifer Mattox (2011).

(when)Young bears play.

They bite each other on the neck and ears.

(if) Monkeys want to play.

They show other monkeys a silly face.

(after) Dolphins blow bubbles.

They swim through them, trying to break them.

(whenever) Animals feel happy.

They like to play.

(when) Polar bears in the zoo find balls floating in the water.

They pounce on them.

Set 2: Cued

Samples gathered from "Games That Travel the World" by Chitra Soundar (2011).

(as) For centuries people traveled.

They took their games to new places.

(when) People came home from their travels.

They brought new games with them.

(although) Chess started in India 1,500 years ago.

People now play it all over the world.

(after) The game weiqi traveled from China to Japan.

The Japanese began calling it go.

(as) Games journey around the world.

They take on new forms.

Set 3: Non-cued

Samples gathered from "Ancient Mound Builders" by E. Barrie Kavasch (2003).

An important warrior or elder died.

His people would place him on a structure made of logs that they burned.

The fire burned down.

They covered this over with earth.

More important people died.

Tribe members placed those bodies on top of the original mound.

These mounds grew higher and higher.

They sometimes connected to other nearby mounds.

Economic development began to destroy the sacred mounds.

State and national parks were established to protect the remaining mounds.

Set 4: Non-cued

Samples gathered from "First Contact With Europeans" by Stephen Currie (2003).

Ponce de Leon believed a Fountain of Youth existed.

Ponce de Leon sailed to the area now known as Florida.

He and his explorers sailed along Florida's southwestern shoreline.

Some Calusa Indians beckoned to them to come ashore.

The explorers dropped anchor.

They sent several men ashore.

The Calusa had never seen such fascinating supplies.

The Calusa began carting away tools and oars.

The Europeans objected.

A brief battle broke out.

Set 5: Non-cued

Samples gathered from "First Contact With Europeans" by Stephen Currie (2003).

Hernando de Soto traveled through the Southeast.

He visited the Indian peoples of Alabama, Georgia, and Mississippi.

The Creek spoke gracious words of friendship.

De Soto did not respond in the same way.

One Creek leader gave DeSoto a beautiful string of pearls.

De Soto treated them with cruelty.

He accepted their gifts.

He demanded they provide food and shelter for his men.

European powers grew.

The Indian cultures rapidly changed.

Set 6: Non-cued

Samples gathered from "No Teepees Here" by Rhonda Fair (2003).

People often think of the teepee as the traditional housing of all American Indians.

The Indians lived in many types of homes.

The Seminoles lived in swampy areas of Florida.

Their pole homes had a raised floor to avoid flooding.

The Seminoles began living in concrete housing.

The Seminoles continued to construct thatched chickees for the summer.

The Witchitas wanted to honor the supreme being, Kinnikasus.

The Witchitas prayed to the spiritual power before thatching the roof.

Europeans influenced the Creeks.

Creek homes had wooden shingle roofs.

Pattern 9: Close With an Adverb Clause

Tip: The subordinator will now introduce the second sentence. The students will need to decide on the correct pronouns to use in the completed combination. Example:

- The swans flew in circles.
- The swans spotted the pond.
- The swans flew in circles when *they* spotted the pond.

Set 1: Cued

Samples gathered from *Ramona Quimby, Age 8* by Beverly Cleary (1981).

Ramona hoped her parents would forget the talking-to.

She did not want anything to spoil her day. (because)

Mrs. Quimby stood back from the sink.

She swished suds in the dishpan. (as)

Mrs. Quimby handed everyone a lunch bag.

They left home. (before)

Mr. Quimby gave each girl a new pink eraser.

They held out their hands. (when)

Mr. Quimby hugged Ramona.

She sighed. (when)

Set 2: Cued

The poacher displayed the jaguar pelts.

He had done nothing wrong. (as if)

The researchers stepped away from the jaguar.

The tranquilizer began to wear off. (as soon as)

The activist lobbied government to create a protected area for the cats.

She had collected disturbing data about jaguars. (after)

Jaguars can bite through a turtle's shell.

They have powerful jaws. (because)

The Paraguay River and its tributaries flooded.

Months of rain had drenched the area. (because)

Set 3: Non-cued

Samples gathered from *The Trumpet of the Swan* by E. B. White (1970).

Sam knew he would return to the pond.

He had seen the nest of a Trumpeter Swan.

Mr. Beaver cautioned Sam to take care.

He walked across the swamps.

A pilot flew Sam and his father to the lake.

They camped for several days.

In the evenings Sam and his father would sit on the porch.

They finished eating supper.

Sam hoped he would see the young swans.

They came out of their eggs.

Set 4: Non-cued

Western Union completed the transcontinental telegraph.

People no longer used the Pony Express.

Reconnaissance balloons enabled Union regiments to fire artillery accurately.

They could not see the enemy from the ground.

The generals on both sides deliberated their next moves.

The soldiers saw little military action.

DeKooning, a penniless artist, stowed away on a freighter.

He dreamed of living in America.

DeKooning married Elaine Fried, a vibrant daredevil.

DeKooning's work showed more vibrancy and movement.

Set 5: Non-cued

Samples gathered from *Getting to Know the World's Greatest Artists: Botticelli* by Mike Venezia (1993).

Alessandro Filiepi became known as Botticelli.

He went to live with his older brother.

People called the brother Botticello, or "little barrel."
The brother had a short round body.

Botticelli met many artists.
Botticelli lived and worked in his brother's workshop.

Botticelli's early paintings looked very much like Lippi's paintings.
Botticelli had worked as Lippi's assistant.

Lorenzo de' Medici encouraged his friends to hire Botticelli.
Lorenzo de' Medici loved Botticelli's paintings.

Set 6: Non-cued

Critics hail Mary Cassatt as a great American artist.
She spent most of her life living and painting in France.

Mr. and Mrs. Cassatt wanted their children to see the sights.
They lived in Paris.

They visited museums and art galleries.

Mary saw her first works of art.

Mary changed her painting style.

She became a close friend of Edgar Degas, an Impressionist painter.

Mary painted tender scenes of mothers and their children.

She never had any children of her own.

Pattern 10: Parallel Items in a Series

Tip: The early sets require students to complete sentences with nouns in a series. Later sets require parallel phrases. Students might have to change the number of a verb or a noun in the completed combination. Example:

- My computer needed a new battery.
- My DS needed a new battery.
- My cell phone needed a new battery.
- Combination: My computer, DS, and cell phone all needed new batteries.

Set 1: Nouns in a Series

Giraffes live in our zoo.

Hippos live in our zoo.

Elephants live in our zoo.

Kangaroos can hop.

Rabbits can hop.

Frogs can hop.

The squirrels played in the big oak tree.

The blue jays played in the big oak tree.

The butterflies played in the big oak tree.

Books entertain me on rainy days.

Movies entertain me on rainy days.

Games entertain me on rainy days.

The thunder frightened the puppy.

The lightening frightened the puppy.

The wind frightened the puppy.

Set 2: Nouns in a Series

My computer needed a new battery.

My DS needed a new battery.

My cell phone needed a new battery.

Snowballs make winter fun.

Sleds make winter fun.

Ice skates make winter fun.

Popcorn makes a healthy after-school snack.

Apples make a healthy after-school snack.

Muffins make a healthy after-school snack.

Egrets suffered because of the oil spill.

Ducks suffered because of the oil spill.

Turtles suffered because of the oil spill.

Plastic bags littered the beach.

Soda cans littered the beach.

Fast-food wrappers littered the beach.

Set 3: Nouns in a Series

Skateboarding requires protective gear.

Rollerblading requires protective gear.

Biking requires protective gear.

Rubies glistened in the king's crown.

Diamonds glistened in the king's crown.

Emeralds glistened in the king's crown.

The marching band had trombones.

The marching band had tubas.

The marching band had trumpets.

In the fall the farmers harvest cranberries.

In the fall the farmers harvest corn.

In the fall the farmers harvest soybeans.

In Egypt my brother visited the Great Pyramids.

In Egypt my brother visited the Sphinx.

In Egypt my brother visited the Cairo Museum.

Set 4: Nouns and Phrases in a Series

Tigers have razor-sharp claws.

Tigers have enormous teeth.

Tigers have tremendous strength.

Tigers like to feast on water buffalo.

Tigers like to feast on wild pigs.

Tigers like to feast on deer.

Tigers like to lie in cool shallow pools to escape from flies.

Tigers like to lie in cool shallow pools to escape from mosquitoes.

Tigers like to lie in cool shallow pools to escape from gnats.

Tigers once roamed in the frozen north of Asia.

Tigers once roamed in the jagged mountains of Asia.

Tigers once roamed in the steamy jungles of Asia.

Male tigers may fight over a hunting territory.

Male tigers may fight over a female.

Set 5: Nouns and Phrases in a Series

Samples gathered from *The Big Book of Trains* by Jane Yorke (1998).

The diesel-electric locomotive hauled freight across the United States.

The diesel-electric locomotive hauled freight from California.

The diesel-electric locomotive hauled freight to Chicago.

The locomotive pulled five freight cars.

The locomotive pulled seventeen coal cars.

The locomotive pulled eleven flatbeds.

During our trip around the world we dined on lechon in Manila.

During our trip around the world we dined on calzone in Naples.

During our trip around the world we dined on macarons in Paris.

At one stop I snapped close-ups of interesting parts of an old steam engine.

I snapped the cowcatcher in the front.

I snapped the sandbox near the wheels.

I snapped the firebox behind the cab. (Hint: End the first sentence with a colon and list the prepositional phrases as appositives.)

Monorail trains run high up off the ground.

Monorail trains run over the tops of buildings.

Monorail trains even run over rivers.

Pattern 11: Parallel Verb Phrases in a Series

Tip: Caution students to make sure the number of the verb agrees with the subject. Most sentences will use *and* to create the parallel structure, but some may use the word *then.*

Set 1

The clown juggled.

The clown tumbled.

The clown turned summersaults.

The sea otters float in the river.

The sea otters dive in the river.

The sea otters swim in the river.

The musician sang.

The musician danced.

The musician played piano.

On Saturday I dusted my room.

On Saturday I vacuumed my room.

On Saturday I straightened up my room.

The baby laughed during the game of peekaboo.

The baby clapped during the game of peekaboo.

The baby hid her face during the game of peekaboo.

Set 2

During recess we ran.

During recess we skipped.

During recess we bounced balls.

The ballerina twirled.

The ballerina leaped.

The ballerina bowed.

The chef at my favorite restaurant stirred the soup.

The chef at my favorite sampled the soup.

The chef at my favorite salted the soup.

The seamstress measured the cloth.

The seamstress marked the cloth.

The seamstress cut the cloth.

The stylist shampooed my hair.

The stylist cut my hair.

The stylist dried my hair.

Set 3

Before going to bed I eat a snack.

Before going to bed I take a bath.

Before going to bed I brush my teeth.

The green goo oozed down the halls.

The green goo flowed out the windows.

The green goo covered the playground.

Millions of gallons of oil seeped from the seafloor.

Millions of gallons of oil floated to the surface.

Millions of gallons of oil created an oil slick.

Leonardo da Vinci painted oil portraits.

Leonardo da Vinci sculpted marble statues.

Leonardo da Vinci designed magnificent bridges.

While vacationing in Charleston, we walked the length of Meeting Street.

While vacationing in Charleston, we toured Fort Sumter.

While vacationing in Charleston, we bought souvenirs at the open air market.

Set 4

From high in the sky, the gannet spies an easy target.

The gannet dives toward the water.

The gannet swallows its prey whole.

The springer spaniel on the beach raced after a seagull.

The springer spaniel on the beach dove into the water.

The springer spaniel on the beach finally gave up the chase.

At the animal hospital the wallabies jump from their cribs.

At the animal hospital the wallabies run down the halls.

At the animal hospital the wallabies chase each other.

The chimpanzee uses sticks as tools.

The chimpanzee digs for bugs.

The chimpanzee chews leaves for the water.

The Pennsylvania farmer plowed the field.

The Pennsylvania farmer planted the summer rye.

The Pennsylvania farmer waited for rain.

Set 5

Dr. Martin Luther King spoke with eloquence.

Dr. Martin Luther King fought for equality.

Dr. Martin Luther King died for his beliefs.

When we visited Disneyland, Minnie Mouse posed for a photo.

When we visited Disneyland, Minnie Mouse waved from the float.

When we visited Disneyland, Minnie Mouse hugged the children.

The space shuttle fired its rockets.

The space shuttle rose from the platform.

The space shuttle broke free of gravity.

To keep tradition alive, the Inuit speak Inukitut.

To keep tradition alive, the Inuit hunt for food.

To keep tradition alive, the Inuit make wood and bone carvings.

In Mexico on the Day of the Dead, markets sell skeletons made of sugar.

In Mexico on the Day of the Dead, people dance in parades.

In Mexico on the Day of the Dead, families decorate altars.

Pattern 12: Open With an Adjective or an Adjective Phrase

Tip: The early sets use a simple adjective but later sets require an adjective phrase. Remind students that the adjectives should be set off with a comma, and the first noun in the sentence must be the word that the adjectives are describing. Example:

- The ocean is free of ice.
- The ocean mirrors the cobalt Arctic sky as we kayak.
- Correct: Free of ice, the ocean mirrors the cobalt Arctic sky as we kayak.
- Incorrect: Free of ice, we kayak on the ocean that mirrors the cobalt Arctic sky.

Set 1

The pony was skittish.

The pony trotted away from the children.

The Gila monster was angry.

The Gila monster challenged the chameleon to a showdown.

The fox was sly.

The fox carried the food to his den.

The bat was graceful.

The bat soared through the night sky to catch insects.

The snake was silent.

The snake lay in the tree waiting for a tasty treat to scamper by.

Set 2

Mexican food is hot and spicy.

Mexican food shows up on my menu at least once a week.

The Maya were powerful.

The Maya built an empire with great cities.

Worry dolls are tiny and bright.

Worry dolls make worries disappear by morning.

The Junkanoo costumes are flamboyant.

The Junkanoo costumes in the parade fascinated me.

The lower slopes of the Andes are rich and fertile.

The lower slopes of the Andes grow corn and coffee.

Set 3

Brazilian music is rhythmical.

The Brazilian music drifted through the streets every evening.

Brasilia is high tech and modern.

Brasilia boasts unique architecture.

A few western European farms are small and traditional.

A few western European farms still have oxen pulling machinery.

Egyptian artwork is ancient.

Egyptian artwork attracts many tourists to Africa every year.

Russian folk tales and fairy tales are magical.

Russian folk tales and fairy tales have been passed down orally for centuries.

Set 4

Brazil is famous for its festivals and music.

Brazil draws tourists from all over the world.

The Panama Canal is important to Central America.

The Panama Canal links the Atlantic Ocean to the Pacific.

Carnivals and festivals are vital to island life.

Carnivals and festivals fill the streets with parades and loud music.

Llamas and alpacas are necessary for transportation.

Llamas and alpacas carry goods across the Andes Mountains.

Homes in Scandinavia are eco-friendly.

Homes in Scandinavia use solar panels and insulation to save energy.

Set 5

Samples gathered from *Lincoln: A Photobiography* by Russell Freedman (1987).

Abraham Lincoln was tall and gangly.

Abraham Lincoln topped his six-foot-four-inch body with a high silk hat.

Abraham Lincoln was witty and talkative in public.

Abraham Lincoln seldom revealed his inner feelings.

Lincoln is legendary but humble.

Lincoln rose from life in a log cabin to serve as president of the United States.

Lincoln was superstitious about dreams, omens, and visions.

Lincoln, nevertheless, had a cool, logical mind.

Lincoln was unpopular during the Civil War.

Lincoln heard critics call him a hick and a stupid baboon.

Set 6

Samples gathered from "Serve Over Ice" by Jonathan B. Tourtellot (2011).

The ocean is free of ice.

The ocean mirrors the cobalt Arctic sky as we kayak.

A meal of liver is rich in vitamin C.

The meal of liver provides the nutrients that the Inuit need.

The native diet is healthy and nutritious.

The native diet has come back into vogue for the Inuit.

The hunter is full of good cheer.

The hunter celebrates his success.

Pattern 13: Open With a Present Participle

Tip: In each set the present participle can be found in the first sentence. In early sets it is in the present participle form. In later sets students must change the form of the verb. Example:

- The tamandua uses its strong stomach muscles.
- The tamandua breaks down the insects it has swallowed whole.
- Using its strong stomach muscles, the tamandua breaks down the insects it has swallowed whole.

Set 1

My baby sister was giggling.

My baby sister took her first steps.

My friend was sleeping for hours.

My friend missed Thanksgiving dinner.

The football player was fumbling the ball.

The football player frowned.

I was hoping for a new bike.

I couldn't wait for my birthday to come.

The sprinter was racing at full speed.

The sprinter passed the other runners.

Set 2

The ranger was teaching us how to spot poison ivy.

The ranger pointed to the vines on the tree.

The children were dreaming about Disneyland.

The children had smiles on their sleeping faces.

We were staring at the TV.

We did not hear Mom call us for dinner.

I was wondering about outer space.

I stared at the stars in the sky.

The artist was painting a portrait.

The artist dabbed his brush in the paint.

Set 3

The tourists were kayaking across the blue water.

The tourists reached the white sand beach.

The tour guide was riding a scooter.

The tour guide arrived at our hotel to begin our tour.

The hiker was climbing the steep rocks.

The hiker grabbed a tree limb for support.

Our point guard eyed up the basket.

Our point guard swished a three-pointer.

The chef drizzled chocolate on the cake.

The chef finished her masterpiece.

Set 4

Samples gathered from *Jungle Animals* (Chancellor, 1992).

The Indian Leaf butterfly is disappearing into the background.

The Indian Leaf butterfly hides from her predators.

The Flame butterfly is settling on a passion flower plant.

The Flame butterfly laid her eggs.

The Queen Alexandria Birdwing flies thirty yards above the ground.

The Queen Alexandria Birdwing shows her wingspan of almost one foot.

The moths fluttered their drab wings.

The moths circled our yard light.

The antennae help the butterfly to balance.

The antennae looked like wisps of silk.

Set 5

Samples gathered from *Jungle Animals* (Chancellor, 1992).

Anteaters use their strong claws.

Anteaters break into a nest of termites.

The tamandua pokes its snout into a nest.

The tamandua used its long sticky tongue to catch his dinner.

The tamandua searches for ants and termites at night.

The tamandua spends most of its life in the trees.

The tamandua uses its strong stomach muscles.

The tamandua breaks down the insects it has swallowed whole.

A pangolin is rolling up tightly and hiding.

A pangolin protects itself from predators.

Set 6

Samples gathered from *Jungle Animals* (Chancellor, 1992).

The baby snake peeks out of its egg.

The baby snake takes its first look at the world.

The Pope's pit viper rubs its mouth against a branch.

The Pope's pit viper loosens its skin and wriggles free.

The Gaboon viper hides in the leaves.

The Gaboon viper waits to poison its prey.

The vine snake hangs in the branches.

The vine snake moves very slowly.

The anaconda weighs 500 pounds.

The anaconda can crush a caiman and swallow it whole.

Pattern 14: Open With a Past Participle

Tip: The past participial phrase can always be found in the first sentence. In some sentences, students will have to determine the correct pronoun and decide on its placement. Example:

- Lines of stress and anxiety were etched in President Lincoln's face.
- Lines of stress and anxiety aged President Lincoln.
- Etched in President Lincoln's face, lines of stress and anxiety aged him.

At times students must change the verb form to make it a past participle. Example:

- Lincoln would wrap himself in bearskins and huddle near the fire.
- Lincoln would read during the long winter nights.
- Wrapped in bearskins and huddled near the fire, Lincoln would read during the long winter nights.

Set 1

My father was shocked.

He scolded my sister for pushing her cousin.

The kitten was trapped.

The kitten struggled to crawl free from the box.

My neighbor was bored.

She decided to dye her hair purple.

My teacher was impressed.

She listened to me reading the difficult book.

Grandpa felt satisfied.

Grandpa plopped down on the couch after Thanksgiving dinner.

Set 2

My brother was covered in a white sheet.

My brother gathered Halloween treats as a ghost.

My brother was frightened by the monster costumes.

My brother raced home.

My brother was relieved to be home.

My brother slammed the door and turned the lock.

My brother was finished with trick or treating.

My brother searched through his bag of candy.

My brother was exhausted.

My brother fell asleep in his costume.

Set 3

Galileo was sentenced to confinement.

Galileo could not leave his villa near Florence.

Kings and queens were enchanted by Mozart's music.

Kings and queens often invited Mozart to visit their castles.

The Wright Brothers were determined to invent the first airplane.

The Wright Brothers worked tirelessly for many years.

Elizabeth Blackwell was rejected by twenty-nine medical schools.

Elizabeth Blackwell refused to give up her dream.

Robert Smalls was elected to the U.S. Congress.

Robert Smalls, a civil war hero, served South Carolina honorably.

Set 4

Samples gathered from *Lincoln: A Photobiography* by Russell Freedman (1987).

Lincoln was born near Hodgenville, Kentucky.

Lincoln grew up in a log cabin with a hard-packed dirt floor.

Lincoln would wrap himself in bearskins and huddle near the fire.

Lincoln would read during the long winter nights.

President Lincoln was absentminded and perpetually late for meals.

President Lincoln sometimes upset his wife.

Lincoln was self-educated through borrowed books and newspapers.

Lincoln developed a sharp mind and keen insights.

Lincoln was thrilled by a biography of George Washington.

Lincoln read the book several times.

Set 5

Samples gathered from *Lincoln: A Photobiography* by Russell Freedman (1987).

Lines of anxiety and stress were etched in President Lincoln's face.

Lines of anxiety and stress aged President Lincoln.

The president's friends worried about his safety.

The president's friends feared that rebel sympathizers would try to kidnap or kill him.

Soldiers camped on the White House lawn.

Soldiers stayed near to escort the president on his afternoon carriage rides.

Mary Todd Lincoln was plagued by imaginary fears.

Mary Todd Lincoln suffered from depression.

Lincoln was relaxed and laughing heartily at the play.

Lincoln sat next to his beloved wife.

Pattern 15: Open With a Present Perfect Participle

Tip: Students can pull the participle from either sentence of the set, but it probably will be easiest for them to use the first sentence to form the present perfect participle. They should add the word *having* to the verb to create the present perfect tense. If the verb is irregular, they must change the form. Example:

- The sod huts shrank from the cold.
- The sod huts now had gaping holes that let the freezing wind blow through.
- Having shrunk from the cold, the sod huts now had gaping holes that let the freezing wind blow through.

Set 1

We saw the Canadian Geese flying south.

We knew that cold weather would soon follow.

My aunt helped to prepare the food.

My aunt looked forward to a dinner of pierogies and cabbage rolls.

I grew up reading romantic tales of the Wild West.

I dreamt of racing mustangs across the open plains.

The paleontologists unearthed a dinosaur bone.

The paleontologists continued to excavate the site.

Square-dancing evolved from the Red River Jig.

Square-dancing has many similar steps.

Set 2

Major General Winfield Scott devised a Union strategy to isolate the enemy.

Major General Winfield Scott shared his plan with the Secretary of War.

The National Archives had undergone a major renovation.

The National Archives could now display many more documents.

The sod huts shrank from the cold.

The sod huts now had gaping holes that let the freezing wind blow through.

My father had read about the famous hot springs in Banff.

My father booked a vacation at Banff Springs Hotel.

The Batonga had lived in the area for centuries.

The Batonga did not want to leave their homes to create the Kariba Dam.

The scientist had developed a hypothesis.

The scientist began his experiments.

Set 3

Benedict Arnold became disillusioned with the Revolution.

Benedict Arnold conspired to help the British capture West Point.

Miss Brown has traveled to all seven continents.

Miss Brown decorates her home with unique souvenirs.

The archaeologists discovered several carvings of women.

The archaeologists drew conclusions about a woman's life in the Tang dynasty.

Mozart mastered the violin as a child.

Mozart went on to play numerous other instruments.

People sold or gave away much of their property before setting sail.

People arrived in America with few belongings.

Pattern 16: Open With an Infinitive Phrase

Tip: The word *to* is the sign of the infinitive. The early sentences use simple infinitives such as "to find work." Later sets use more complex infinitive phrases such as "to make better lives for themselves and their families." In most sets it will be easiest for the students to create the infinitive from the first sentence. They often will need to change the verb form before adding *to*. Example:

- The code talkers communicated military secrets.
- The code talkers sent messages in the Navajo language.
- To communicate military secrets, the code talkers sent messages in the Navajo language.

Set 1

People needed to find work.

People migrated to California.

Countries needed to fight the Axis power.

The United States, Great Britain, Russia, and China formed an alliance.

Disney taught Americans how to support the war.

Disney showed cartoon characters saving and recycling household goods.

The code talkers communicated military secrets.

The code talkers sent messages in the Navajo language.

Blimps were used to hunt for enemy submarines.

Blimps flew over the Pacific Ocean.

Set 2

The green anaconda swallows large prey.

The green anaconda can unhinge its jaws.

The anaconda must survive the brutal heat of the dry season.

The anaconda flees to mud holes.

The chef seals in flavors.

The chef wraps the beef, cornmeal, and spices in banana leaves.

We wanted to reach the cave where the bats lived.

We waded through jet-black water that reached to our shoulders.

Capybara keep their front teeth short.

Capybara need to chew on willow or birch branches.

Set 3

The settlers protected themselves from the winter weather.

The settlers needed to build shelters quickly.

The settlers needed to prevent drafts.

The settlers filled the holes in the cabin walls with rocks, wood, and clay.

The Scandinavians wanted to make better lives for themselves and their families.

The Scandinavians sailed to America in the 1800s.

The children celebrated the holidays.

The children made woven heart baskets filled with treats.

Peter Stuyvesant reestablished Dutch control in the New World.

Peter Stuyvesant took seven warships down the Delaware River.

Pattern 17: Restrictive Adjective Clauses

Tip: Remember, restrictive means the clause is needed; therefore, no commas are used. The students need to determine which idea should be used to create the adjective clause. In some sentences the intent will be clear. In others, some discussion may be needed to determine the intent. It can change depending on which idea is used as an adjective. Examples:

- The football team claimed their seventh victory of the season.
- My brother captains that football team.
- The football team that my brother captains claimed their seventh victory of the season.
- The football team that claimed their seventh victory of the season has my brother as their captain.

- The hikers hugged their families.
- The hikers finished a trek across the United States.
- The hikers who hugged their families finished a trek across the United States.
- The hikers who finished a trek across the United States hugged their families.

Set 1

The speaker encouraged all people to volunteer to help the Special Olympics.

The people played sports.

The mounds flanked the plaza.

The mounds served as platforms for houses of nobility.

The store filed for bankruptcy.

The store sold all of its furniture at a 75 percent discount.

The football team claimed their seventh victory of the season.

My brother captains that football team.

The golfer played eighteen holes of golf today.

The golfer had broken his wrist last year.

Set 2

The hikers hugged their families.

The hikers finished a trek across the United States.

The protestors slept on cardboard boxes.

The protestors refused to leave the plaza.

The students need help with their application forms.

The students should wait in the cafeteria.

The artist uses empty soda cans to make flowers.

The artist also makes vases from pickle jars.

The singer wore a necklace worth a million dollars.

The singer won three Grammys last year.

Set 3

I wanted to wear a sweater.

The sweater had two missing buttons.

The ring cost me a week's wages.

I discovered that the ring had a fake diamond.

The squadron operates eight aircraft.

The squadron also provides aeromedical evacuation support.

Military working dogs deploy overseas with their handlers.

Military working dogs complete ninety days of training.

The honor guard participates in ceremonies.

The ceremonies honor the life and service of Air Force members.

Pattern 18: Nonrestrictive Adjective Clauses

Tip: Remember a nonrestrictive restrictive adjective clause is not needed for clarity so it should be set off with commas. Students can think of commas as little handles that may be used to pick up the nonrestrictive clause and throw it away. The pronoun *that* should not be used to create any of these combinations; students should use *who, whose,* and *which.* Example:

- The ethnographers traveled to the Carpathian Mountains.
- Ethnographers study individual cultures.
- The ethnographers, who study individual cultures, traveled to the Carpathian Mountains.

Set 1

The farmer thought he had hit a rock with his shovel.

The farmer actually found a basalt carving from the Olmec civilization.

The people lived in small villages.

The people built homes with thatched roofs and pole walls.

The architects planned a new city.

The architects chose an area overlooking the confluence of three rivers.

The Olmecs created the first civilization in ancient America.

The Olmecs migrated from Siberia into Northern America.

Walter Mondale served as vice president under Jimmy Carter.

Walter Mondale ran for president in 1984.

Set 2

The ethnographers traveled to the Carpathian Mountains.

Ethnographers study individual cultures.

In 1993 my grandmother returned to Borysław, Poland.

My grandmother grew up in Borysław, Poland.

Flowers and flying geese decorate the ornate tea basket.

The tea basket held the leaves for making medicinal tea.

Mozart could play the harpsichord at the age of four.

Mozart gave concerts at the imperial courts in Vienna.

The National Archives features images by Matthew Brady.

Matthew Brady took thousands of photos of the Civil War.

Set 3

Earl Warren served as chief justice of the U.S. Supreme Court.

Earl Warren died in 1974.

The Daughters of Liberty worked to make the colonies more self-sufficient.

The Daughters of Liberty spun thread and wove cloth to replace British imports.

Sacagawea's name means "bird woman."

Sacagawea taught Lewis and Clark how to find edible plants.

Penguins live in the wild only in the Southern Hemisphere.

Penguins raise their young on the icy shore of Antarctica.

The Amazon River begins in Peru.

The Amazon River flows across South America to empty into the Atlantic Ocean.

Pattern 19: Compound Sentence With a Semicolon

Tip: The semicolon connects two complete sentences. Those sentences must have a close relationship. Students must make decisions about pronouns and select the correct one to replace repetitious nouns. Example:

- The female emu lays dark green eggs in a nest.
- The male emu keeps the eggs warm.
- The female emu lays dark green eggs in a nest; the male emu keeps *them* warm.

Set 1

An octopus can lie flat on the ocean floor.

An octopus's predators cannot see it.

The female emu lays dark green eggs in a nest.

The male emu keeps the eggs warm.

Baby emus face great danger.

Foxes love to hunt them for food.

Worker ants gather food.

Worker ants feed the entire colony.

Set 2

We searched for a Tasmanian devil during the day.

Tasmanian devils hunt at night.

I visualized Tas, the funny cartoon character.

The real Tas has pointed teeth, bone-crushing jaws, and a terrifying scream.

Female Tasmanian devils can give birth to fifty joeys.

Only about four of the joeys survive.

The Tasmanian devil's diet sounds gross.

Tasmanian devils dine on carrion, no matter how old or rotten.

Set 3

People fear black widow spiders.

The black widow can inject killing poison.

The Thorny Devil has an unusual defense mechanism.

The Thorny Devil can pop up a fake head and hide its real one.

A hungry Thorny Devil can eat an astonishing number of ants.

A Thorny Devil will devour 3,000 ants in one meal.

Snakes have powerful hinged jaws.

Snakes can pull their prey into their mouth.

Pattern 20: Compound Sentence With an Elliptical Expression

Tip: Look for identical words in the two sentences. These repetitions should be replaced by a comma or a pronoun substitute. The repeating verb is most often replaced by the comma. In most cases, no changes need to be made to the first sentence. It can be helpful to read the final sentence aloud and listen for clarity and rhythm. Examples (read the combinations aloud to decide which of the two examples has better clarity and rhythm):

- Paintings of horses and bison covered the walls of the first cave.
- Paintings of complex circles and triangles covered the walls of the second cave.
- Paintings of horses and bison covered the walls of the first cave; complex circles and triangles, the second one.
- Paintings of horses and bison covered the walls of the first cave; complex circles and triangles, the second.

Set 1

In China I toured the Great Wall.

In Egypt I toured the Great Pyramids.

Don Henley sings the blues.

Eva Cassidy sings ballads.

The emu's body has long droopy feathers.

The emu's head has short pointy feathers.

Paintings of horses and bison covered the walls of the first cave.

Paintings of complex circles and triangles covered the walls of the second cave.

Set 2

In Peru, for dinner I enjoyed ceviche.

In Peru, for dessert I enjoyed flan.

Emperor Qin Shi Huang oversaw the first phase of the Great Wall.

Emperor Wu Di, a great Han ruler, oversaw the second phase of building.

Mao Zedong ordered the destruction of the Great Wall.

Deng Xiaoping ordered the restoration of the Great Wall.

The Nile is the longest river in the world.

The Amazon is the second-longest river in the world.

Set 3

In New York, tourists enjoy the beauty of Central Park.

In Newark, tourists enjoy the beauty of Weequahic Park.

In literature class we read novels.

In social studies we read biographies.

Abraham Lincoln served as president of the United States.

Jefferson Davis served as president of the Confederate States of America.

In the summer I enjoy swimming, hiking, and baseball.

In the winter I enjoy skiing, ice skating, and basketball.

Pattern 21: Opening With Absolutes

Tip: The information in the absolute can be found in the first sentence. Often the verb form needs to change. Sometimes an adjective or a possessive pronoun precedes the noun, but remember an absolute always has a *noun* followed by modifiers. Example:

- The barn's roof was riddled with holes.
- The barn provided little shelter from the rain.
- Its *roof* riddled with holes, the barn provided little shelter from the rain.

- His fingers searched for a secure hold.
- The climber balanced on the side of the cliff before moving higher.
- *Fingers* searching for a secure hold, the climber balanced on the side of the cliff before moving higher.

Some students may find it difficult to see the difference between Pattern 21 and Pattern 13, which opens with a present participle. The final sentence in the set above is an example of Pattern 21; the one below, an example of Pattern 13:

- Searching for a secure hold, the climber balanced on the side of the cliff before moving higher.

Explain to students that Pattern 21 must open with a noun or an adjective noun. Pattern 13 opens with an *ing* word—a present participle that describes the first noun behind the comma.

Set 1

Her hands covered her mouth.

The child giggled as the clown created a balloon animal for her.

The bear used its massive paws to tear and slash the garbage bags.

The bear searched the landfill for a tasty meal.

The barn's roof was riddled with holes.

The barn provided little shelter from the rain.

The oak tree's limbs were split by the massive sheets of ice.

The oak tree would not survive the winter.

Set 2

The puppy's tail wagged nonstop.

The puppy yipped a friendly greeting when I came home from work.

His fingers searched for a secure hold.

The climber balanced on the side of the cliff before moving higher.

General Washington had his sword drawn and pointed at the enemy.

General Washington led his troops into the battle.

Flames roared from rooftops and danced at the windows.

The fire destroyed the city of Atlanta during Sherman's March.

Pattern 22: Adjectives Moved Behind a Noun

Tip: The adjectives to be manipulated are supplied in the opening sentence. If more than two adjectives are given, students should experiment with the words to decide on their final placement. Reading the combinations aloud will help them to hear if the sentence has rhythm and clarity. All of the following combinations are grammatically correct, but reading them aloud will help students to decide which one best serves the writer's intent. Example:

- Langston Hughes was fiery, talented, and eloquent.
- Langston Hughes encouraged artists and musicians to honor their culture.
- The fiery Langston Hughes, talented and eloquent, encouraged artists and musicians to honor their culture.
- The talented Langston Hughes, fiery and eloquent, encouraged artists and musicians to honor their culture.
- The eloquent Langston Hughes, talented and fiery, encouraged artists and musicians to honor their culture.

In some sets only two adjectives are provided. In addition, the adjectives might need to be placed behind a direct object rather than a subject. Example:

- For years scientists have visited Easter Island to study the statues.
- The statues are huge and mysterious.
- For years scientists have visited Easter Island to study the statues, huge and mysterious.

Set 1

The soldiers were weary and wounded.

The soldiers called to the nurses and doctors for help.

The nation was shocked and disillusioned.

The nation demanded to know the truth about the Teapot Dome scandal.

Langston Hughes was fiery, talented, and eloquent.

Langston Hughes encouraged artists and musicians to honor their culture.

Phar Lap was huge and lightning-fast.

Phar Lap won races in Australia and Mexico, but developed a fatal case of colic from eating unfamiliar grass.

The carrion might be rotten and foul.

Vultures love to dine on carrion.

Set 2

The mountain beaver is hungry but patient.

The mountain beaver munches on the nutrient-rich dung.

Beetles are miniscule but destructive.

Beetles slip unnoticed into any place they might find food.

Stonehenge is ancient and mysterious.

Stonehenge tracks the movements of the sun and the moon.

Maria Belleville was punctual and reliable.

Maria Belleville gathered information from the Royal Observatory at Greenwich.

John Harrison was persistent and creative but scientific.

John Harrison built the first chronometer, a clock that worked at sea.

Pattern 23: Open With a Parallel Structure

Tip: The three introductory words can be found in the first sentence of each pair. Students have a tendency to open the sentence with the words *these are.* Model how to use the information in the sentences to avoid the empty constructs of *there are* or *these are.* The second sentence usually can be used exactly as it is written. The combination exercise is intended to help students write sentences that they can then read aloud to hear the rhythm of the pattern. Example:

- The sequoias are massive, ancient, and impressive.
- Giant sequoias grace the California coastline.
- Massive, ancient, and impressive—giant sequoias grace the California coastline.

Set 1

The flappers sported bobbed hair, shortened hemlines, and silk stockings.

The flappers' new style represented women's newfound freedoms.

By the 1928 Olympics, American women competed in skiing, basketball, and archery.

By the 1928 Olympics, American women competed in several new sports.

Lincoln, Washington, Roosevelt, and Jefferson are on Mount Rushmore.

Four presidents grace Mount Rushmore, the monument designed by Gutzon Borglum.

Flying upside down, wing walking, and changing planes in midair were among the stunts that barnstormers did.

The death defying stunts of the barnstormers thrilled the crowds.

The Cartwright brothers were Adam, Hoss, and Little Joe.

The Cartwright brothers always spoke respectfully to their Pa.

Set 2

In the 1920s the gangsters were brutal, greedy, and organized.

The gangsters in the 1920s controlled cities like Chicago and New York.

Babe Ruth became known as the Sultan of Swat and the Great Bambino.

Babe Ruth led New York to win seven American League pennants.

Wimbledon, the U.S. National, and the Davis Cup are famous tennis championships.

Big Bill Tilden won each of these tennis championships.

I like crosswords, hink pinks, and word searches.

Every morning I solve three word puzzles.

Some insects eat books, blankets, and baskets.

Household items can make a tasty snack for many insects.

Pattern 24: Using Conjunctive Adverbs to Connect Two Sentences

Tip: Students must select the conjunctive adverb that most accurately expresses the relationship between the two sentences. (See Table 3.7 in the previous chapter for a partial list of conjunctive adverbs.) The conjunctive adverb should always be placed in the second sentence. Students must make decisions about the appropriate use of pronouns to avoid repeating nouns. Example:

- At extreme altitudes, mountain climbers breathe in less oxygen.
- They can suffer brain damage.

- At extreme altitudes, mountain climbers breathe in less oxygen. They can, therefore, suffer brain damage. (with an accurate conjunctive adverb)
- At extreme altitudes, mountain climbers breathe in less oxygen. They can, nevertheless, suffer brain damage. (with an inaccurate conjunctive adverb)

Set 1

The foul-smelling carrion crawled with maggots.

The vulture tore into the rotting meat.

At extreme altitudes, mountain climbers breathe in less oxygen.

They can suffer brain damage.

Sherpas take in more air per minute than people living at lower levels.

Sherpas have amazing stamina when leading mountain climbing expeditions.

Therapy dogs can help people deal with depression and loneliness.

Therapy dogs distract people from their pain or illness.

Frida Kahlo never wavered in her determination to recover from a near-fatal accident.

She suffered excruciating pain and underwent more than thirty operations.

Set 2

The USS Monitor featured a spinning gun turret and an armor belt that circled the ship.

Impressed by these innovations, engineers modeled more ships on its design.

For more than 100 years, the USS Monitor lay on the bottom of the Atlantic Ocean.

The U.S. Navy brought sections of it to the surface.

Bats choose roosts inside hollow trees, caves, or the walls of buildings.

Some bats even roost inside leaves or under tree bark.

Mary, Queen of the Scots, married Lord Darnley, a handsome charmer.

Darnley plotted the murder of Mary's trusted advisor David Riccio.

No one will ever know if Mary, Queen of Scots, actually loved any of her husbands.

She did love her son and her closest friends.

SENTENCE COMBINATIONS: PART 2

The sentence combination exercises in this section offer a different set of challenges. First, none of the exercises in this section are cued, nor are they tied to any specific patterns. Encourage the students to play with each set and listen to the possible combinations. Once they hear a combination that has rhythm and clarity, they can write the completed combination. By working slowly, they will create a range of structures. Some of the structures that they create will be patterns they have already practiced. Other combinations will be variations of patterns. Rather than opening a sentence with a present participle, the students might move that structure to a different location. Students are capable of doing this using the "wealth of linguistic power" that they have developed over the years of exposure to language (Strong, 1973).

Allowing the students to linger over the combinations helps them to hear the rhythm of the prose. Learning how to manipulate the language through the patterns is an important basic skill. But learning how to manipulate the patterns to create a fluid paragraph with cohesion teaches the students a great deal about the skills needed by writers.

In this section, students are given three to five sets of sentences. I never assign more than that because I want students to feel free to linger over the sentences and manipulate these "kernels." Each set consist of kernels that must be combined to create a sentence. Discussing the final combinations is crucial to the learning. Do not ask students to determine which pattern they have created nor to name the parts of speech. Do not ask students to memorize grammar and punctuation rules. But do celebrate with students as they create sentences that have specific nouns, vivid verbs, clarity, and rhythm. Grammatical errors can and should be discussed once the sentences are complete.

At first it might help the students to walk through the sentences one by one. Students will learn to eliminate repetition and to embed "jewelry" or modifiers into the first kernel. Model the steps for combining.

1. Work through the sentences one by one and eliminate repetition.
   o The rabbit nibbled on the carrots.
   o ~~The rabbit was~~ white.
   o ~~The carrots were~~ juicy.
   o ~~The carrots were~~ growing in the garden.

2. Look at the remaining words and decide where to embed the words or phrases.
    ○ The white rabbit nibbled on the juicy carrots growing in the garden.

Some students might anchor the modifiers to the wrong noun. Discuss the kernels and model how to determine the placement of the modifiers. Since the second kernel says that the rabbit was white, the adjective must be anchored to that noun *rabbit*. In this sentence, the placement of a modifier is incorrect:

- The rabbit nibbled on the juicy white carrots growing in the garden.

I also find it valuable with less experienced writers to have the "less is more" discussion. Let's look at the following combination.

- The dolphin leaped.
- ~~The dolphin was~~ gray.
- ~~The dolphin was~~ in the aquarium.
- ~~The dolphin leaped~~ through a hoop.
- ~~The hoop was~~ plastic.
- ~~The dolphin leaped~~ gracefully.
- Examples of possible combinations:
- The gray dolphin in the aquarium leaped gracefully through a plastic hoop.
- Gracefully, the gray dolphin in the aquarium leaped through a plastic hoop.
- In the aquarium the gray dolphin leaped through a plastic hoop gracefully.

Through this type of combination, students can learn a valuable revision tool: deleting words and phrases. The samples above are excellent examples of combinations based on the kernel sentences. The combinations include all of the kernel elements, but, for that very reason, the final combinations are wordy. Ask the students if any of the words can be eliminated to create a tighter sentence.

We discuss the fact that most people would know that dolphins are gray so the adjective is unnecessary. Also, saying that the dolphin leaped gracefully seems redundant. Has anyone ever seen a clumsy dolphin? And is it important to know that the hoop was plastic? A flaming hoop might be important enough to mention since it adds an element of danger for the dolphin. But the fact that the hoop is plastic does not do much to encourage a reader to visualize. Good writers make decisions.

- The ~~gray~~ dolphin in the aquarium leaped ~~gracefully~~ through a ~~plastic~~ hoop.
- In the aquarium the ~~gray~~ dolphin leaped through a ~~plastic~~ hoop ~~gracefully~~.

Subsequent kernels are more complex and allow for greater variety in the final combinations. Even at this stage, many students find that drawing a line through the repetitious material makes the combination task more manageable. Be sure to explain to students that they must add conjunctions or prepositions to create the final sentences.

- The students covered the books.
- ~~They were~~ science books.
- ~~They~~ used white paper.
- ~~The paper was~~ splashed with flowers.

Examples of some possible combinations:

1. The students covered the science books with white paper splashed with flowers.

2. The students covered the science books with white, flower-splashed paper.

3. Using white paper splashed with flowers, the students covered the science books.

4. The students covered the science books, and they used white paper splashed with flowers.

5. To cover the science books, the students used white paper splashed with flowers.

6. The white, flower-splashed paper was used by the students to cover the science books.

Find an efficient way to display the work of several students. Prior to having tools such as LCD projectors or document cameras, I had three or four students go to the board at once and write their combinations. Glancing at their papers enabled me to select three students who had combined differently. When one group was at the board writing, I quickly chose three sentences for the second set by highlighting sentences I wanted on the board. When we finished discussing one set of sentences, students with highlighted sentences quickly moved to the board to erase and write their examples.

This gave us an opportunity to look at the decisions made by students and to discuss those decisions. We did discuss errors in punctuation and mechanics, but we spent more time listening to the rhythm of the sentences and discussing placement of modifiers. For example, Sentence 4 in the above samples is grammatically correct, but it is wordy compared to the other options. Sentence 6 uses a dreaded form of *be*, resulting in passive voice.

Having a discussion about these sentences allows students to see that there is no one right answer. They begin to savor the power they have as writers—the power to make choices. If students complete three sentences in one exercise, they might decide to try three different patterns. It might be possible to combine every sentence in an exercise by beginning with a preposition. For the sake of variety, students might opt to begin one of the sentences with an adverb or a participle. Again, this does not mean that the student who has used three prepositions has made an error. It means the writers have made different choices.

The following exercises offer sentences in sets. When the students have finished, they will have three to five separate sentences. Later sets require that the complete combinations make a short paragraph. I have not always broken the sentence sets into the simplest kernels. Encourage students to try different structures: Use coordinating or subordinate conjunctions. Open with prepositional phrases, adverbs, participles, or infinitives.

In some of the exercises, an author is cited because the information in the set was gathered from an article or a book, but the kernel sentences have not been copied from the original. The authors have been cited to honor their work, and so that teachers and students can refer to the articles for additional information if they find the topic to be interesting.

Exercise 1: Simple Sentences

- The dolphin leaped.
- The dolphin was gray.
- The dolphin was in the aquarium.
- The dolphin leaped through a hoop.
- The hoop was plastic.

- The puppet danced.
- The puppet is red.
- The puppet danced on the table.
- The puppet did this yesterday.

- Dad did something during the football game.
- He baked a turkey.
- The turkey was huge.
- He baked it with dressing.
- He baked it for Thanksgiving dinner.

Exercise 2: More Simple Sentences

- A turtle raced.
- He raced this afternoon.
- The turtle was wearing a green helmet.
- He raced across the road.
- The road was dusty.

- The turtle swam.
- The turtle swam this morning.
- The turtle was huge.
- The turtle was green.
- The turtle swam in the pond.

- Groups of bats hibernate.
- These groups are large.
- They hibernate during winter.
- The bats hibernate in cool places.
- The bats hibernate in dry places.

Exercise 3: Bat Facts

- Some bats migrate.
- They migrate to warmer areas.
- They do this in the fall.
- These areas have plenty of food.

- Bats can fold their wings.
- The wings are around their bodies.
- They do these to stay dry.
- They do this to stay warm.

- Bats can move like an acrobat.
- Bats can chase insects.
- They can chase through a maze.
- The maze is made up of tree branches.

Exercise 4: Redwood Facts

- Some salamanders live.
- They live in the redwood canopy.
- They live there their entire lives.
- They never see the forest floor.

- Fire can hollow out a cavern.
- The cavern is in a redwood trunk.
- The redwood continues to grow.
- Early settlers made pens.
- They made the pens in the redwood caverns.
- They kept geese in the pens.

Exercise 5: Tree Farms

- Growers shear tree branches.
- They do this in the summer.
- The shearing encourages new branches to grow.

- Some growers cut down trees.
- They do this in the fall.

- They put the trees in storage.
- The storage is cold.
- The do this so the trees stay fresh.
- They stay fresh until the holidays.

- Other farms let people come.
- They come to cut their own trees.
- They come to buy wreaths.
- The wreaths are for their homes.

Exercise 6: Chestnut Trees

Samples gathered from "Gone Today, Here Tomorrow?" by Rebecca Hirsch (2011).

- Chestnut trees were giants.
- They sprawled across 200 million acres.
- They sprawled from Maine.
- They sprawled to Mississippi.
- They sprawled during the nineteenth century.

- The chestnut tree is American.
- The chestnut tree is majestic.
- The chestnut tree met an enemy.
- It met the enemy at the end of the nineteenth century.

- An Asian fungus hitched a ride.
- It rode into America.
- It attacked chestnut trees.
- It did this at the Bronx Zoo.

Exercise 7: Chestnut Trees

Samples gathered from "Gone Today, Here Tomorrow?" by Rebecca Hirsch (2011).

- Puffs of fungus spores sailed.
- They sailed on the wind.
- They clung to the fur.
- They clung to the feathers.
- The fur and feathers were of animals.

- The spores landed.
- They landed in cracks.
- The cracks were in the chestnut's bark.
- The fungus began to grow.

- The fungus ate the bark.
- The bark was growing.
- It grew around the tree's trunk.
- This strangled the tree.

Exercise 8: Anatomy Facts

- The skull houses the brain.
- The skull protects the brain.
- The skull protects the organs for sight and hearing.
- The skull protects the organs for smell and taste.

- George Stubbs was an eighteenth century painter.
- He painted animals.
- He spent two years studying horse anatomy.

- The badger has thick-boned limbs.
- It has strong feet.
- It has long claws.
- These things enable the badger to dig tunnels.

Exercise 9: Jungle Animal Facts

- An iguana is looking for a snack.
- The snack is tasty.
- An iguana can catch insects.
- It does this in the branches.
- The branches are leafy.
- The branches are on jungle trees.

- Otters swim in rivers.
- The rivers are in jungles.
- The otters feed on small fish.
- The otters feed on mammals.
- The otters feed on birds.

- Macaws eat fruit.
- The macaws are scarlet.
- The macaws spread the seeds.
- It does this so that trees can grow.
- The trees are new.
- The trees grow in the jungle.

Exercise 10: More Jungle Animal Facts

- Butterflies carry pollen.
- The butterflies are Morpho.
- They carry it between flowers.

- They do this to help make seeds.
- The seeds are new.
- The tamandua shoots out its tongue.
- The tongue is long.
- The tongue is sticky.
- It does this to catch insects.
- The insects are escaping.
- They are escaping from a nest.

- Anteaters have tails.
- The tails are prehensile.
- The tails are long.
- The tail helps the anteater.
- The tail helps it to climb.
- They climb high up.
- They climb into the trees.

Exercise 11: Reptile Eggs

- Reptile eggs have hard shells.
- These keep the babies safe.
- These provide lots of food.
- The food is there to help them grow.

- Reptiles lay their eggs.
- They do not take care of them.

- Baby reptiles need moisture.
- They need this to keep alive.

- The shell is tough.
- The shell is leathery.
- The shell keeps moisture inside.
- So the mother buries the eggs.
- She does this to keep the eggs safe from predators.

- The eggs are buried under layers of leaves.
- The eggs are buried under layers of dirt.
- The egg stays warm.
- It stays that way until the baby hatches.

Exercise 12: Reptile Facts

- The outside of the egg looks solid.
- The egg is a reptile's.
- It has tiny holes in it.
- These holes let oxygen flow in.
- These holes let carbon dioxide flow out.

- The reptile body is like a fire.
- The body needs oxygen to burn food.
- So reptiles breathe in oxygen.

- Reptiles must keep their bodies warm.
- They need warmth in order to metabolize.
- Metabolize means change food into energy.
- Food energy helps the body to grow.
- Food energy helps the body make new cells.
- Food energy makes the muscles work.

- Reptiles live in all the parts of the world.
- The parts of the world are warmer.

Exercise 13: Vampire Bat Facts

Samples gathered from *Animals Eat the Weirdest Things* by Diane Swanson (1998).

- Vampire bats fly low.
- They fly in search of blood.
- They fly during night.
- They fly during the darkest hours.

- They sip blood.
- They sip from sleeping pigs.
- They sip from goats.
- They sip from horses.
- They sip from cows.

- A vampire bat swoops closer.
- Its sense of smell helps.
- Its sense of smell is super.
- It helps it zero in.
- It finds its target.

- The vampire bat uses its teeth.
- The teeth are supersharp.
- It makes a tiny cut.
- The cut is in a horse's neck.
- The cut is in a horse's shoulder.
- Or the cut is in the horse's rump.

- The blood starts to flow.
- The bat laps it up.
- The bat is mouse-sized.

Exercise 14: Vampire Bat Facts

Samples gathered from *Animals Eat the Weirdest Things* by Diane Swanson (1998).

- The bat has grooves on its tongue.
- The bat has grooves on its bottom lip.
- The grooves direct the blood.
- The blood goes to its throat.
- The blood goes to the back.

- Chemicals keep the blood from doing something.
- The blood does not clot.
- The chemicals are in the bat's saliva.

- Another bat or two will join it.
- This happens sometimes.
- They lap at the same cut.
- They might do this for up to half an hour.

- Its stomach bulges.
- It bulges with blood.
- The bat returns.
- It goes to its hollow tree.
- Or it goes to its cave.

- The vampire bat fails to feed.
- This happens for two or three nights.
- If this happens something else could happen.
- The bat could die.

Exercise 15: Vampire Bat Facts

Samples gathered from *Animals Eat the Weirdest Things* by Diane Swanson (1998).

- Bats live in colonies.
- The colonies are large.
- Bats form bonds.
- The bonds are important.
- The bonds are with other bats.

- A bat might have a poor night of hunting.
- If this happens something else happens.
- She will lick her buddy.
- This is to ask her to share.
- They share blood.

- The buddy brings up some of her meal.
- The meal is blood.

- She passes it to the other bat.
- They do this mouth to mouth.

- The bat will return the favor.
- She will do this if her buddy returns hungry.
- She will do this on another night.

- Every night vampire bats need blood.
- The need half of their body weight.
- They need this to stay alive.

SENTENCE COMBINATIONS: PART 3

The following combination exercises are the most difficult since the sentences are not clustered into sets. Students need to determine which sentences to group together to create the sentences of a paragraph. The original paragraph is provided to help if students are confused about the content. The teacher can explain relationships such as cause and effect or comparison and contrast. It is also interesting to compare the students' final versions to the original paragraph. I have had many students who felt that their final paragraph was better than the paragraph written by the professional author. I do not discourage that confidence booster, but I do remind students that they are seeing only one paragraph from a text. Many factors played a part in the author's final decisions: audience, surrounding text, personal style.

These exercises will help your students to understand that the word *something* is often used as a placeholder and can be deleted from the final sentence. Example:

- I remembered something.
- I remembered it later.
- It was that Kayla had a fear.
- Her fear was deep-seated.
- Her fear was of snakes.

From this set, students may create: Later I remembered that Kayla had a deep-seated fear of snakes.

Also, students will need to manipulate verb tense in order to make cohesive paragraphs. And they should give careful consideration to pronoun usage. Again, encourage students to play with the elements and try a range of patterns.

Exercise 1: *The Wednesday Surprise* by Eve Bunting

Original text from *The Wednesday Surprise* (Bunting, 1989, p. 23):

Dad blows out the birthday candles and we give him his gifts. Then Grandma shoots a glance in my direction and I go for the big bag and drag it across to the table. I settle it on the floor between us.

Kernels to be combined:

- Dad blows out the candles.
- They are birthday ones.
- We give him his gifts.
- Then Grandma shoots a glance.
- It is in my direction.
- I go for the bag.
- It is big.
- I drag it across.
- I drag it to the table.
- I settle it on the floor.
- It is between us.

Exercise 2: *Mr. Lincoln's Whiskers* by Karen B. Winnick

Original text from *Mr. Lincoln's Whiskers* (Winnick, 1996, p. 12):

In the morning, Grace hurried to mail the letter before going to school. She kept it hidden under her cape. If Levant knew she had written to Mr. Lincoln, he would laugh.

Kernels to be combined:

- Grace hurried.
- She did that in the morning.
- She had to mail the letter.
- She would do that before going to school.
- She kept it hidden.
- It was under her cape.
- She had written to Mr. Lincoln.
- Levant would laugh.
- He would do that if he knew about her letter.

Exercise 3: *Cactus Café: A Story of the Sonoran Desert* by Kathleen Weidner Zoehfeld

Original text from *Cactus Café* (Zoehfeld, 1997):

A pair of Gila Woodpeckers has pecked out a hollow in one of the great saguaro's arms. Snuggled safely inside, their newly hatched babies peep for food.

Kernels to be combined:

- A pair of woodpeckers has pecked.
- They are Gila Woodpeckers.
- They pecked out a hollow.
- It is in one of the saguaro's arms.
- The saguaro is great.
- Babies are snuggled inside.
- They are snuggled safely.
- They are newly hatched.
- They peep for food.

Exercise 4: *Jacob I Have Loved* by Katherine Paterson

Original text from *Jacob I Have Loved* (Paterson, 1980, p. 47):

One day I had talked Call into exploring the house with me, but just as we stepped onto the porch, a huge orange-colored tomcat came shrieking out a broken window at us. It was the only time in our lives that Call outran me. We sat gasping for breath on my front stoop.

Kernels to be combined:

- I had talked Call into something.
- I did that one day.
- I talked him into exploring the house with me.
- Just as we stepped onto the porch something happened.
- A tomcat came shrieking.
- It was huge.
- It was orange-colored.
- It came out a window.
- The window was broken.
- It came at us.
- It was the only time in our lives that something happened.
- Call outran me.
- We sat.
- We gasped for breath.
- We sat on the stoop.
- The stoop was in the front.

Exercise 5: *One-Eyed Cat* by Paula Fox

Original text from *One-Eyed Cat* (Fox, 1984, pp. 4–5):

Until two months ago, Sunday breakfasts had been quiet. Ned's Papa always wore his amethyst tiepin in his black silk tie, his black trousers with the satin stripe down each side, and the cutaway jacket with back panels that looked like a beetle's folded wings, and he had his Sunday look, thinking about his sermon, Ned knew. The only noise had been their spoons hitting the sides of the cereal bowls.

Kernels to be combined:

- Sunday breakfasts had been quiet.
- This was until two months ago.
- Ned's Papa always wore something.
- He wore his amethyst tiepin.
- He wore it in his tie.
- The tie was black silk.
- He wore his black trousers.
- The trousers had a satin stripe down each side.
- He wore the cutaway jacket.
- It had back panels.
- The panels looked like a beetle's wings.
- The wings were folded.
- And Papa had a Sunday look.
- The look was him thinking.
- He was thinking about his sermon.
- The only noise had been their spoons.
- The spoons were hitting the sides of the bowls.
- The bowls were for cereal.

Exercise 6: *Red Scarf Girl* by Ji Li Jiang

Original text from *Red Scarf Girl* (Jiang, 1997, pp. 121–22):

I remembered coming home from kindergarten and showing Grandma the songs and dances we had learned. Grandma sat before us with her knitting, nodding her head in time to the music. Sometimes we insisted that she sing with us, and she would join in with an unsteady pitch and heavy Tianjin accent, wagging her head and moving her arms just as we did.

Kernels to be combined:

- I remembered coming home.
- I came home from kindergarten.
- I showed Grandma the songs.
- I showed Grandma the dances.
- We had learned them.
- Grandma sat before us.
- She sat with her knitting.
- She was nodding her head.
- She did that in time to the music.

- Sometimes we insisted on something.
- We insisted that she sing with us.
- She would join in.
- She did it with an unsteady pitch.
- She did it with an accent.
- The accent was heavy.
- The accent was Tianjin.
- She was wagging her head.
- She was moving her arms.
- She did it just as we did.

Exercise 7: *More Perfect Than the Moon* by Patricia MacLachlan

Original text from *More Perfect Than the Moon* (MacLachlan, 2004, p. 62):

Rose drew a picture of Caleb and Violet, their faces pointed up, mouths open, looking like howling dogs. This made me laugh. It felt strange to laugh. I hadn't laughed in a long time, and Mama looked over at me and smiled. Papa smiled, too, and Maggie brought out a tall, white, frosted cake with strawberries.

Kernels to be combined:

- Rose drew a picture.
- It had Caleb and Violet.
- Their faces pointed up.
- Their mouths were open.
- They looked like howling dogs.
- This made me laugh.
- It felt strange to laugh.
- I had not laughed in a long time.
- Mama looked over at me.
- She smiled.
- Papa smiled too.
- Maggie brought out a frosted cake.
- It was tall and white.
- It had strawberries.

Exercise 8: *When Pigasso met Mootisse* by Nina Laden

Original text from *When Pigasso met Mootisse* (Laden, 1998, p. 25):

Then, curious to see what Mootisse had been doing, Pigasso sprinted around to the other side. At the same time, Mootisse galloped over to Pigasso's side. The silence was broken as the two artists began laughing at their amazing works of heart.

Kernels to be combined:

- Mootisse was curious.
- He wanted to see what Mootisse had been doing.
- Pigasso sprinted around.
- He did this to the other side of the fence.
- Mootisse galloped over.
- He did this to Pigasso's side.
- He did this at the same time.
- The silence was broken.
- The two artists began laughing.
- They laughed at their works of heart.
- The works were amazing.

Exercise 9: *Sing Down the Moon* by Scott O'Dell

Original text from *Sing Down the Moon* (O'Dell, 1970, p. 12):

With the first flash of sun on the canyon wall, the men rode out of the meadow. Tall Boy led the way, moving briskly on his white pony. He did not look to either side, nor at those who had come to wish the warriors farewell, nor at me. He looked straight in front of him, his bold chin thrust out and his mouth drawn tight.

Kernels to be combined:

- There was the first flash of sun.
- It was on the canyon wall.
- The men rode out of the meadow.
- Tall Boy led the way.
- He moved briskly.
- He was on his white pony.
- He did not look to either side.
- He did not look at those who had come.
- They came to wish the warriors farewell.
- He did not look at me.
- He looked straight.
- He looked in front of himself.
- His bold chin thrust out.
- His mouth was drawn tight.

Exercise 10: *Beauty and the Beast* by Willard and Moser

Original text from *Beauty and the Beast* (Willard & Moser, 1992, p. 51):

The shadows of the trees stretched like lazy cats in the afternoon sun. Beauty had forgotten to eat her lunch, and it would soon be time to meet the Beast for dinner; she gathered up her lunch pail and trowel. Suddenly a thorn from the roses raked her hand and opened a bloody seam along her knuckles.

Kernels to be combined:

- The shadows stretched.
- They were tree shadows.
- They stretched like cats in the sun.
- The cats were lazy.
- The sun was in the afternoon.
- Beauty had forgotten something.
- She had not eaten her lunch.
- It would soon be time for something.
- She had to meet the Beast for dinner.
- She gathered up her lunch pail.
- She gathered up her trowel.
- A thorn raked her hand.
- This happened suddenly.
- The thorn was from the roses.
- It opened a seam.
- The seam was bloody.
- It was along her knuckles.

MORE RESOURCES FOR SENTENCE COMBINING

For junior high or high school teachers looking for more sentence combining exercises, I would recommend any of the sentence combining books by William Strong (1973, 1986). In addition, *Sentence-Combining Workbook* by Pam Altman and others (2007), as well as Killgallon's (1997) books on sentence composing, have excellent combining exercises.

Remember, the discussion of the final combination is the most important part of sentence combining work. Students need to discuss the decisions that an author makes to bring rhythm and clarity to a piece of text. The Common Core State Standards state that students will be required to "Develop and strengthen writing as needed by planning, revising, editing, rewriting, or trying a new approach" (National Governors Association Center for Best Practices and Council of Chief State School Officers, 2010, CC.K-12.W.R.5. All rights reserved.). Sentence combination work will help students to develop those skills.

The next chapter provides activities for students needing extra practice with the patterns.

Activities for Students Needing Extra Practice

5

Students will assemble grammatically correct sentences by manipulating chunks of sentences from professional authors.

I have provided activities using text from various authors. Each activity has two sets. Set 1 shows the original sentences and pattern numbers. Some of the sentences actually follow more than one pattern or might be variations of a pattern. I tried to identify the pattern that I felt would be most helpful. Set 2 includes the same sentences, but each one is broken down into chunks separated by slash marks. Students will work with these sentence chunks. I found that giving students chunks of three to five sentences works well. If I give more than five sentences, the students do not have sufficient time to discuss the sentences and experiment with structure. The sentences have been selected from various pages of each book. The goal is not to create a complete paragraph, but to manipulate sentence chunks. Each sentence will stand individually when completed.

DIRECTIONS AND HELPFUL HINTS

You will need five different colors of paper. Make copies of the sentences found in Set 2, the ones with the slash marks. Cut out the sentences and then cut them apart on the slash marks so that students will have sentence chunks to reassemble. Each sentence should be copied onto a different color paper so that students can quickly sort the sentence chunks into separate piles. Give students a bag with the sentence chunks and the following directions.

1. Sort the sentence pieces by color. You should have five stacks of sentences parts, one of each color.

2. Reassemble the parts to make five complete sentences. Each sentence will be one color, but you will have five sentences when finished.

3. Once you have arranged the pieces to create a sentence, stop and read it aloud. Listen closely. Does the arrangement have clarity? Does the sentence flow smoothly as you read? Does the sentence have a rhythm? Experiment with a new arrangement and then listen to that one.

4. Determine the punctuation and capitalization needed for the final sentence.

5. When finished, you will have five complete sentences.

Unscrambling sentences has many benefits. Students develop the following skills and understandings:

- An understanding of how sentence parts fit together
- A realization that sentences can be constructed several ways; there is not just one correct arrangement
- A realization that authors make choices about sentence structure, word choice, and punctuation
- A realization that they already have a great deal of grammar knowledge
- Development of an ear for rhythm, clarity, and fluency
- Vocabulary development
- An understanding that punctuation is not a set of rules to be memorized, but a courtesy that writers provide for readers. Punctuation is a tool that writers use to help convey a message.

It is not necessary that students have already studied the patterns. The goal is to let them use their internal grammar to construct a sentence. The goal is to have intelligent discussions about sentence structure and an author's decisions. But simply creating a sentence and assigning a pattern number is not the goal. I have shared pattern numbers in Set 1 to provide teachers with additional information that might help them.

The discussion about the sentence structure and an author's decisions is valuable. Let's look at a sentence from *Leola and the Honeybears* (Rosales, 1999):

Original Sentence:	Leola sang out as she struggled to pull the biggest, wettest bedsheet from the laundry basket.
Sentence Chunks:	Leola sang out / as she struggled / to pull / the biggest wettest bedsheet / from the laundry basket
Possible Sentences:	As she struggled to pull the biggest, wettest bedsheet from the laundry basket, Leola sang out.
	Leola sang out from the laundry basket as she struggled to pull the biggest, wettest bedsheet.
	Leola sang out as she struggled to pull from the laundry basket the biggest, wettest bedsheet.

The second sentence does have an error; Leola is not in the laundry basket. Give students an opportunity to explain why they created each particular sentence. What is the student visualizing? Why does that sentence seem logical to the student? I want students to understand two big points with this activity. First, authors make decisions, and those decisions are based on the entire text. For example, the first and the third possible sentences both have clarity and rhythm. But if the author has already used some sentences that open with the adverb clause, she might not want to start another sentence in that pattern. And that ties in to the second big lesson: The chunks (elements) that make up a sentence can be manipulated to create a range of grammatically correct patterns.

Another valuable discussion often occurs when students look at the author's original text. While studying the patterns, students learn some very specific demands concerning punctuation. While reading, students will discover that professional authors seem to break grammar rules willy-nilly. When I teach sentence Pattern 13, open with a present participle, I want students to set the participial phrase off with a comma and to keep the phrase anchored to the noun it describes. But look at the following sentence from Karen Hesse's *Sable* (1994): "Mam and Pap sat at the kitchen table, looking exhausted." The participial phrase "looking exhausted" clearly describes Mam and Pap, yet it is "anchored" to the noun *table*.

Students must realize that they are looking at the work of professional authors who have studied grammar and writing for years. They have paid their dues and have reached a point where they work with several editors and publishers. They make decisions that will tell their story or communicate information most effectively. It may look like a grammar violation to us, but the authors are professional writers making responsible decisions.

I want my students to be grounded in the grammar rules before they begin making decisions to bend the rules. Grammar is a courtesy, and good grammar should be taken seriously. But that does not mean memorizing rules; it means listening to text and making decisions.

Set 1: It is not necessary that the students create the exact sentences as those in Set 1 since many sentence chunks can be moved to several locations in a sentence. In fact, with some classes I have avoided ever giving students the original sentences since many students seem to think that creating a structure different from the original means their sentence is incorrect. If a student has created a grammatically correct structure, honor it. If the student has created a sentence that has errors—such as dangling participles or misplaced modifiers—discuss the errors and provide them a second chance.

Set 2: Copy each sentence from this set onto a different color paper. Cut the sentences into pieces. I cut on the slash marks in order to eliminate the marks. Some students try to use the slashes to assemble the pieces. I want students to read the sentence chunks and listen to the words as they assemble complete sentences.

Punctuation and beginning capitalization have been eliminated from the sentence chunks. Once the students have assembled a sentence, they will need to discuss what punctuation and capitalization is needed.

Some teachers retype the sentences so they can enlarge the font and create larger sentence strips. Others have enlarged the sentences on a copy machine. For some students, the larger sentence strips are easier to work with. And the larger strips are not as easily lost.

Store the strips in ziplock baggies. Number the bag and number the back of each sentence strip. Every piece is returned to bag with the corresponding number. When sentence strips are found lying on the floor at the end of class, it is a simple task to return them to the correct bags.

EXERCISE 1: *LEOLA AND THE HONEYBEARS* BY MELODYE BENSON ROSALES

Set 1: Original sentences from *Leola and the Honeybears* (Rosales, 1999)

1. Leola sang out as she struggled to pull the biggest, wettest bedsheet from the laundry basket. (Pattern 9: Close with an adverb clause)

2. When Leola got her way, she could be as sweet as brown sugar. (Pattern 8: Open with an adverb clause)

3. Suddenly, Leola caught sight of some milkweed seeds blowing in the breeze across the meadow. (Pattern 4: Open with an adverb)

4. She turned around full circle, but she couldn't tell which way was home. (Pattern 6: Compound sentence with a coordinating conjunction)

5. They dined on delicious daily delights like dandelion stew, double-dipped daffodil custard, and sweet daisy-dough cakes. (Pattern 10: Parallel items in a series)

Set 2: Sentence chunks to be copied onto colored paper

1. Leola sang out / as she struggled / to pull / the biggest wettest bedsheet / from the laundry basket

2. when Leola / got her way / she could be / as sweet as brown sugar

3. suddenly / Leola caught sight / of some milkweed seeds / blowing in the breeze / across the meadow

4. she / turned around full circle / but / she couldn't tell / which way was home

5. they dined / on delicious daily delights / like dandelion stew / double-dipped daffodil custard / and / sweet daisy-dough cakes

EXERCISE 2: *SABLE* BY KAREN HESSE

Set 1: Original sentences from *Sable* (Hesse, 1994)

1. The Cobbs' hound, Truman, sat on the steps beside me. (Pattern 7: An appositive behind a noun)

2. Peering through the gate, my eyes searched for signs of Sable. (Pattern 13: Open with a present participle)

3. Standing in his front hall, I dripped onto the pale patterned rug. (Pattern 13: Open with a present participle)

4. Between the dishes and the saw, I didn't hear the chug of a motor until the car had nearly reached the top of our driveway. (Pattern 9: Close with an adverb clause)

5. Mam walked over, reached down, and touched Sable. (Pattern 11: Parallel verb phrases in a series)

Set 2: Sentence chunks to be copied on colored paper

1. the Cobbs' hound / Truman / sat on the steps / beside me

2. peering through the gate / my eyes / searched for signs / of Sable

3. standing in his front hall / I dripped / onto the pale patterned rug

4. between the dishes and the saw / I didn't hear / the chug of a motor / until / the car had nearly reached / the top of our driveway

5. Mam / walked over / reached down / and touched Sable

EXERCISE 3: *SUPERFUDGE* BY JUDY BLUME

Set 1: Original sentences from *Superfudge* (Blume, 1980)

1. He rested his head on Mom's shoulder, shoved his fingers into his mouth, and slurped on them. (Pattern 11: Parallel verb phrases in a series)

2. Fudge fell asleep before I'd finished the book. (Pattern 9: Close with an adverb clause)

3. My mother and father call the house *fantastic, fabulous, unbelievable.* (Pattern 10: Parallel items in a series)

4. My mother, who had been reading the morning paper, looked up. (Pattern 18: Nonrestrictive adjective clauses)

5. So now she had plums all over her face, plums drooling down on to her bib, plums stuck in her hair and plums covering her rattle, which she banged on her tray as she laughed. (Pattern 10: Parallel items in a series, and Pattern 18: Nonrestrictive adjective clauses)

Set 2: Sentence chunks to be copied onto colored paper

1. he rested his head / on Mom's shoulder / shoved his fingers into his mouth / and / slurped on them

2. Fudge fell asleep / before / I'd finished the book

3. my mother and father / call the house / *fantastic* / *fabulous* / *unbelievable*

4. my mother / who had been reading the morning paper / looked up

5. so now she had plums all over her face / plums drooling down on to her bib / plums stuck in her hair / and / plums covering her rattle / which she banged on her tray / as she laughed

EXERCISE 4: *MAMA, I'LL GIVE YOU THE WORLD* BY RONI SCHOTTER

Set 1: Original sentences from *Mama, I'll Give You the World* (Schotter, 2006)

1. She works hard every day at Walter's World of Beauty, cutting, coloring, and curling. (Pattern 10: Parallel items in a series)

2. While Mama, like a magician, turns Mrs. Koo's dark hair the color of sunset, Walter, Georges, and Rupa cut and comb. (Pattern 8: Open with an adverb clause)

3. Then she writes a story for English about a girl with a magic brush that brushes people's cares away. (Pattern 17: Restrictive adjective clauses)

4. In between customers, Mama rests in her chair and lets Luisa brush her long, thick curls. (Pattern 5: Open with a prepositional phrase, and Pattern 6: Compound sentence with a coordinating conjunction)

5. Under the dryers, the ladies loudly whisper their secrets, but Luisa has a secret of her own. (Pattern 5: Open with a prepositional phrase, and Pattern 6: Compound sentence with a coordinating conjunction)

Set 2: Sentence chunks to be copied on colored paper

1. she works hard / every day / at Walter's World of Beauty / cutting / coloring / and curling

2. while Mama / like a magician / turns Mrs. Koo's dark hair the color of sunset / Walter / Georges / and Rupa cut and comb

3. then she writes a story / for English / about a girl / with a magic brush / that brushes people's cares away

4. in between customers / Mama rests / in her chair / and lets Luisa brush / her / long / thick / curls

5. under the dryers / the ladies / loudly whisper their secrets / but / Luisa has a secret of her own

EXERCISE 5: *THE JUNKYARD WONDERS* BY PATRICIA POLACCO

Set 1: Original sentences from *The Junkyard Wonders* (Polacco, 2010)

1. Short and stout, she seemed a little scary, brusque. (Pattern 12: Open with an adjective or an adjective phrase)

2. Some of you smell like lemons, some cinnamon, some almonds. (Pattern 10: Parallel items in a series)

3. We removed all the outer skin, built in new balsa struts, and repaired a lot of the skeleton. (Pattern 11: Parallel verb phrases in a series)

4. Maybe Mr. Weeks, the janitor, could help us get to the roof. (Pattern 7: An appositive behind a noun)

5. We huddled together out on the playground, chattering about our plans for the launch. (A variation of Pattern 13: Open with a present participle)

Set 2: Sentence chunks to be copied onto colored paper

1. short and stout / she seemed a little scary / brusque

2. some of you smell like lemons / some cinnamon / some almonds

3. we / removed all the outer skin / built in new balsa struts / and / repaired a lot of the skeleton

4. maybe / Mr. Weeks / the janitor / could help us get to the roof

5. we huddled together / out on the playground / chattering about our plans / for the launch

EXERCISE 6: *THE COWBOY AND THE BLACK-EYED PEA* BY TONY JOHNSTON

Set 1: Original sentences from *The Cowboy and the Black-Eyed Pea* (Johnston, 1992)

1. The cowboy set out, mustache a-jouncing, spurs a-jingling. (A variation of Pattern 21: Opening with an absolute)

2. He wore tooled leather boots, an overgrown neckerchief, and fringes galore. (Pattern 10: Parallel items in a series)

3. In the midst of the downpour, a young man knocked at the door. (Pattern 5: Open with a prepositional phrase)

4. As he rode along, he twisted and twitched. (Pattern 8: Open with an adverb clause)

5. Lightning sizzles across the sky. (Pattern 1: Specific noun–vivid verb)

Set 2: Sentence chunks to be copied onto colored paper

1. the cowboy set out / mustache a-jouncing / spurs a-jingling

2. he wore / tooled leather boots / an overgrown neckerchief / and / fringes galore

3. in the midst of the downpour / a young man / knocked at the door

4. as / he rode along / he twisted and twitched

5. lightning sizzles / across the sky

EXERCISE 7: *THE WAINSCOTT WEASEL* BY TOR SEIDLER

Set 1: Original sentences from *The Wainscott Weasel* (Seidler, 1993)

1. This nymph, this ugly creature of the swamp, transformed herself into a big, beautiful dragonfly. (Pattern 7: An appositive behind a noun)

2. Dragonflies have six legs, which hang like a basket to scoop up other flying bugs. (Pattern 18: Nonrestrictive adjective clause)

3. Every thump of my heart, every breath, every moment, stretched as if time didn't exist. (Pattern 10: Parallel items in a series)

4. I trembled for a moment. (Pattern 1: Specific noun–vivid verb)

5. We saw a great blue heron stalking in the shallows for minnows and frogs. (A variation of Pattern 13: Open with a present participle—this sentence places the present participle behind a direct object)

Set 2: Sentence chunks to be copied on colored paper

1. this nymph / this ugly creature of the swamp / transformed herself / into a big beautiful dragonfly

2. dragonflies have six legs / which hang like a basket / to scoop up other flying bugs

3. every thump of my heart / every breath / every moment / stretched as if time didn't exist

4. I trembled / for a moment

5. we saw a great blue heron / stalking in the shallows / for minnows and frogs

EXERCISE 8: *THE LOTUS SEED* BY SHERRY GARLAND

Set 1: Original sentences from *The Lotus Seed* (Garland, 1993)

1. My grandmother saw the emperor cry the day he lost his golden dragon throne. (Pattern 17: Restrictive adjective clause)

2. Whenever she felt sad or lonely, she took out the seed and thought of the brave young emperor. (Pattern 8: Open with an adverb clause)

3. One terrible day her family scrambled into a crowded boat and set out on a stormy sea. (Pattern 4: Open with an adverb)

4. Then one day in the spring my grandmother shouted, and we all ran to the garden and saw a beautiful pink lotus unfurling its petals, so creamy and soft. (Pattern 6: Compound sentence with a coordinating conjunction)

5. I wrapped my seed in a piece of silk and hid it in a secret place. (Pattern 1: Specific noun–vivid verb)

Set 2: Sentence chunks to be copied onto colored paper

1. my grandmother / saw / the emperor cry / the day / he lost / his golden dragon throne

2. whenever / she felt / sad or lonely / she took out the seed / and thought of / the brave young emperor

3. one terrible day / her family / scrambled / into a crowded boat / and set out / on a stormy sea

4. then one day / in the spring / my grandmother / shouted / and we all ran / to the garden / and saw a beautiful pink lotus / unfurling its petals / so creamy and soft

5. I wrapped my seed / in a piece of silk / and hid it / in a secret place

EXERCISE 9: *LIFE IN THE OCEANS* BY LUCY BAKER

Set 1: Original sentences from *Life in the Oceans* (Baker, 1990)

1. Beneath the world's oceans lie rugged mountains, active volcanoes, vast plateaus, and almost bottomless trenches. (Pattern 5: Open with a prepositional phrase, and Pattern 10: Parallel items in a series)

2. The deepest trenches could easily swallow up the tallest mountains on land. (Pattern 2: Noun-verb-noun)

3. Seen from above, the world's oceans appear empty and unchanging, but beneath the surface hides a unique world where water takes the place of air. (Pattern 6: Compound sentence with a coordinating conjunction)

4. A fantastic and rich assortment of plants and animals lives in these waters, from the microscopic plankton to the giant blue whale. (Pattern 1: Specific noun–vivid verb)

5. Although oceans dominate the world map, we have only just begun to explore their hidden depths. (Pattern 8: Open with an adverb clause)

Set 2: Sentence chunks to be copied onto colored paper

1. beneath the world's oceans / lie rugged mountains / active volcanoes / vast plateaus / and almost bottomless trenches

2. the deepest trenches / could easily swallow up / the tallest mountains on land

3. seen from above / the world's oceans / appear empty and unchanging / but / beneath the surface / hides a unique world / where water takes the place of air

4. a fantastic and rich assortment / of plants and animals / lives in these waters / from the microscopic plankton / to the giant blue whale

5. although oceans / dominate the world map / we have only just begun / to explore their hidden depths

EXERCISE 10: *CHEYENNE MEDICINE HAT* BY BRIAN HEINZ

Set 1: Original sentences from *Cheyenne Medicine Hat* (Heinz, 2006)

1. The stallion flattened his ears and reared as two lariats swept through the air, fell around his neck, and tightened. (Pattern 11: Parallel verb phrases in a series)

2. Panic set in and his eyes rolled white. (Pattern 6: Compound sentence with a coordinating conjunction)

3. A half-ton of fury, he struggled against the taut ropes and lashed out with powerful kicks from his hindquarters. (Pattern 21: Open with an absolute)

4. Two mares whinnied in alarm and fell to the same fate. (Pattern 1: Specific noun–vivid verb)

5. The wranglers forced them upriver toward a makeshift corral, while their confused foals followed silently, refusing to abandon their mothers. (Pattern 9: Close with an adverb clause)

Set 2: Sentence chunks to be copied onto colored paper

1. the stallion / flattened his ears / and / reared / as two lariats swept through the air / fell around his neck / and tightened.

2. panic set in / and / his eyes rolled white

3. a half-ton of fury / he struggled / against the taut ropes / and / lashed out with powerful kicks / from his hindquarters

4. two mares / whinnied in alarm / and / fell to the same fate

5. the wranglers / forced them upriver / toward a makeshift corral / while their confused foals / followed silently / refusing to abandon their mothers

The discussion following the reconstruction activities is valuable. Look at the various ways that a sentence could be reconstructed and discuss the decisions that went into the final choices. For students who still need practice, Chapter 6 offers more ideas.

Extra Practice With Patterns

6

Students have been learning one pattern per week. Some students might be practicing sentence combining or sentence reconstruction activities. The new patterns should be appearing in essays, narratives, and other assignments. This chapter provides five more activities that can be used to help students understand and use the patterns.

EXTRA PRACTICE ACTIVITIES

MARKER BOARDS

Materials

- One marker board per student
- One dry erase marker per student
- One eraser per student
- Binders of sentence patterns

Educational supply catalogs have small marker boards available. I have found that a stack of scrap paper and markers works well too.

Procedure

Without a doubt, marker board day was my students' favorite class session. Students cheered if they walked into the classroom, and they saw me at the front of the room with the milk crate that held the marker boards. They lost no time getting into their groups and counting off. Keep this activity fun and moving fast. The goal is to build automaticity in sentence production and to reinforce patterns.

Students work in groups of three. Each student should number off, one-two-three, and remember his or her number. Ask all of the number ones to gather materials for their team: three marker boards, three erasers, and three dry markers.

Students must understand the rules of marker board day.

1. All students on a team will write the exact same sentence on their board and make sure to check each other's work.

2. Write large enough to fill the entire board so that sentences can be read from a distance.

3. The teacher will call out the following phrase, "Number _____, please stand up." At that point, all writing and all talking must stop and one student from each group will be standing up with the marker board facing the teacher.

4. The teacher will circulate the room, read each sentence aloud, and award points. If anyone in a group talks or causes a disturbance during the reading of sentences, that team will lose five points. Any team with a negative score will be given a sentence-combination assignment for homework.

5. Each group will be responsible to keep track of their points by making hatch marks on the bottom of one board. I have found that my students were amazingly honest about keeping track of their own points.

6. Each team will receive one point for creating a perfect sentence: no CUPS (capitalization, usage, punctuation, spelling) errors. Another point is awarded for creating the correct pattern. Teams can receive bonus points by using specific nouns and vivid verbs. These points are awarded by whimsy and any argument or opposition to the teacher's decision will result in a five-point loss.

7. Occasionally, teams might be given an additional challenge. If they can meet the challenge, they will win an additional point.

Now the fun begins. The teacher's job is to provide a sentence challenge for the students. Sometimes I tell the students, "Today we will be working on one pattern. Every sentence you write today must be Pattern 7" (or whatever pattern you select to practice). Immediately, students open their binders to see which pattern they will be creating. Most days, I challenge them with a different pattern every round.

I also give the students a word that I want to appear in the sentence. I might say, "Please write a sentence in Pattern 7, and somewhere in the sentence I want you to use the word *football*." This assures me that they will create an original sentence rather than simply copy a sentence from their binder. Some students will use a sentence from their binder and simply change a few words. That is perfectly fine. Remember, the goal is to reinforce the patterns and to build automaticity. Students will learn to write the patterns by imitating a model and through constant practice.

Give the students time to write the sentences and then call out, "All number threes please stand up." Students never know what number you will be calling. I might call for number three again on the next round. I might call for another number. Some groups will groan because they did not finish. Other groups have a quick flurry of checking the work of student number three. Soon every group has one student standing. Circle the room, read the sentences, and award points. Praise their accomplishments and point out errors. But keep it fun and lighthearted.

Having the students work in numbered groups of three keeps every one engaged. If students worked individually, and I called on one student to stand up to read a sentence, the rest of the class would begin daydreaming because I am working with only that student. By having students in groups of three that compete, I can keep everyone involved. In a class of thirty students, I have ten students standing with an answer. They all listen to hear how many points their team has earned. In addition, since they do not know which number I will call, they are careful to check the work on everyone's boards.

The following list shows some of the challenges I have given to students.

- Please write a Pattern 8 and use alliteration only in the adverb clause.
- Please write a Pattern 7 and include the name of the author of *Miz Berlin Walks.*
- Please write a Pattern 17 and include something you learned in science this week.
- Please write a Pattern 6 and use the name of the current vice president of the United States.
- Please write a Pattern 21 and use the name of a character from a book you are currently reading.
- Please write a Pattern 19 and include a strong context clue to the meaning of the word *revolution.*
- Please write a Pattern 15 and include a simile.

The game is fun but very challenging. Students enjoy the competition and it reinforces students on many levels: kinesthetic, auditory, visual. I do demand total silence as I read the sentences because I want all of the students to hear the pattern. I want them to absorb the rhythms of the language and hear the vocabulary.

PICTURE WALK

Materials

- Interesting pictures from magazines, calendars, and the like. Pictures with a lot of activity will work best. You will need one picture for each student.
- A paper attached to each picture. At the top of the paper, write one of the sentence patterns that describes something in the picture. For example,

let's imagine you have a picture of a young boy playing outside with a dog. You might attach any one of the following patterns to the picture:

- o Pattern 6: The boy tossed the ball, and the German shepherd scurried to retrieve it.
- o Pattern 21: His tail wagging, the German shepherd waited to fetch the ball.
- o Pattern 7: The dog, a German shepherd, chased the ball.

- Just create one sentence with specific nouns and vivid verbs for each picture.

Procedure

- Spread these pictures with target sentences attached around the perimeter of the room.
- One student stands by each picture.
- Students look at the picture, read the target sentence, and write another sentence that imitates that pattern and comments on the picture. Finally, students write their initials by their sentence.
- Give students some time to write a sentence and then give a signal for everyone to move to their right and stop at the next picture. Students look at the new picture, read the sentences, write a new sentence, and put initials by the sentence they have written.
- The goal is not to create a story or a sequence. The goal is to imitate and practice a range of patterns.

PICTURES INTO WORDS

Materials

- The graphic organizer shown below
- Several pictures with lots of action
- A document camera or some way of displaying the pictures for the entire class
- Strips of paper in four colors to use as points
- Sample sentences to explain points

Procedure

Students will work in teams of three. Give each student a graphic organizer. I number the organizers so that each member of the team has a different one.

Explain that students will be writing sentences based on a picture. Each member of the team will write the same sentence. During each round, students will have an opportunity to earn points for the sentences that they write. The samples in Table 6.1 show the types of sentences that can earn points. Let's say that I have shown students a picture of a boy ready to bat in a baseball game.

In Figure 6.1 is a sample of the graphic organizer that the students will use to write their sentences. The spaces to the right must of course be made larger so that the students can write sentences.

Table 6.1

Points	Possible Sentences	Explanation of Score
0	The boy is ready to bat. The boy looks nervous. The boy is determined to get a hit.	Each of these sentences has a weak verb.
1	The nervous boy stared. The tall, gangly boy swung the heavy wooden bat. The sweaty tall muscular boy waited patiently for the pitch.	Too many adjectives and adverbs are used to create a visualization.
2	The boy swung at the first pitch. The batter knocked the stuffing out of the ball. The batter clobbered the first pitch.	Vivid verbs create a visualization for the reader.
5	Waiting for the pitch, the batter stared down the pitcher. The batter, tall and lanky, strode to the plate with an air of confidence. Hands clutching the bat, my brother waited for the perfect pitch.	Vivid verbs and interesting sentence patterns create a strong visualization.

Figure 6.1   Graphic Organizer for Writing Sentences

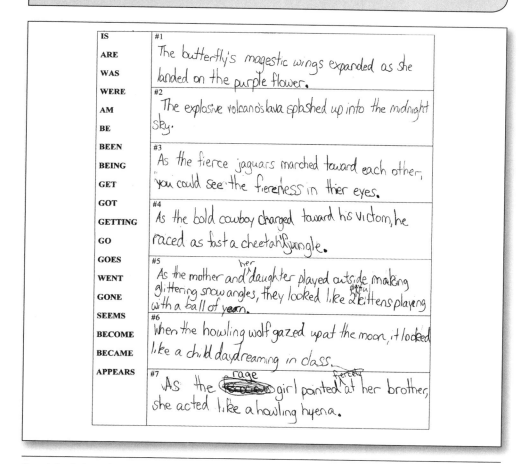

Show the first picture and give the teams time to create a sentence based on that picture. Circulate about the room and read the sentences of each team. To keep track of points, I give each team a colored square or strip of paper: yellow = 0 points, blue = 1 point, orange = 2 points, red = 5 points. Explain why you have awarded the points. Have students reread the sentences that are excellent. Point out vivid verbs, use of similes, and interesting structures. Students learn to write by imitation; they will imitate these sentences as the game progresses.

I recently worked with a group of fifth graders who had not studied sentence patterns. The students had been asked to write an opinion paragraph about their favorite vacation spot. Their teacher and I were concerned because a typical paragraph, even after two days of modeling work, sounded like this:

> I love Florida. It is the coolest place to vacation. It is so exciting. The beaches are so beautiful. The hotels are awesome. The food is delicious. The swimming pools are awesome too. We have a lot of fun in Florida. Now you know why Florida is my favorite vacation spot.

I explained several times that they were writing telling sentences rather than sentences that show. I modeled how to write sentences with vivid verbs and specific nouns. I tried visualization activities. Nothing could shake this class free of the sentences loaded with forms of *be,* reliance on the word *so,* and empty words like *cool* and *awesome.* On the third day, I brought in seven action pictures to put on the document camera. Using the sample sentences, I modeled how they could earn points. Notice on the samples of student work in Figures 6.2, 6.3 and 6.4 how their sentences grew progressively stronger. The students began to move away from trite adjectives. They began to try more complex patterns. In a few short minutes, the students were beginning to produce sentences that gave the reader a chance to visualize.

Notice the first two sentences written by the team in Figure 6.2. This team begins both sentences with the article *the* and they rely heavily on adjectives to create a picture. By the sixth sentence, this team is opening the sentence with a subordinator and using a simile to create a picture. They still rely on a few adjectives but they are not using the trite *beautiful, pretty,* and *awesome.*

The team in Figure 6.3 continued to open their sentences with an article, but by the sixth and seventh sentences they were using vivid verbs: *howled* and *glared.* The work completed by the team in Figure 6.4 shows that they too began to move away from reliance on adjectives to create images. In their early sentences they use the trite adjectives *beautiful* and *hot.* They rely on adverbs—*harshfully.* By the fourth sentence they are moving into stronger verbs and imagery. They repeated the idea of "the heart pounded." But remember, the students had a limited amount of time to complete the sentences, which explains why they began repeating a verb they liked.

In a forty-minute session we completed seven sentences. It took five minutes to explain the rules and to model the various points for each sentence. That left five minutes for teams to write a sentence. Each of the seven teams then read their sentence aloud, and I awarded points. I also offered explanations for points as I went along. The explanation moved students toward the type of writing I wanted: specific nouns, vivid verbs, and more complex structures. This is a fast-paced activity designed to build automaticity and awareness of word

Figure 6.2 Sample Student Sentences: Team 1

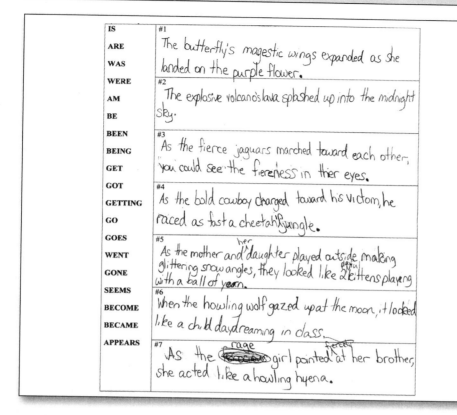

Figure 6.3 Sample Student Sentences: Team 2

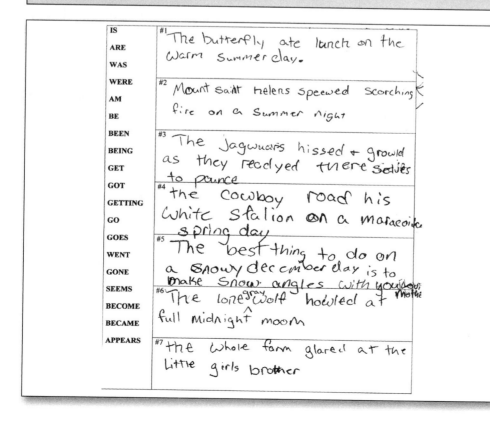

Figure 6.4 Sample Student Sentences: Team 3

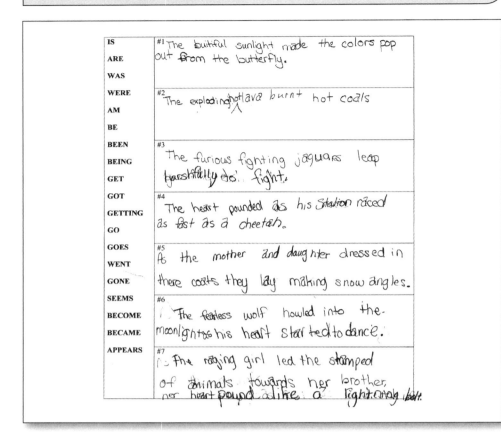

choice. Unlike marker boards, where I insist on accuracy in spelling and punctuation, this activity focuses on speed, word choice to create an image, and sentence complexity.

SENTENCE EXPANSION

Materials

- One worksheet per student.
- Samples of a worksheet follow.

Procedure

Students begin with a simple N-V or N-V-N sentence. They add one new element to the sentence at each step. Be sure to always keep the previous sentence, but always add one new element. Always underline or italicize the new element.

The worksheet provided to the students would have only the information in bold in Table 6.2. The sentences in the right-hand column have been provided to use as models for the activity.

Table 6.2

Embed the Following	New Sentence
	The squirrel scampered.
Prepositional Phrase	*In the morning* the squirrel scampered.
Two Modifiers	In the morning the *brown* squirrel scampered *playfully.*
Revise	In the morning the brown squirrel scampered.

In this activity, students are learning to embed sentence elements to a basic pattern. This task can be made easy or challenging, depending on the number of steps and the requested elements. Obviously, one cannot request them to embed an element if it has not yet been taught. In other words, do not ask a student to add an absolute if they have not yet studied and practiced Pattern 21.

The final step on this activity is always to revise the sentence. Students understand that revision means they can add information, delete information, or rearrange the sentence. I want students to look at the sentence and make decisions about modifiers and sentence arrangement. The original expansion activity may have asked them to add two modifiers, but in the final sentence those modifiers might be redundant.

For a variation of the sentence expansion activity see Killgallon's *Sentence Composing for Middle School* (1997).

The examples in Figure 6.5 show some variations of the expansion activity.

Figure 6.5 Sample Expansion Activity Worksheets

Embed the Following	New Sentence
	The clown entertained us.
Prepositional Phrase	The clown *at the circus* entertained us.
Present Participle	*Juggling three fire sticks,* the clown at the circus entertained us.
Subordinate Clause	Juggling three fire sticks, the clown at the circus entertained us *as the workers led the lions into a cage.*
Two Modifiers	Juggling three *flaming* fire sticks, the clown at the circus entertained us as the workers led the *roaring* lions into a cage.
Revise	Juggling three flaming sticks, the clown entertained us as the workers led the roaring lions into a cage.

Embed the Following	New Sentence
	The dog howled.
Adverb	*Yesterday* the dog howled.
Prepositional Phrase	Yesterday the dog *in the backyard* howled.
Revise	The dog in the backyard howled yesterday.

Embed the Following	New Sentence
	Leonardo painted portraits.
Modifier	Leonardo painted *beautiful* portraits.
Prepositional Phrase With Series of Nouns	Leonardo painted beautiful portraits *of saints, citizens, and royalty.*
Subordinate Clause	*When he lived in Florence,* Leonardo painted beautiful portraits of saints, citizens, and royalty.
Appositive	When he lived in Florence, Leonardo, a *Renaissance artist,* painted beautiful portraits of saints, citizens, and royalty.
Revision	Leonardo, a Renaissance artist, painted portraits of saints, citizens, and royalty.

Embed the Following	New Sentence
	The monster slimed our yard.
A Prepositional Phrase	The monster slimed our yard *on Halloween.*
Absolute	*Glop flowing from his mouth,* the monster slimed our yard on Halloween.
Adjective Clause	Glop flowing from his mouth, the monster, *who towered taller than the trees,* slimed our yard on Halloween.
Appositive	Glop flowing from his mouth, the monster, who towered taller than the trees, slimed our yard on Halloween, *the scariest night of the year.*
Revision	Glop flowing from his mouth, the monster towered over the trees and slimed our yard on Halloween night.

Embed the Following	New Sentence
	Butterflies flit.
Prepositional Phrase	Butterflies flit *among the flowers.*
Present Participle	*Taking sips of nectar,* butterflies flit among the flowers.
A Modifier	Taking sips of nectar, *giant* butterflies flit among the flowers.
Coordinating Conjunction and Clause	Taking sips of nectar, giant butterflies flit among the flowers, *but their predators do not see them.*
Revision	Flitting among the flowers, giant butterflies take sips of nectar, but their predators do not spot them.

COLOR-CODED SENTENCES

Materials

- One bag of color-coded sentence strips per team
- Color-coded signs
- Paper in a range of colors: white, blue, pink, yellow, orange, green
- Laminator

Procedure

It will take a bit of work to assemble this activity, but it will reap benefits. You will need to make signs as indicated below. I used a word processing program set to the largest font and printed the signs. I put a bulleted list on the back of each sign to help me remember what I want to say during the activity. The list is not intended to be a script; it is merely a reminder of hints to help the students. No list is needed for the white sign since the white strips will always be the first step.

Color of Signs and Sentence Strips	Words on Sign
White	Noun-Verb Noun-Verb-Noun
Blue	Adverb
Pink	Prepositional Phrase
Yellow	Coordinating Conjunction
Orange	Subordinator
Green	Participial Phrase

Blue List

- The blue words are adverbs.
- Can you make a blue-white sentence?
- This is sentence Pattern 4.
- Adverbs can bounce in a sentence.
- Adverbs tell us how, when, where, why something happens.
- Can you move the blue word to another part of the sentence?

Pink List

- The pink words are prepositional phrases.
- Can you make a pink-white sentence?
- This is a sentence Pattern 5.
- Can you move the prepositional phrase?
- If you can move it, what type of phrase is it? An adverb phrase.
- If you can move the phrase, how is the phrase functioning? As an adverb.
- The form of the phrase is a preposition at the beginning and a noun or pronoun at the end.
- Prepositional phrases never have verbs.

Yellow List

- The yellow words are coordinating conjunctions.
- We have seven coordinating conjunctions: *so, and, but, or, nor, for,* and *yet.*
- Can you make a white-yellow-white sentence?
- Coordinating conjunctions join two things of equal value.
- We will use them today to join two sentences together.
- If you have a complete sentence on both sides of a coordinating conjunction, you will need a comma.

Orange List

- The orange words are subordinators.
- We will use the subordinators to join two sentences together.
- Can you make an orange-white-white sentence?
- This is sentence Pattern 8.
- If you remove the second white strip, will the orange and one white make a complete sentence? No.
- One orange and one white makes a dependent clause.
- Another name for a dependent clause is a subordinate clause.
- Can you bounce that dependent clause? Yes.
- If a clause can bounce, how is it functioning? As an adverb; it is an adverb clause.
- When you make a white-orange-white sentence, you have made sentence Pattern 9.
- If the orange word is the first word in a sentence, you will need a comma in that sentence. Can anyone read their sentence and tell me where to put the comma?
- If the orange word is in the middle of the two white sentences, you do not need a comma.

Green List

- The words on the green strips are present participial phrases.
- Present participles always start with an *ing* word. That is one way to recognize their form.
- Present participial phrases function as adjectives.
- That means the phrase must be anchored to the noun it describes.

To create the bags of sentence strips for the students, select words and phrases from the following lists and copy these onto the colors that correspond to the signs. Enlarge the font and put spaces between the lines before copying since these will be cut into strips for the students.

Copy some of the N-V and N-V-N sentences from Table 6.3 onto white paper.

Table 6.3

Noun-Verb	Noun-Verb-Noun
The windows rattled.	The farmer drove his tractor.
The astronaut signaled.	The green frog swallowed a fly.
The baby cried.	The butcher sliced the bacon.
The chair collapsed.	The hungry boy ate a cookie.
The baseball flew.	The dentist pulled my tooth.
The paint smeared.	The spider scraped her knees.
The crowd cheered.	The worker fixed the computer.
Our secretary typed.	The officer wrote a ticket.
The train chugged.	The president signed the bill.
The ice cream melted.	The spider stretched her legs.
My sister danced.	The puppy woke our neighbors.
The river flooded.	The runner beat the tag.
The pig squealed.	My grandparents bought a puppy.
The paper tore.	The toddler hugged her friend.
Our neighbors waved.	The mail carrier sprained her ankle.
The horse whinnied.	Smoke stings the firefighter's eyes.
The wind roared.	Lightning hit the dry grass.
The cup shattered.	Students carry heavy backpacks.
The ballerina twirled.	The helicopters dropped water.
The monkey spat.	Helicopters deliver equipment.
The magician escaped.	The magician swallowed twenty-four swords.
The leaves danced.	The team lifted the trophy.
The train left.	The rock star played his guitar.
The car raced.	My sister caught the bouquet.
The rain fell.	The donkey jumped the fence.
The blender whirred.	The plumber stopped the leak.
The paint will dry.	The bat ate the bugs.
The swimmer dove.	The driver won the race.
My bike chain broke.	The secretary typed a memo.
The golfer cheered.	The catcher tagged the runner.
My dad raced.	The rocker smashed his guitar.
The spider skipped.	The child wanted french fries.
The nurse frowned.	My friends share their toys.
The spider tripped.	Grandma called the eye doctor.
The wind roared.	My parents rode the Ferris wheel.
The phone rang.	My brother woke our neighbors.
The computer crashed.	The lions and tigers dozed.
My brother smiled.	The lion tamer thrilled the audience.
The team played.	The stuntwoman dazzled the audience.
The microphone squealed.	My neighbor cut our grass.
My teacher laughed.	The artist painted a portrait.
The stars twinkled.	The ants carried the bread crumbs.
The check bounced.	The orthodontist adjusted my braces.
The groom fainted.	The skier jumped the ramp.
Hundreds of people stared.	We bought a new cell phone.
The tightrope walker paused.	The dust covered my car.
	The scientists studied the mold.
	The noise frightened me.

Copy some of the adverbs from Table 6.4 onto blue paper.

Table 6.4

Again	Accidentally
Annually	Blissfully
Carefully	Cautiously
Eagerly	Eventually
Finally	Foolishly
Hopefully	Frequently
Immediately	Furiously
Mechanically	Gently
Noisily	Gracefully
Often	Innocently
Patiently	Instantly
Quickly	Last night
Quietly	Merely
Silently	Recently
Suddenly	Slowly
Timidly	Sometimes
Today	Tomorrow
Yesterday	Unfortunately
Tenderly	Willfully

Copy some of the prepositional phrases from Table 6.5 onto pink paper.

Table 6.5

After school	After the wedding
At 6:45 a.m.	Around the block
At me	Around the corner
At the age of 63	Around the curve
At the school picnic	At Christmas
Because of the bumpy road	At noon
Because of the earthquake	At the gym
Behind the barn	At the picnic
Down the garden path	At the wedding
During the game	At the zoo
During the last quarter	Because of the rain
During the opening ceremony	Before lunch
During the parade	Down the hill
In my pool	For five minutes
In the basement	In spite of the rain
In the morning	In the evening
In the rugged mountains	In the grass
Like Cookie Monster	In the sun
Near the fire	In the window

Off the platform	Into the lake
On her walk	Like a tornado
On stage	On her feet
Since Friday	On stage
Under the table	On the cell phone
Up the hill	On the ground
Up the mountain	Over the wall
Up the spout	Through the air
With a click of the mouse	Through the field
With a cracked screen	With enthusiasm
With a crooked tail	With great care
With a magic marker	With one gulp
With a piece of bubble gum	Without warning

Copy all of the coordinating conjunctions onto yellow paper. Every student bag needs all seven of the coordinating conjunctions.

1. So

2. And

3. But

4. Or

5. Not

6. For

7. Yet

Copy all of the following subordinators onto orange paper. Every student bag should have all of the subordinators.

After	Even though	Until
Although	If	When
As	Just as	Whenever
As if	Since	Wherever
Because	So that	Whether
Before	Unless	While

Copy some of the following present participial phrases onto green paper.

Amazing everyone in the crowd	Balancing on a thin cable
Balancing on her tiptoes	By selling her piano
Breaking her glasses	Crossing the street
Chopping down shrubs and trees	Cuddling the kitten
Destroying nearly 7 million acres	Dreaming up new stunts
Fighting the raging fires	Fearing nothing

Flying through the air	Giggling at Mickey Mouse
Hoping to please her parents	Hoping for a win
Howling at the moon	Leaping into cages
Protecting the forests	Licking his lips
Pumping water	Matching wits with the animals
Refusing to eat the broccoli	Petting the dog
Risking their own lives	Riding her bicycle
Sinking the putt	Sliding into second base
Stumbling on the ice	Spilling the glass of milk
Trying to set a new record	Spying a penny under the desk
Typing twenty words a minute	Stepping into the cage
Waving to the crowd	Swimming with the sharks
Working long shifts	Baking a dozen cakes
Folding all the laundry	Sharpening the pencils
While playing video games	

1. Give each team of three or four students a bag of the multicolored sentence pieces.

2. Have the students sort the strips of paper by color. Hold up the signs for the type of sentence you want them to create. For example, hold up a blue adverb sign and a white N-V or N-V-N sign and say, "Please create a blue-white sentence."

3. Students then select a blue piece and a white piece to create a sentence. Here are some samples of the types of sentences students might create:

   - Eventually the chair collapsed.
   - Yesterday the mail carrier sprained her ankle.
   - Mechanically the officer wrote a ticket.

4. Give students a few minutes to create a sentence or two. Next, ask a few students to read one of their sentences.

5. Teach the punctuation by saying, "If the blue word ends in an *ly*, it should be set off by a comma." Have two or three more groups read their sentences but say "comma" where their sentence needs it.

6. Ask the students if they can bounce the blue word. Most of them can. "If the word bounces, it is probably functioning as an _____." Students respond, "adverb."

That is the procedure you will follow. Select colored signs for a new sentence. You can hold the signs up or use magnets to hold the signs to a board. Use the information that you have printed on the back of the signs as a reminder of things you want to teach. The following are examples of Pattern 8 sentences: Open with an adverb clause. Change them to white-orange-white to create Pattern 9.

Orange-White-White

- When my grandparents bought a puppy, my sister danced.
- Before the check bounced, the dentist pulled my tooth.
- Since the runner beat the tag, my brother smiled.

Ask students where they would use a comma in an orange-white-white sentence. Have them read the sentences and say the word *comma* where it belongs.

Ask students to remove the second white strip. They should have the following:

- When my grandparents bought a puppy
- Before the check bounced
- Since the runner beat the tag

Ask if the remaining pieces make a sentence. Of course they don't. Explain that this is a subordinate clause. Return the white strip and ask if they can bounce the first orange-white pieces. They should have the following:

- My sister danced when my grandparents bought a puppy.
- The dentist pulled my tooth before the check bounced.
- My brother smiled since the runner beat the tag.

Since the clause can bounce, it is an adverb clause. Explain that since the orange word appears in the middle, they do not need to use a comma.

Many of the sentence patterns can be created by manipulating the color-coded signs. The colors help students to see the various elements of a sentence.

Pattern 5: Open with a prepositional phrase

Pink-White

- Without warning lightning hit the dry grass.
- Because of the rain, the scientists studied the mold.
- During the parade the dust covered my car.

Pattern 6: Compound sentence with a coordinating conjunction

White-Yellow-White

- The lions and tigers dozed, but the lion tamer thrilled the audience.
- The wind roared, so the leaves danced.
- The magician swallowed twenty-four swords, and the green frog swallowed a fly.

Pattern 13: Open with a present participle

<u>Green-White</u>

- Balancing on a thin cable, the tightrope walker paused.
- Protecting the forests, the helicopters dropped water.
- Sliding into second base, the runner beat the tag.

Color-coded sentences is another activity that I like to keep moving quickly. I do the entire activity orally because my main goal is to have students see how the sentence elements work together. I also want the students to hear the patterns. But I know several teachers who place bags of sentence strips in the writing center. They then post color-coded signs on a board, and students working at the center create several sentences that follow the required pattern. The students then copy the sentences on paper to practice punctuation and capitalization.

USE OF THE ACTIVITIES

This chapter provided activities that teachers could use with small groups that need extra help. The activities also could be used by the whole class to provide a fun but worthwhile break from writing workshop. Chapter 7 focuses on short writing assignments that encourage students to use a variety of sentence patterns.

Short Writing Assignments 7

Practicing the sentence patterns will help students to develop automaticity and fluency. Students who write daily develop fluency and endurance skills necessary to exceed on high-stakes tests. Daily writing is the path to developing higher order thinking and endurance (Routman, 2005). Short writing assignments give students an opportunity to manipulate the patterns and make decisions about how and when to use a pattern.

This chapter provides two types of short assignments: nongraded opening activities and targeted skill-builders. Both types of activities are designed to build fluency with the patterns and demonstrate the power of revision. In addition, both types of activities are fun. As I visit schools across the country, my heart breaks when I see the intense focus on writing to the test. Joy and creativity have been replaced with ridiculous prompts and rigid rubrics aligned to a formula. The irony of this situation is that the tests do not require formula writing. Yes, students might pass a test with a formula, but they learn nothing about the nuances of good writing. The myth of formula writing as the silver bullet needs to be replaced with the truth.

Students should learn writing skills, not writing formulas. Sentence construction, coherence, cohesion, powerful openings and closings, vivid vocabulary—to develop these skills, students need to make constant cognitive decisions. Allowing students to make those decisions can bring back the joy to writing. Writing is an extremely complex process that develops through constant practice and decision making.

It is not necessary, or even possible, to assign grades to everything students write. "If you are reading everything your students write, they're not writing enough" (Routman, 2005, p. 65). The quick group pieces that students do are not graded. A read-around to allow groups to share meets the goals of the work. Students can hear the rhythm of the sentences; they can visualize when specific nouns and vivid verbs are used. Students understand that the group pieces are practice pieces. They provide a perfect opportunity for students to take risks with their writing.

OPENING ACTIVITIES

The following activities can be completed in five to ten minutes. They work well as class openers to get students settled in and working. The fast-paced and lighthearted work energizes the students as they move from this work into writing workshop. These rapid-fire, nongraded activities will need to be modeled and explained the first time they are used in class. Later, the students can tackle the activity more quickly.

PERSONAL DESCRIPTIONS

Materials

Writing material and a list of nouns such as the following:

Guitar	Garmin	Books
Book	Brussel sprouts	Rap music
Soda	Running shoe	Poetry
Refrigerator	Treadmill	Thumbtack
Microwave	Computer	Cell phone
Flowers	Cola	Remote control car
Printer	Eye glasses	Pencil

Procedure

- Form teams of three.
- Each team selects one noun from the list—do this quickly.
- Each person on the team will work alone to write a personal description of the chosen word. The description must be a complete sentence but should be lighthearted. We are not looking for a dictionary definition but for a personal description.
- Once every one on the team has completed a personal description, take all three descriptions and combine them into one sentence.
- Teams will have five minutes to complete this task.

Example 1: Describe a dog.

Student 1: A dog is a family pet.

Student 2: A dog is an animal that barks when cars pull into our yard.

Student 3: A dog is an animal that loves to chase cats.

Combined Descriptions: Dogs make great family pets because they bark when cars pull into the yard, and they chase away cats.

Example 2: Describe a remote control.

Student 1: A remote control is a device that turns people into couch potatoes.

Student 2: A remote control is a black plastic thing that hides in strange places in my living room.

Student 3: A remote control is a tool that lets me plop down on the couch and watch three shows at one time.

Combined Descriptions: Hiding in my living room, the remote control is a black plastic device that turns me into a couch potato as I plop down to watch three shows at one time.

WRITE-EMBED-REVISE

Materials

A list of sentences such as the following:

- The animal played in our yard.
- The children enjoyed the cake.
- The musician entertained the crowd.
- The team drank the refreshing drink.
- The man ruined the book.
- The thief stole the jewelry.
- The boys ate sandwiches for lunch.
- The couple danced in the room.
- My sister cried over the mess.

Procedure

- Students work with one partner.
- Each student selects a sentence from the list.
- Rewrite the sentence to embed an overload of "jewelry" (i.e., adjectives, adverbs, and prepositional phrases). Many students have been taught to add lots of adjectives to make a sentence better. The new sentence will be overloaded with bling and glitz.
- Swap papers with your partner.
- Use revision skills to rewrite the sentence to make it a powerful sentence. Delete, add, change, and rearrange until you have one strong sentence with specific nouns and vivid verbs. Do not change the meaning of the original sentence.

Example 1

1. The squirrel climbed up the tree. (original sentence)

2. The furry, frisky, bushy-tailed brown squirrel climbed quickly to the top of the towering old oak tree loaded with acorns in the neighbor's yard. (sentence with embedded modifiers)

3. In search of acorns, the squirrel scampered to the top of my neighbor's tree. (revised sentence)

Take note of the decisions made to create the final sentence. Unnecessary adjectives were eliminated. Squirrels are bushy-tailed and furry so the adjectives are redundant. If the squirrel scampered, we can infer that it climbed quickly. And since the squirrel is in search of acorns, we know the tree is oak. Students have used the revision skills of deleting and changing.

Example 2

1. The thief stole the jewelry.

2. The sneaky, grubby, mean thief quickly and quietly stole the jewelry lying on the dresser and then ran away.

3. The burglar slipped into the bedroom, slid a diamond ring and several gold chains into his pocket, and then fled into the night.

Variation: Rather than have the students select a sentence from a list, post one sentence. Every student works individually to embed modifiers and then exchanges sentences with a revision partner. When several students share their revised sentences, the students can hear the power of making good decisions as they revise. Each sentence is different because of the decisions students made.

Q IS FOR DUCK

Materials

Q Is for Duck by Elting and Folsom (1980)

Procedure

- Read *Q Is for Duck.*
- Discuss the format of the book. Make sure that students understand that the letter Q represents a characteristic of a duck.
- Select a topic, such as fairy tales, inventors, historical figures, or presidents.
- Brainstorm about the topic.
- Using ideas from the brainstorming, ask students to create sentences.
- Revise the original sentences as needed.
- The revised sentences can be assembled into a class book. (Polette, 2005)

Example 1: Fairy Tales

1. *G* is for Rumplestiltskin because he makes *gold.*

2. *G* is for Rumplestiltskin because he spins *gold* from straw.

3. *R* is for Cinderella because her clothes are *rags.*

4. *R* is for Cinderella because she wears *raggy* clothes.

5. *B* is for Red Riding Hood because she has a *basket*.

6. *B* is for Red Riding Hood because she skips through the forest to bring a *basket* of goodies to Grandma's house.

Example 2: Explorers

1. *P* is for Balboa because he was the first European to see the eastern *Pacific* Ocean after he crossed the Isthmus of *Panama*.

2. *A* is for Daniel Boone because he founded the first U.S. settlement west of the *Appalachian* Mountains.

3. *K* is for Marco Polo because he visited the *Kublai Khan* in Beijing.

4. *C* is for Dr. Sally Ride, the first American woman in space, because she was aboard the *Challenger*.

5. *Q* is for Samuel de Champlain, a French explorer and navigator, who founded the city of *Quebec* as a center of the fur trade.

FLOODLIGHT-FLASHLIGHT SENTENCES

Materials

A floodlight-flashlight chart like one in Figure 7.1

Figure 7.1 Sample Floodlight-Flashlight Chart

Floodlight	Flashlight	Sentence
Actor		
Car		
Flower		
Book		
Artist		
Scientist		

Procedure

- Give every student the floodlight-flashlight chart with the floodlight words provided.
- Students fill in the flashlight word.
- Write a sentence that uses the floodlight word and the flashlight word.

Examples

Floodlight	Flashlight	Sentence
Actor	Pierce Brosnan	Pierce Brosnan, my favorite actor, starred in several James Bond movies.
Car	Corvette	When my old car died, I bought a yellow Corvette.
Flower	rose	Each bridesmaid carried a single yellow rose, the state flower of Texas.
Book	Tuck Everlasting	I liked the movie *Tuck Everlasting*, but I enjoyed the book even more.
Artist	Picasso	Chicago features several sculptures by the artist Picasso.
Scientist	Einstein	Many people consider Einstein the greatest scientist of all time.

Variation: Students can keep this chart in their sentence pattern folders and work on it whenever they have a few extra minutes of time. Once they complete ten sentences, they can hand them in for a grade or bonus points.

HELP ME VISUALIZE

Materials

Interesting pictures that can be displayed. The Internet has numerous sites with free, public domain pictures. Posters and old calendars also serve the purpose.

Procedure

- Display an interesting picture so that all students can see it.
- Students write a sentence that uses specific nouns and vivid verbs.

Students need only a few minutes to do this. When they finish, let a few students share their sentences. This is a great time to let struggling writers shine and receive some sincere praise for constructing a great sentence.

Example: If you have displayed a picture of a turtle walking through a garden, students might write the following sentences.

- The turtle plodded through the garden.
- My family watched the turtle tread across the lawn.
- The tortoise lumbered across the lawn, under the bridge, and into the lake.

To encourage time on task, I like to have an activity ready for students as they come into the classroom after lunch break or when they are returning from music or PE. After the activity has been explained the first time, students know exactly what to do upon entering the classroom, so time is not wasted. They know that they will have very little time to write a sentence, so the activity helps to build fluency and automaticity. It also builds vocabulary as they hear other sentences. When students work to create an original sentence, they are working at the higher levels of Bloom's taxonomy.

TARGETED ACTIVITIES

Students are introduced to one new pattern a week, which I prefer to teach on the first day of the week. On the remaining days, students participate in writing workshop to create essays, narratives, poetry, short assignments, or other projects.

Most assignments that I give to students are accompanied with a rubric, because a well-designed rubric provides focus, in addition to eliminating confusion and the question, "How long does it have to be?" A strong rubric lets students know the goals and requirements up front.

The rubric for short assignments is simple and focused so that students will taste success, a strong motivator as they tackle longer assignments. Keeping the rubric simple gives students room to experiment and allows the teacher to focus on the student. But rubrics can be a two-edged sword. If used with consistency, rubrics can assure validity and reliability. On the other hand, rigid rubrics aligned to a formula can stifle the writing process and discourage discussion.

The rubric in Figure 7.2 demands that the students focus on sentence construction. No points are awarded for strong openings or closings, coherence, or cohesion. Those elements will be dealt with in longer assignments.

Figure 7.2 Sample Sentence Construction Rubric

	☺	😐	☹
Specific Nouns			
Vivid Verbs			
Sentence Variety: Length and Pattern			
4 to 10 Sentences			
Powerful Conventions			
	A = 4 or 5 smiles/no frowns B = 3 smiles/no frowns C = 1 or 2 smiles/no frowns		

This simple rubric, which targets one skill, optimizes every student's chance for success. Students who can write six to ten strong sentences will score well on the short assignments. Students who do not succeed on these short assignments can easily tackle a revision. They do not feel overwhelmed by a plethora of mistakes. Revision is quick and simple because of the focused target. So, not only do the students develop sentence writing skills, they develop skills in editing and revision.

As students tackle more complex assignments, the taste of success from these short assignments will provide motivation. Success leads to more success. The short assignments do not have the level of stress often associated with more complex tasks. These assignments are quick and easy to grade, which means the students receive immediate feedback. With slight adjustments, the rubric in Figure 7.2 can be used with each of the following activities.

LITERATURE IN THE PAPERS

Materials

Newspapers or magazines

Procedure

- Select a focus for the activity, such as mythology, characters in literature, or fables.
- Each student selects one character that they want to relate to the papers or magazines. For some students it is easier to find a picture or article first and then connect it to a character.
- Students select a picture or article that can be connected to a literary character.
- Using the above rubric, write an explanation that demonstrates the connection between the newspaper or magazine and the character you have chosen.

Suggestions: Students could write a paragraph that connects *Tuck Everlasting* (Babbitt, 1975) to an advertisement for wrinkle creams. Coffee advertisements could be connected to the mother in *Across Five Aprils* (Hunt, 1964) who suffered headaches because of a lack of coffee. A picture of a wristwatch might be related to Ray Bradbury's widely anthologized short story "All Summer in a Day."

Example: Mythology in the papers using a picture of Marilyn vos Savant.

Athena, the goddess of wisdom, helped Theseus solve his problem of battling the Minotaur. She also looked out for the wily Odysseus, who outwitted Cyclops, the Sirens, and Circe on his return to Ithaca.

Marilyn vos Savant, listed in *Guinness World Records* as having the highest IQ, also helps people to solve problems: math problems, logic problems, and various puzzles. Unlike Athena, Marilyn did not spring forth from her father's head in a full suit of armor.

SENTENCE PATTERNS FOR THE GENERATIONS

Materials

3 × 5 cards (write one abstract noun on each card)

Suggested Abstract Nouns		
Love	Faith	Hope
Anxiety	Courage	Charity
Fear	Teamwork	Despair
Joy	Laziness	Anger
Spirit	Pride	Failure
Success	Loyalty	Humor
Boredom	Wisdom	Worry
Confidence	Generosity	Greed
Determination	Talent	Contentment
Selfishness	Prudence	Intelligence

A list of discussion questions such as the following:

- How would you define the word?
- How can it be encouraged?
- What causes it?
- What might destroy it?
- Where can it be seen? (concrete examples)
- What are some synonyms?
- With what is it associated?

Procedure

Procedure for first day:

- Students work in teams of three or four.
- Give one 3 × 5 card to each team.
- Give teams time to discuss their word using the discussion questions—about ten to fifteen minutes.
- Give each team a few minutes to share their most important discussion points.
- Each team then writes a short definition of their word.

Procedure for second day:

- Using their definition from the previous day, students discuss the word and provide examples. For example, if a team defined *bravery* on the first day, they would then answer the following questions:
  - What would bravery look like for a child?
  - What would bravery look life for a teen?
  - What would bravery look like for an adult?
  - What would bravery look life for a senior citizen?

- Students revise their definition: add, delete, change, rearrange.
- Post the final definition to a bulletin board.

- Every student selects one word. They can choose the word that they have been working with or they may choose a different word.
- Each student writes four sentences about the word, one sentence for each of the age groups—child, teen, adult, senior.
- Each sentence must be a different pattern and give an example of the word for a different age group.
- The sentence does not have to include the word; it can be inferred from the actions.

Variation: Students must search the newspapers to find an example of their word for each age group and then write one sentence for each example.

Example: Boredom
Boredom for a child:

The ring bearer, bored at the wedding reception, plopped himself down in the middle of the crowd. (Pattern 14: Open with a past participle)

Boredom for a teen:

Leading 9 to 0 in the final inning, the players in the dugout lost interest in the softball game. (Pattern 13: Open with a present participle)

Boredom for an adult:

The soldier grew weary of waiting to hear if he had qualified during target practice. (Pattern 9: Close with an adverb clause)

Boredom for a senior:

Since my grandparents joined the exercise classes at the senior center, they never feel bored. (Pattern 8: Open with an adverb clause)

The preparation time for this activity takes at least two days, which might seem like a lot of preparation time to write four sentences. But the students gain valuable insights into character traits, which will help them during reading. That information enables them to make better inferences and to draw conclusions about characters they meet in literature. Students also learn that courage, wisdom, and greed are character traits common to all people, but that those traits might look different based on age. With age, we develop a deeper understanding of the traits.

A variation of this activity, called A Dictionary for All, can be found in *Ideas Plus, Book Four* (Sauvie, 1986).

VOCABULARY PEOPLE

Materials

- A list of slightly uncommon adjectives that describe people
- Magazines with lots of pictures

Acerbic	Altruistic	Apathetic
Acrimonious	Demure	Angelic
Laconic	Impertinent	Avaricious
Legendary	Indolent	Bellicose
Parsimonious	Insipid	Erudite
Pensive	Intrepid	Garrulous
Placid	Jocose	Incorrigible
Pugnacious	Lethargic	Ostentatious
Querulous	Loquacious	Sullen
Reticent	Magnanimous	Taciturn
Sagacious	Mendacious	Truculent
Sinister	Meticulous	Vivacious

Procedure

- Each student selects one adjective from the list.
- Students research to develop an understanding of the denotation and connotation of their words.
- Students look through magazines to find a picture of someone that their word might describe.
- Each student then writes a short paragraph that provides strong clues to the meaning of the word.
- They create an alliterative title that uses the word plus a name.
- Post all of the pictures and paragraphs on the board. Students can scan the pictures so that the stories and pictures print out on one page.
- Number each paragraph and picture.
- Give the students a list of all the adjectives that have been used.
- Challenge the students to read the paragraphs and then write a simple definition for each of the words.

Example 1: Ostentatious Oscar

Ostentatious Oscar loves to display his huge muscles. Every day at the gym he practices his boxing. Oscar always uses the practice mats near the front door to make sure that everyone can see him. His neon-colored clothes, covered with rhinestones and pearls, sparkle even in the dark. Other people walk into a room, but Ostentatious Oscar struts into a room. (This might be accompanied with a picture of a wrestler or of Mr. Clean from an advertisement.)

Example 2: Mendacious Myrtle

"Hello, Mr. Jones? This is Myrtle." (cough, cough)

"What's the matter, Myrtle? You don't sound so good."

"I'm really sick. I'm in bed with a fever of 104, and I have this cough. I'm not going to be able to make it to work today."

"What's that noise in the background, Myrtle? It sounds like a cash register."

"Oh, ummm, I have the TV on. That's an old rerun of CSI that you hear. Um, I plan on going to the doctor later today. I'm sure if I get some medicine, I should be able to come back to work on Monday."

"Well, I'll tell you what, Myrtle. Don't bother coming back on Monday. I think I can find someone else to do your job. Someone who is not MENDACIOUS. You're fired." (This could be accompanied by someone standing on a street and talking on a phone.)

BUILD A SENTENCE

Materials

Word lists like those below

Procedure

- Select several sentences from a piece of text that the students will be reading. The material can be fiction or informational.
- Select some words from each sentence and give the words to the students.
- Students are to construct a grammatically correct sentence using every word in the order that they are listed.
- Compare student sentences to the original. The goal is not to create the same sentence as the story; that would be impossible. It is just to expose them to some of the vocabulary and give them an opportunity to practice sentence patterns.
- Once students have the original sentences, they can make predictions about the text.

Example 1: Word lists from *The Griffin and the Minor Canon* by Frank R. Stockton (1986).

morning   monster   stone   over   grasped   powerful

Possible student sentence: This morning a monster made of stone jumped over the river and grasped a fish in his powerful jaws.

Original sentence: This morning a green monster made of stone leaped over the garden fence and grasped a yellow rose in his powerful paw.

Here are more sets of words from *The Griffin and the Minor Canon.*

when	desolate	ledge	cave	home	forest
picking	carrying	flew	marsh	roots	beneficial
admirable	leisure	gaze	noble	cowardly	selfish
appearance	morning	citizens	enthusiasm	truly	wonderful
if	visit	little	but	great	over
town	dreadful	scarcely	dwelt	image	door
never	mirror	streams	turbulent	of	reflect

who	subordinate	finished	services	aged	weekday
sculptor	figure	evidently	pleased	ground	curious
sculptures	outside	grotesque	nobody	because	exactly

Example 2: To make the activity easier, provide fewer words or use an easier text. This is example is taken from *Leola and the Honeybears* by Melodye Benson Rosales (1999).

Variation: Do a picture walk of the book prior to the writing exercise to help students develop ideas. Many of the students will try to use the words in the first part of the sentence. Model sentences that demonstrate using the words in various locations.

1.	small	cottage	woods
2.	today	nothing	fun
3.	dined	delicious	stew
4.	chatter	laughter	always
5.	plopped	damp	ground

Possible sentences:

- Leola walked until she came to a *small cottage* in the *woods.*
- *Today* Leola hoped to do *nothing* and have lots of *fun.*
- The bears who lived in the cottage *dined* on a *delicious stew.*
- *Chatter* and *laughter* could *always* be heard in the bears' cottage.
- Leola ran and ran until she finally *plopped* down onto the *damp ground.*

From Patterns to Essays

8

Teachers often ask what a week in the classroom might look like if the students work on patterns the first day of the week. What happens on the remaining days? The answer: writing workshop. Present a power lesson that addresses one writing skill. After the power lesson, students spend the remaining time writing, editing, or revising. That is an overly simple explanation of writing workshop. But I feel that writing workshop is crucial if students are to have sufficient time to focus on writing as a communication skill. "Composition is very hard and takes years of experience to learn to do well" (Ray & Laminack, 2001, pp. 21–22). For those who have never taught writing workshop, I recommend reading one of the many excellent books that explain how to set up and manage a writing workshop. Two of my favorite authors for writing workshop are Katie Wood Ray and Ralph Fletcher. Writing workshop requires clear procedures and goals that will help the students to make decisions and work independently.

Writing workshop also will help students to reach the demands of the Common Core State Standards, which require that students "write routinely over extended time frames (time for research, reflection, and revision) and shorter time frames (a single sitting or a day or two) for a range of tasks, purposes, and audiences" (National Governors Association Center for Best Practices and Council of Chief State School Officers, 2010, CC.K-12.W.R.10. All rights reserved.). Writing workshop will help students to develop the required writing stamina. Students also learn how to manage time as they tackle short and lengthier tasks.

It is not necessary to have taught all of the patterns before moving the students into writing workshop. Students will begin using more complex forms that they have read or heard. Once the pattern is taught, the students will refine their work. To develop writing stamina and decision-making skills, students need to begin working on lengthier texts. I prefer to move students into writing expository essays before narratives because they can use content knowledge from core classes. Rather than having students write to a prompt, I have them select their writing topics. This assures that they will have content knowledge and it increases motivation because students will be writing about a topic of their choice.

In addition, the Common Core State Standards (National Governors Association Center for Best Practices and Council of Chief State School Officers, 2010. All rights reserved.) require that students write lengthier texts.

CC.K-12.W.R.2 Text Types and Purposes: Write informative/explanatory texts to examine and convey complex ideas and information clearly and accurately through the effective selection, organization, and analysis of content.

Providing students with an opportunity to analyze strong and weak essays will help them to understand organization patterns.

STUDENT-MADE RUBRICS AND THE PATTERNS

Before moving students into writing expository essays, I have them spend time reading numerous examples of essays, which can be found easily in the appendix of the Common Core State Standards and in textbooks. In addition, exemplar essays from previous classes, with student names removed, can be used. A carousel walk with time to read and discuss helps students understand the nature of an expository essay.

First collect twenty to thirty essays in a range of quality. Some essays will be strong and others will be weaker. The weaker essays might lack specific content or follow poor organization patterns. Enter each essay into a word processing program so that each one can be printed in the same font. In addition, make sure that none of the essays have errors in capitalization, usage, punctuation, or spelling. The students will be reading these essays and making decisions about quality based on the content, sentence structures, and organization patterns. An essay might have wonderful content and organization, but if it is riddled with spelling and grammar errors, students automatically will mark it as weak. The purpose of this activity is to have students focus on the content and structure of the essays and not to dismiss an essay for errors.

Post the essays around the room and give these instructions:

- Walk about the room and read each essay.
- Discuss the essays with other students.
- Decide which essays are strong and which are weak.
- If you feel an essay is strong, mark it with an *S* (or a green dot).
- If you feel an essay is weak, mark it with a *W* (or a red dot).
- Do not be influenced by the decisions of other students. You might come to an essay that everyone has marked as weak. If you feel it is a strong essay, mark it as strong.

Give the students ample time to read and discuss the essays. Once they have marked all of the essays, separate the essays into two groups: weak essays and strong essays. Then have the students work in small groups to complete a

T-chart. On one side of the chart, they are to list the characteristics of a strong essay. On the other side of the chart, they should list the characteristics of a weak essay. Encourage them to return to the essays and discuss them as they create their lists. Once students have had time to discuss the essays and make their lists, lead a full-class discussion about the qualities of a good essay and the characteristics of a weak essay. Allowing students to discuss essays and create the lists will help them to understand the characteristics of a good essay more effectively than if they sat through a lecture about essays. The student observations can then be used to create a writing rubric.

The rubric in Figure 8.1 was created following student discussions about expository essays. Student comments that reflect the characteristics of a good essay are aligned under headings *Focus, Support,* and *Organization.* If the students did not discuss conventions, and they often do not since the model essays have been corrected, that feature will need to be added. Determine a point range for grades A, B, C, and D.

The rubric in Figure 8.1 reflects the lessons of sentence patterns. Students realize that good writing has sentence variety, specific nouns and vivid verbs, and power punctuation, and that the writing sounds human rather than robotic.

Figure 8.1   Sample Rubric for Expository Essays

This expository essay demonstrates the following characteristics:				
FOCUS				
The opening attempts to spark some curiosity in the reader.	4	3	2	1
The conclusion makes a point and gives a sense of ending.	4	3	2	1
It stays with the important points—all the sentences fit together.	4	3	2	1
SUPPORT				
Specific nouns and vivid verbs make it sound like a human wrote it.	4	3	2	1
Enough details let readers see and hear—they can visualize.	4	3	2	1
ORGANIZATION				
It has a variety of sentence patterns and sentence length for cohesion.	4	3	2	1
It moves smoothly from one paragraph to the next (coherence).	4	3	2	1
Transitions do not stick out like a red flag but show how ideas connect.	4	3	2	1
CONVENTIONS				
Powerful conventions help the reader understand the ideas.	4	3	2	1
TOTAL POINTS				

The rubric in Figure 8.2 was developed following a discussion about persuasive essays. The students involved in this discussion had been writing expository essays and were ready to tackle persuasive essays. To develop this rubric, the students read two excellent persuasive essays and discussed how persuasive essays and expository essays are similar and how they are different. The rubric reflects student discoveries. They realized that all essays need sentence variety, powerful conventions, and smooth transitions. But persuasive essays have a different focus. The opening needs to express a clear opinion.

Figure 8.2 Sample Rubric for Persuasive Essays

This persuasive essay demonstrates the following characteristics:				
IDEAS				
The opening takes a stand and works to spark some curiosity in the reader.	4	3	2	1
The conclusion makes a point and gives a sense of ending.	4	3	2	1
Sentences stay with the important points—they fit together.	4	3	2	1
WORD CHOICE				
Specific nouns and vivid verbs are used.	4	3	2	1
Enough ideas let readers see and hear (visualization).	4	3	2	1
VOICE				
It sounds as though a human wrote it and not a robot.	4	3	2	1
ORGANIZATION				
Ideas flow from paragraph to paragraph (coherence).	4	3	2	1
Transitions do not stick out; they show how ideas connect.	4	3	2	1
SENTENCE FLUENCY				
Sentence length and smooth openings give flow and rhythm.	4	3	2	1
CONVENTIONS				
Powerful conventions help the reader understand the author.	4	3	2	1
TOTAL POINTS				

The student-designed rubric shown in Figure 8.3 reflects the qualities of a good narrative. Again, the students read two excellent narratives and then had a discussion about the similarities and differences between narratives and expository essays. The students realized that all writing needs strong sentences, specific nouns and vivid verbs, and power punctuation. The modes of writing need strong openings and closings. They realized that personal narratives follow a different organization pattern that usually moves through time. They also noted that the personal narratives showed emotion.

Figure 8.3 Sample Rubric for Narratives

This personal narrative demonstrates the following characteristics:				
FOCUS				
The opening works to spark some curiosity in the reader.	4	3	2	1
The conclusion wraps up the story and recaps the emotions.	4	3	2	1
All the sentences fit together—they do not go off on bunny trails.	4	3	2	1
ELABORATION and VOICE				
Specific nouns and vivid verbs are used.	4	3	2	1
Enough ideas let readers see and hear (visualization).	4	3	2	1
It sounds as though a human wrote it and not a robot.	4	3	2	1
ORGANIZATION				
Events flow from paragraph to paragraph.	4	3	2	1
Transitions move through time and do not scream at the reader.	4	3	2	1
Sentence length and smooth openings give flow and rhythm.	4	3	2	1
CONVENTIONS				
Powerful conventions help the reader to enjoy and follow along.	4	3	2	1
TOTAL POINTS				

Reading and discussing the various types of writing will help students to understand that a wide range of skills are needed to create a strong text. The ability to write effective sentences puts them on the path to effective writing. The power of pattern study is evident in the categories of support or elaboration and conventions. Students recognize the need for sentence variety and strong vocabulary. But the students also begin to understand that the patterns will help with organization because the patterns provide smooth transitions. Students who know the patterns do not need to use formulaic transitions such as *first, second,* and *finally.* Rather they can use adverb clauses, prepositional phrases, or adverbs to create a smooth transition. The use of smooth transitions is a requirement in the Common Core State Standards. By third grade, students are required to "Use linking words and phrases (e.g., because, therefore, since, for example) to connect opinion and reasons" (National Governors Association Center for Best Practices and Council of Chief State School Officers, 2010, CC.3.W.1.c. All rights reserved.). By sixth grade they must "Use appropriate transitions to clarify the relationships among ideas and concepts." (CC.6.W.2.c) Students who understand the patterns do not need to write dull openings and closings. Their openings can spark interest through sentence variety and a strong vocabulary.

The prevalence of high-stakes testing has led many schools to feel that all student writing must evolve from prompts. In Chapter 1 I shared some problems that teachers have cited when trying to teach writing: Students lack (1.) motivation, (2.) basic writing skills, and (3.) content knowledge or information for writing topics. I think that the overuse of prompts is one reason for lack of motivation and lack of content knowledge. Students will be more motivated to write about a topic of their choice. In addition, selecting their own topic will ensure that students have content knowledge. Studying the patterns will give the students basic writing skills. So by eliminating daily prompts and introducing the patterns, three problems can be circumvented.

As I work with schools across the country, I find a great deal of resistance to the idea of eliminating prompts. I agree that the prompts should not be eliminated completely. After all, learning how to read and respond to a prompt is a test-taking skill that students need. But do students need to write to prompts every day to develop that skill? The ability to read and respond to a prompt can be taught in one strong lesson followed by some reinforcement. Prompts can be used for a formal assessment. Using a prompt assures that students will develop the skill of reading and responding to a prompt. In addition, using a prompt for assessment reduces the number of variables introduced into assessment, which will make it easier to determine which skills still need to be reinforced.

What will students write about if they are not given a prompt? They can write about personal interests or content area classes. Have the students create an expert list. At first they will balk and say they are not experts at anything, but they are. Ask: "How many of you eat at fast-food restaurants? Then you are expert enough to write an expository essay about which one is the best or about the advantages and disadvantages of eating fast food. What are your hobbies? What are your interests? Where have you traveled? How do you spend your holidays?"

I remember well one student who doubted that I would let him write about his interests. He said, "I have every Batman comic book ever published. Are you saying I can write about that?" I assured him that he could, and he produced wonderful essays and narratives. He wrote expository essays about Batman's special powers. He wrote comparison and contrast studies about Batman and his enemies, and personal narratives about how he earned the money to purchase the comic books. He argued that reading Batman had a positive effect on a child's character development. His essays had interesting content, and he was highly motivated to write about this topic. More importantly, as he worked on the essays he developed skills. He used sentence variety, developed organization patterns, and supplied secondary support. He then used those skills during assessments when he was given a prompt.

Another important source for student topics comes from the material they study in other classes. I have had students use their class notes from history to discuss the causes of the Civil War, notes from art class to explain tessellations, and notes from science to write about the dangers of pollution. Let students select their topic and they will be more motivated and have content knowledge.

PROCESS FOR OPINION PAPERS AND COMMON CORE STANDARDS

I recently worked with a group of fourth-grade students whose teacher wanted students to write an opinion paper as required in the following:

CC.4.W.1 Text Types and Purposes: Write opinion pieces on topics or texts, supporting a point of view with reasons and information (National Governors Association Center for Best Practices and Council of Chief State School Officers, 2010. All rights reserved.).

These students had studied the first eight or nine sentence patterns.

First, I modeled how to complete a graphic organizer. I explained that I had to choose something to write about. Figure 8.4 shows that I decided to focus on my trip to Egypt. I needed to narrow it and decide what two ideas or floodlight points I wanted to share with my readers. I chose to discuss the pyramids and the Nile River. Once I had selected my points, I had to brainstorm some flashlight details that I could write about in my essay. I pointed out to students that at this point, I was not writing complete sentences. I only needed bullet points to help me remember my brainstorming. Anyone reading the organizer probably would not understand some of my bullet points, such as the word *kites*. But to me the bullet provides very specific information that I might want to share.

Figure 8.4   Sample Graphic Organizer: Egypt

FOCUS EGYPT	
FLOODLIGH GReat PYRAMID WAS IMPRESSIVE	FLOODLIGHT NILE R. was beautiful
FLASHLIGHT • oveR 4000 yRs old • tomb — Khufu • oveR 2 million stones • 2 – 15 tons • 20 yRs – 20,000 laboRoRs • Kites • aiRshaft	FLASHLIGHT • longest – 4000 miles • sunRise – plants – diamonds • Aswan – CaiRo • sunset – Red-oRange – yellow-puRple • long stRetches of gReen • bRown deseRt

For the next step we completed a whole class organizer, as seen in Figure 8.5. I chose the topic that we would write about: trees. Students contributed ideas for the floodlight points that we would make and for the supporting details or flashlights. Again, I stressed to the students that this step is brainstorming and that when we write the final essay, we might not use all of the supporting details.

Then the students completed an organizer in small teams of four as seen in Figure 8.6. I circled to the seven groups of students as they worked in order to make sure that they were on track and understood how to list specific details or flashlight statements. The work represented in Figures 8.4 through 8.6 took forty-five minutes to complete.

Figure 8.5 Sample Graphic Organizer: Trees

FOCUS TREES

FLOODLIGHT	FLOODLIGHT
Help keep us healthy	food
FLASHLIGHT	FLASHLIGHT
• create oxygen	• fruits / veggies
• take in carbon dioxide	• syrups
• provide fruits / (food) vegetables?	• nuts
• shade —	
• paper	
• provide animal homes	
• exercise	
• warmth - wood	
• shelter	
• medicine	

Figure 8.6 Sample Graphic Organizer: Halloween

FOCUS Halloween is the Best holiday (forms)

FLOODLIGHT Halloween is Scary	FLOODLIGHT Yummy treats
FLASHLIGHT	
Being Scary — Scaring people	geting yummy candy — Sweet, Soar, red, Orange, green, and More
geting scared	giving out candy
Scary comstumes	
Scary Decorations — Spiders, mummys, Vampires, ghost, and more	geting free treats — Jolly ranchers, twizers, mints, suckers, Gum and more

The following day, I spent about five minutes reviewing the use of the graphic organizer. I then explained that each student would select one focus from a suggested list and complete a graphic organizer individually. I gave the students the following six choices:

- My school is the best school in the world.
- _____ is my favorite athlete.
- _____ is my favorite day of the year.
- Living in the country has many advantages.
- Living in town has many advantages.
- _____ is a wonderful vacation spot.

Figure 8.7 shows one student's completed organizer. It took the students between twenty and twenty-five minutes to complete the organizer.

Figure 8.7 Graphic Organizer: Tom Brady

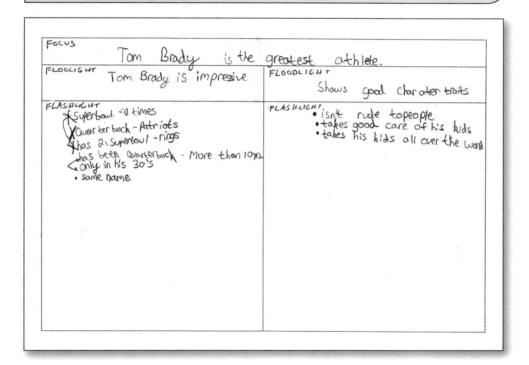

During the next lesson, I modeled for the students how to write strong sentences that would allow the reader to visualize the bullet points or flashlight details. In other words, we would use specific nouns and vivid verbs to create flashlight sentences. I explained that they might need to write anywhere from two to four sentences about select bullet points in order to create a strong visualization. They might decide to combine some bullet points, they might add a few points, or they might have bullet points that they decide not to use at all. Using the student work in Figure 8.8, I asked the student if she had any points she wanted to combine, and she selected warm sand and building sand castles. We wrote the sentence: "I enjoy building castles in the warm sand." I next asked the student to form a picture of this in her head. What could you say that would help us to see what you are picturing? Working together, we created the following sentences: "My mom helps me to carry buckets and buckets of sand and water. Soon enormous white sand towers, walls, and doors take shape on my castle."

Figure 8.8   Sample Graphic Organizer: Florida

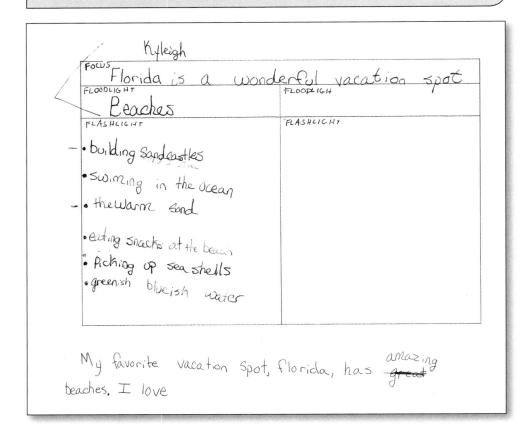

The students returned to teamwork. Using the bullet point about scary costumes on Halloween, the students worked to write several sentences that would help readers to see the scary costumes. In Figure 8.9 are samples sentences the teams expanded one simple bullet point. We shared the work on the document camera. The students were impressed to see the numerous ways that a bullet could be expanded. I stressed to them that good writers make many decisions and take some risks as they work.

The students were ready to tackle writing an opinion paragraph. Since we had a limited amount of time, I chose to have the students write one simple paragraph rather than a full essay, even though they had enough material to write a four-paragraph essay. They could have used their focus statement and the two floodlight points to create a simple mapping paragraph to open the essay. Each floodlight would then become a paragraph by using the flashlight details. And a closing would be the fourth paragraph. To expand an essay, they simply needed to add another column and address another floodlight point with supporting flashlight details.

Figure 8.9 Sample Sentences: Halloween Costumes

(1)

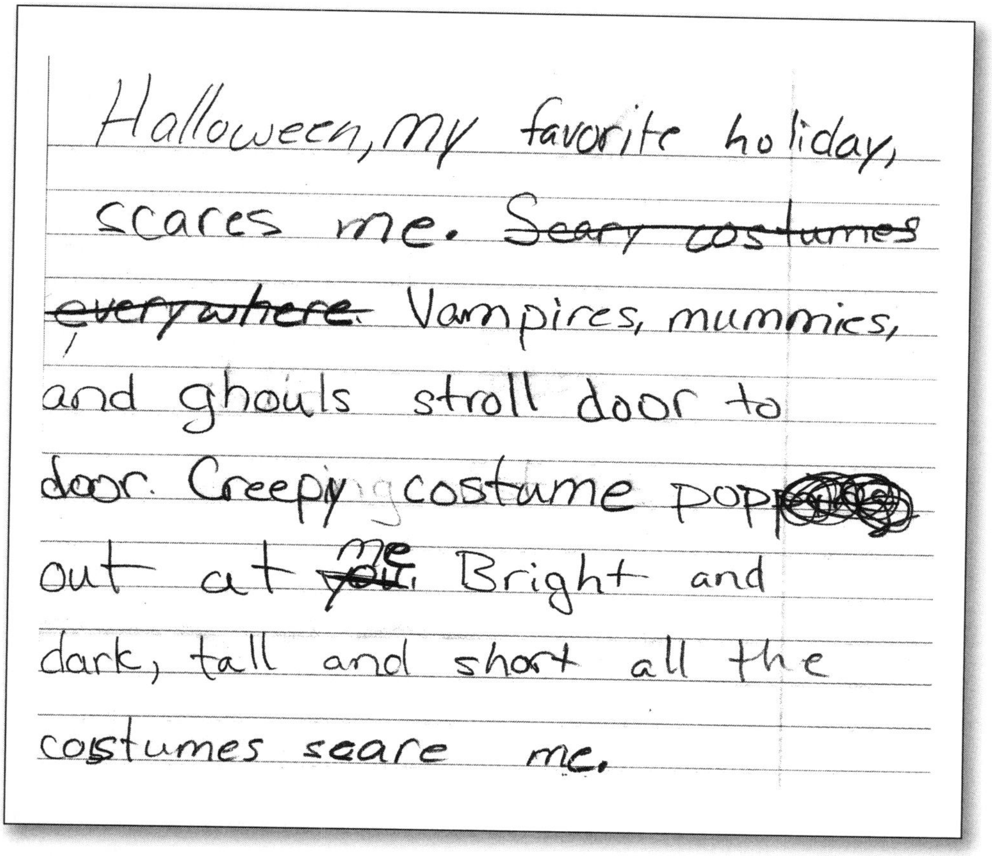

Halloween, my favorite holiday, scares me. ~~Scary costumes everywhere~~. Vampires, mummics, and ghouls stroll door to door. Creepy costume pop~~ped~~ out at ~~you~~ me. Bright and dark, tall and short all the costumes seare me.

(2)

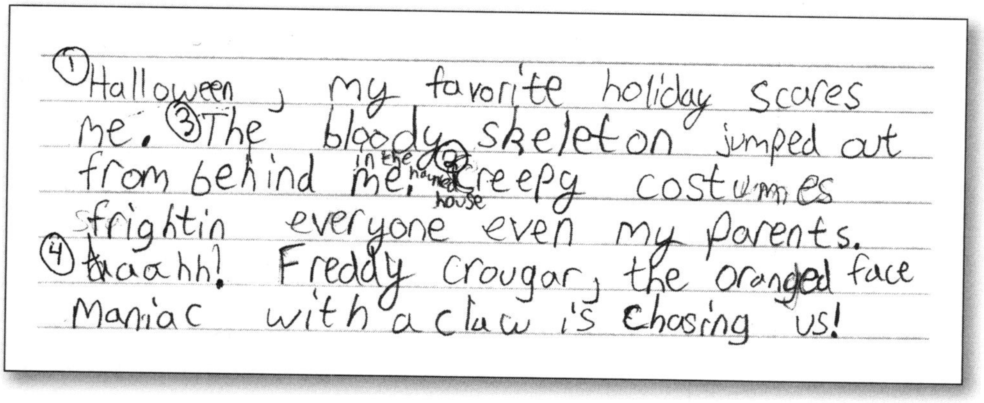

① Halloween, my favorite holiday scares me. ③ The bloody skeleton jumped out from behind me in the haunted house. ② Creepy costumes frightin everyone even my parents. ④ aaahh! Freddy Crougar, the oranged face maniac with a claw is chasing us!

(3)

> From ghosts and ghouls to vampires and witches, costumes of all kinds visit my house for candy. Jumping out of the shadows, scaring younger trick-or-treaters with their horrifying costumes, teenagers enjoy scaring me.

Figure 8.10 shows two days of work for one of the students. He chose to write a paragraph expressing his opinion that Tom Brady is the greatest athlete. Notice that the student uses an appositive to create a focus sentence. He followed his graphic organizer closely to create the first draft of his paragraph. On the following day, I praised him for his strong opening sentence and his original closing. I then suggested to him that he could make his essay stronger if he would combine the following sentences: "His rings are solid gold with diamonds in the middle. They are worth more than one million dollars." Since this student relied heavily on forms of *be* throughout his paragraph, combining these two sentences would eliminate one of them and give him some variety in sentence structures and sentence length. He created the following combination: "He has two solid gold rings with sparkling diamonds in the middle, worth two million dollars each."

When I left class that day, this young man was working on rewriting the sentence one more time, since he realized that the phrase "worth two million dollars each" was not anchored properly. He said, "I want to say that the rings are worth two million dollars each, but this sounds like the diamonds are worth two million dollars each." I did not have a chance to return to that classroom, but felt quite confident that this author would work until he created the sentence that he wanted. He had been studying patterns and had the tools he needed to create the sentence that he wanted.

Had time allowed, I would have had the students try one more revision trick with highlighters. Ask students to highlight the first three words of every sentence in a piece of text they have produced. Two things will become evident. If every sentence begins with a noun-verb, the essay lacks sentence variety. But if

Figure 8.10 Sample Paragraph: Tom Brady

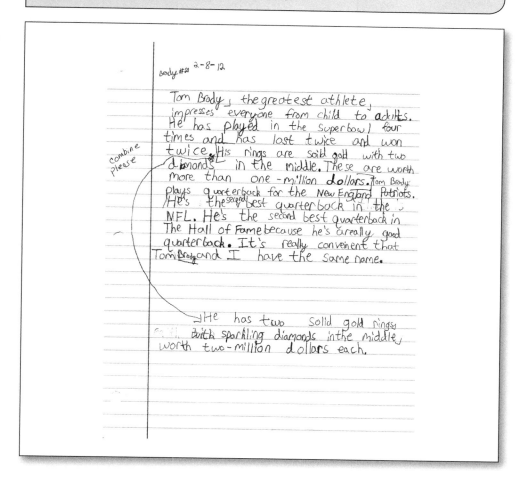

the highlighting reveals a few prepositional phrases, subordinators, or adverbs, the essay has sentence variety. By reading through and listening closely, students can hear if they have used a range of patterns. They do not need to make every sentence a different pattern; no professional writer would do that. They simply need to use an occasional opening other than noun-verb.

The highlighting also will help students to see the length of each sentence. If the highlighting is close and frequent, they have too many short sentences. They can revise by combining two or three of those sentences. If they find that they have a section that lacks highlighting for several lines, they might have a run-on sentence or a comma splice that needs to be repaired.

Some teachers want step-by-step lessons sequenced from the beginning of the year to the end. But I find that difficult to do for writing because the daily lessons need to address students' needs. Following a rigid series of lessons means that assessment is not driving instruction. If the students have completed an essay and the assessment shows that the students are having difficulties with providing supporting details, then that determines the power lessons that should be taught. If the assessment shows that students do not use transition devices, then mini-lessons on transition devices need to be presented. If a rigid series of lessons drives the curriculum, students might be working on strong openings when it is a skill they already have. Assessment needs to drive instruction.

CONCLUSION

I hope that the material presented in this book helps teachers and students to develop basic writing skills. More than anything, though, I hope that working with the patterns and the supporting activities will bring a sense of joy and excitement back to writing. Make writing a daily activity in the classroom. Use writing to communicate, to learn, and to explore.

References

Altman, P., Caro, M., Metge-Egan, L., & Roberts, L. (2007). *Sentence combining workbook* (2nd ed.). Boston: Wadsworth.

Anderson, J. (2005). *Mechanically inclined: Building grammar, usage, and style into writer's workshop.* Portland, ME: Stenhouse.

Babbitt, N. (1975). *Tuck everlasting.* New York: Macmillan.

Baker, L. (1990). *Life in the oceans: Animals, people, plants.* New York: Scholastic.

Bavaria, S. (2011). Arabian horses—from the family tent to the 4-H ring. *Appleseeds, 13*(8), 24–25.

Benjamin, A., & Berger, J. (2010). *Teaching grammar: What really works.* Larchmont, NY: Eye on Education.

Benjamin, A., & Oliva, T. (2007). *Engaging grammar: Practical advice for real classrooms.* Urbana, IL: National Council of Teachers of English.

Biel, T. L. (1992). *Tigers.* Zoobooks series, vol. 9, no. 10. Mankato, MN: Wildlife Education.

Blume, J. (1980). *Superfudge.* New York: Bantam Doubleday Dell Books for Young Readers.

Bruning, R. H., Schraw, G. J., & Ronning, R. (1999). *Cognitive psychology and instruction.* Upper Saddle River, NJ: Prentice Hall.

Buckley, S. (Ed.). (2011). John Muir, nature boy. *Appleseeds, 13*(7).

Bunting, E. (1989). *The Wednesday surprise.* New York: Trumpet Club.

Chancellor, D. (Ed.) (1992). *Jungle animals.* New York: DK.

Cleary, B. (1981). *Ramona Quimby, age 8.* New York: Harper Trophy.

Cleary, B. P. (2000). *Hairy, scary, ordinary: What is an adjective?* Minneapolis: Carolrhoda Books.

Currie, S. (2003). First contact with Europeans. *Indians of the Southeast, 24*(7), 17–21.

Elting, M., & Folsom, M. L. (1980). *Q is for duck.* New York: Clarion Books.

Fair, R. S. (2003). No teepees here. *Indians of the Southeast, 24*(7), 22–23.

Fox, P. (1984). *One-eyed cat.* New York: Aladdin.

Freedman, R. (1987). *Lincoln: A photobiography.* New York: Clarion Books.

Garland, S. (1993). *The lotus seed.* New York: Harcourt Brace.

Gray, L. M. (1995). *My mama had a dancing heart.* New York: Orchard Books.

Heinz, B. (2006). *Cheyenne medicine hat.* Mankato, MN: Creative Editions.

Heller, R. (1989). *Many luscious lollipops.* New York: Scholastic.

Hesse, K. (1994). *Sable.* New York: Scholastic.

Hirsch, R. (2011). Gone today, here tomorrow? *So Tall! Trees, Odyssey, 20*(4), 24–27.

Hunt, I. (1964). *Across five Aprils.* New York: Berkley Books.

Jiang, J. L. (1997). *Red scarf girl.* New York: HarperCollins.

Johnston, T. (1992). *The cowboy and the black-eyed pea.* New York: G. P. Putnam's Sons.

Kavasch, E. B. (2003). Ancient mound builders. *Indians of the Southeast, 24*(7), 6–9.

Killgallon, D. (1997). *Sentence composing for middle school.* Portsmouth, NH: Boynton/ Cook Heinemann.

King, S. (2000). *On writing.* New York: Scribner.

Kutiper, K. (1983). *Idea exchange for English teachers.* Urbana, IL: National Council for Teachers of English.

Laden, N. (1998). *When Pigasso met Mootisse.* San Francisco: Chronicle Books.

Lusted, M. A., & Derby, T. (2011). So you want to work with horses. *Appleseeds, 13*(8), 15–17.

MacLachlan, P. (2004). *More perfect than the moon.* New York: Joanna Cotler Books.

Mattox, J. (2011). Animals at play. *Appleseeds, 13*(9), 5–7.

Miller, J., & Lusted, M. A. (2011). Extreme mustang makeover. *Appleseeds, 13*(8), 28–29.

National Governors Association Center for Best Practices and Council of Chief State School Officers. (2010). *Common core state standards: English language arts standards.* Washington DC: National Governors Association Center for Best Practices and Council of Chief State School Officers. Retrieved from http://www.corestandards.org/ the-standards/english-language-arts-standards

Noden, H. R. (1999). *Image grammar: Using grammatical structures to teach writing.* Portsmouth, NH: Boynton/Cook Heinemann.

O'Dell, S. (1970). *Sing down the moon.* New York: Dell Laurel-Leaf.

Paterson, K. (1980). *Jacob I have loved.* New York: Thomas Y. Crowell.

Polacco, P. (2010). *The junkyard wonders.* New York: Penguin.

Polette, K. (2005). *Read & write it out loud: Guided oral literacy strategies.* New York: Pearson.

Polette, K. (2012). *Teaching grammar through writing: Activities to develop writer's craft in all students in grades 4–12.* Boston: Pearson.

Poorman, D. (2011). Let's get to know one another. *Appleseeds, 13*(8), 4–6.

Provost, G. (2001). *Make your words work: Proven techniques for effective writing—for fiction and nonfiction.* Lincoln, NE: iUniverse.com.

Ray, K. W. (1999). *Wondrous words: Writers and writing in the elementary classroom.* Urbana, IL: National Council of Teachers of English.

Ray, K. W., & Laminack, L. (2001). *The writing workshop: Working through the hard parts (and they're all hard parts).* Urbana, IL: National Council of Teachers of English.

Rickitt, R. (2003). Magic in Middle-Earth. *Muse, 7*(9), 19–27.

Rosales, M. B. (1999). *Leola and the honeybears.* New York: Scholastic.

Routman, R. (2005). *Writing essentials: Raising expectations and results while simplifying teaching.* Portsmouth, NH: Heinemann.

Sauvie, M. (1986). *Ideas plus, book four.* Urbana, IL: National Council for Teachers of English.

Schotter, R. (2006). *Mama, I'll give you the world.* New York: Schwartz & Wade Books.

Schuster, E. H. (2003). *Breaking the rules: Liberating writers through innovative grammar instruction.* Portsmouth, NH: Heinemann.

Seidler, T. (1993). *The Wainscott weasel.* New York: Harper Collins/Micahel DeCapua Books.

Smith, M. C. (2011). Buttons are fasten-ating. *Appleseeds, 13*(5), 9.

Soundar, C. (2011). Games that travel the world. *Appleseeds, 13*(9), 24–25.

Sparks, J. E. (1982). *Write for power.* Los Angeles: Communication Associates.

Sprenger, M. (2005). *How to teach so students remember.* Alexandria, VA: Association for Supervision and Curriculum Development.

Stockton, F. R. (1986). *The griffin and the minor canon.* New York: HarperCollins.

Strong, W. (1973). *Sentence combining: A composing book.* New York: Random House.

Strong, W. (1986). *Creative approaches to sentence combining.* Urbana, IL: ERIC Clearinghouse on Reading and Communication Skills and the National Council of Teachers of English.

Swanson, D. (1998). *Animals eat the weirdest things.* New York: Henry Holt.

Tourtellot, J. B. (2011). Serve over ice. *National Geographic Traveler, 28,* 73.

University of Chicago Press. (2003). *The Chicago manual of style* (15th ed.). Chicago: University of Chicago Press.

Venezia, M. (1993). *Getting to know the world's greatest artists: Botticelli.* Chicago: Children's Press.

Weaver, C. (1996). *Teaching grammar in context.* Portsmouth, NH: Boynton/Cook Heinemann.

Weaver, C. (2007). *The grammar plan book: A guide to smart teaching.* Portsmouth, NH: Heinemann.

White, E. B. (1970). *The trumpet of the swan.* New York: Scholastic.

Willard, N., & Moser, B. (1992). *Beauty and the beast.* San Diego: Harcourt Brace Jovanovich.

Winnick, K. B. (1996). *Mr. Lincoln's whiskers.* Honesdale, PA: Boyds Mills Press.

Yagoda, B. (2007). *When you catch an adjective, kill it: The parts of speech, for better and/or worse.* New York: Broadway Books.

Yim, N. (2011). Horses helping others. *Appleseeds, 13*(8), 20–21.

Yolen, J. (1997). *Miz Berlin walks.* New York: Puffin Books, a Division of Penguin Groups.

Yorke, J. (Ed.). (1998). *The big book of trains.* New York: DK.

Zinsser, W. (2001). *On writing well* (25th anniv. ed.). New York: HarperCollins.

Zoehfeld, K. W. (1997). *Cactus café: A story of the Sonoran desert.* Norwalk, CT: Soundprints.

Index

CORWIN

A SAGE Company

The Corwin logo—a raven striding across an open book—represents the union of courage and learning. Corwin is committed to improving education for all learners by publishing books and other professional development resources for those serving the field of PreK–12 education. By providing practical, hands-on materials, Corwin continues to carry out the promise of its motto: **"Helping Educators Do Their Work Better."**